One's Own Sweet Way

A Novel About Anxiety Disorder

C M Riddle

One's Own Sweet Way is based on real-life experiences and is considered a work of fictionalized memoir. For the comfort of family and friends the character names, places, and incidences are used fictitiously, and any resemblance to real persons, living or dead is purely coincidental.

No part of this book may be reproduced, stored in a retrieval system, or transmitted in any form or by any means, electronic, mechanical, photocopying, recording, or otherwise, without the prior written permission of the author.

Cover Photo by: Tanya Constantine Photography
tanyaconstantine.com

Dedicated to **NataliE**, **AL**exis, and mi**A**
The world is a better place because you ask us
stop, look, and listen, and to appreciate the world around us
And to Lorenzo, Maya, and Tt for always being there.

FORWARD

Once a taboo subject, conversations around anxiety disorders have risen above whispers and have earned a clear and necessary voice. I had no idea the path that my daughter, Mia, and I would venture on when I first witnessed anxiety consume her.

Mia had high anxiety most of her life, but it became a glaring disorder when she entered high school. The dragon had emerged, and it would not quickly become domesticated.

Thus began the five-year journey in which to travel alongside the dragon. We sought help from professionals, school officials, our community, and we held belief in the power of family, love, and faith.

Since the first release of One's Own Sweet Way, several parents, teachers, students, grandparents, business professionals, and family members reached out to me. They encouraged me to continue sharing this story so others, both those who suffer from an anxiety, and those who love them, would have a reference to start conversations and to explore the many facets of this invisible, yet remarkable, disability.

The experiences in this story are true. The names, locations, and timeline in this story are fictional. I did this for the comfort and respect of our family, friends, and community. Some characters personify the feelings of negative attitudes toward anxiety or invisible disease. They are representative of feelings and reactions to those mindsets.

It is with honor that I share this experience, and the ability to extract some positive insight from a difficult time for our family. It's my hope to inspire other families.

I am glad you have found your way to this book. If you, or someone you love, suffers from debilitating anxiety, I hope this story helps you. I also encourage you to further explore options beyond the realms of this text so you will succeed in your own sweet, perfect way.

CM Riddle

CHAPTER ONE

NEALA

I scrambled down the embankment toward the shore of San Francisco Bay unaware of the impending doom shadowing me. The cars above clanged as they crossed the Golden Gate Bridge. The gentle roll of the tide peacefully hit the shoreline, and sparkled waves reached across the Bay to Alcatraz.

Although the sun baked the sand, the pylon cast shadows on the beach's rocks. I saw a spot big enough for Rachel and me to have lunch.

"Hey, over here." I waved my hand to catch Rachel's attention. "It's cooler in the shade." I guess she didn't hear me because she started walking toward Julie and Amanda. "Rachel."

The roar of cars whizzing across the bridge seemed to suck my voice in before the words reached her. "Rachel!" I yelled again.

Nothing.

It was clear I'd have to head toward the group, but a sudden heaviness stopped me. As if something had clamped around my neck, my shoulders ached with an unfamiliar burden. It became a challenge to move. Rolling thunder silenced the whoosh of the traffic and everything blurred.

The ocean, once smooth and melodic, gasped with every wave. Dark clouds ate the sun, and the threat of darkness hung in the sky like a funeral shroud. I tried to take a slow breath, but the air seemed too thick. Above me, the bridge moaned. The swinging cables struggled to hold the weight of the tottering bridge.

"Run!" I screamed. The bridge above me rattled fiercely. "Run!" A strong wind whipped my hair across my eyes, my knees trembled, and my feet felt stuck in cement. I prepared to run, but I wasn't sure where to go. My heart clamored. Clouds pushed against my vision.

I gasped and sucked in air. Without realizing it, I had stopped breathing while listening, waiting for what would happen next. I wanted to run, but I couldn't move my body.

The world seemed to close in.

I scanned the students, parents, and teachers, but no one else looked distressed. Two eighth-graders peered at a tide pool, and a group of rowdy boys climbed jagged rocks near the base of the bridge. I looked for my Parent Leader, Kat. Standing near the shore, she and another volunteer kept students from going into the water.

Mr. Patterson, our docent, lifted his clipboard.

This is it, he's gonna tell us we have to get out of here quick.

"All right, everyone, gather 'round," Mr. Patterson said as if he couldn't see the world crumbling around him. "Take your field notes and put them in your backpacks. Put your packs and anything else you don't want to carry into your Parent Leader's car. We're going to walk across the Golden Gate Bridge before heading home. And take any litter from the beach even if it is not yours."

Harsh silence overcame me, and my world flipped back. The ominous clouds had dissipated, and the ocean had smoothed. I felt as if I'd just stepped off a merry-go-round. Dizzy. Nauseous. Not sure what to do, I stumbled toward Kat.

"You look seasick, Neala, are you okay?"

I didn't know what to say. I'd never felt so creepy in my life. "I don't want to walk across the bridge, Kat. I don't feel good." I folded my arms over my belly. "Is it okay to stay in your car until we go home?"

In my mind, I screamed for my mom and my dog. I felt terrified, like something terrible was about to happen. "I can't wait to get home," I said. Nothing was more real than that.

Mr. Patterson said I couldn't be left alone, so I sat in the car with Kat. She tried to talk, but I pretended to be sleepy. After a few tries, she grabbed her phone and messed with it.

I wish I had a phone—Dad said I have to wait until high school. Being in the eighth grade bummed me out. My parents expected me to do so much stuff and be responsible for everything. I was old enough for that. Right? But a phone? No way.

On the way home, I sat between classmates Jessica and Ally. To distract myself from their gibberish, I tried to figure out what had happened on the beach. The panic went away, but a weird electric sensation still coursed through me.

Peeking in Kat's rearview mirror, my green eyes reflected back. I looked normal. My heartbeat had quieted. One glance at the sun high in the sky showed that everything seemed as it should be. Had I imagined the whole thing?

Kat drove back to the school. My stomach lurched when I saw Mom's blue Intrepid in the parking lot. Riding to the house, I would have to listen to the carpool girls, Nikki and Sam, talk about the day. Maybe Mom would pay attention to them and wouldn't ask me about the field trip.

Mom's curly ponytail caught my eye, and I felt relief. She stood by the front office, waiting with the other parents.

Wearing her customary red vest, she stood out. I couldn't wait to be near her. I tapped my foot in anticipation when the Parent Leader cars lined up at the curb, and kids got out. I had to wait for Jessica to grab all her stuff before she could scoot out of the car. My fist curled. Why did she have to buy so many souvenirs at the Marine Museum? Just get out of the dumb vehicle!

By the time I slid out of Kat's car, Mom was at my side. She tried to hug me, but I dodged her just in time. I don't like public affection, so I handed her my backpack instead of a hug. She gave me a funny look—did she notice my still heavy pack from the lunch I hadn't eaten?

Nikki and Sam came running over to us, "Mrs. Byrnes, we had so much fun. We wish you could have come."

Gag me, I thought, heading to Mom's car.

Nikki and Sam talked the entire trip home. Mom didn't say much. She glanced in the mirror and winked at me. I half-smiled back.

After we dropped the girls off, I let the silence in the car surround me. I couldn't wait to pull into our driveway and though I was relieved to be home and near Mom, I couldn't wait to get away from her. I didn't know what had happened earlier—that soul-sinking feeling that the world would end, yet no one else had noticed. I decided not to talk about it.

When I opened the garage door, Lady, our golden retriever, came bounding out. I wanted to hurry to my room for safety, but first, I had to get Lady a cookie. The clink of the treat jar caused her ears to raise. She wagged her tail and trotted toward me.

"Come on, Lady," I said, tossing the cookie to her. She caught it with a quick snap, and I patted her head. "Good girl." Lady licked my hand. "Let's take a nap."

I planned to stay in my room at the end of the hall where it's quiet. It faces the south, so I had Mom get some blackout curtains to keep it dark. She won't let me paint the walls black, but I'd finagled the black drapes and bedsheets.

I'd be safe in my room, surrounded by my Marvel Superhero and *Supernatural* posters, until dinner time. Dad would want to talk about the field trip. He'd crossed the Golden Gate Bridge for work often, so he'd want to get the goods. I'd be careful to stick to the facts.

Tomorrow would be a new day, and with luck, this craziness will have disappeared never to return.

CLAIRE

The smell of strawberry shampoo with a faint odor of seashore penetrated the air when Neala, along with Nikki and Sam, piled into the car. Neala, who was taller than the other girls, sat in the front, stuffing her backpack between her feet. The girls in the back chatted about the field trip. I noticed Neala didn't offer much; then again, it wasn't unusual.

I learned my lesson as a chauffeur with my older daughter, Sarah. Since she'd started middle school, I wasn't to participate in chitchat and definitely not allowed to sing along with the radio. I was there to drive. Period. As miles accrued, I grabbed opportunities to eavesdrop on real happenings in their lives.

Neala appeared skittish. She pushed the radio buttons repeatedly as if looking, but not finding, a particular station. Clearly she tried to avoid me. After the other girls got out of the car, Neala gazed out her window until we approached our house.

Keeping my eyes on the road, I heard her seatbelt unclick. As I put the car in park, Neala lunged out of the car without her stuff. "Hey! Don't forget your backpack; it will stink to high heaven if you leave it in here overnight," I called.

"Okay," Neala bemoaned, flipping her long hair and stepping back. Reaching into the car to get it, she added, "I'm tired, I'm taking Lady to my room."

"Empty out your lunch box, and don't leave your homework until too late," I said as the door from the garage into the family room slammed shut.

After hanging my keys on the hook, I surveyed the family room. It appeared mostly tidy, except for the clean laundry piled on the opened reclining section of the couch that needed folding. An empty beer bottle sat on the glass coffee table. As I scooped up the laundry and headed to clean the table, I stopped myself midstride. Not my bottle, not my problem, I thought. I'd learned to recognize codependency traits after marriage counseling with my ex.

I used to take on everyone's problems, especially my ex's, which resulted in not paying adequate attention to my own. I thought being a good wife meant putting him first. Now, I practice keeping that dysfunction in check. I think of the flight attendant's message while on the plane—put your own oxygen mask on first. Then you can help others.

I left the bottle.

Taking laundry to the kitchen, I caught wafting, savory smells from the vegetables I'd put in the oven earlier. In a couple of hours, everyone would be home for dinner. I folded the clothes. Soon, the evening routine would begin, which would lead into another day, just like the one before.

CHAPTER TWO

CLAIRE

Neala, my youngest, with her quick smile and keen sense of humor, made my days enjoyable. She liked solitude, spending time alone with her toy animals and books. She had Kane's height, dark hair, my fair complexion and a compulsion for honesty. She's self-conscious, cautious, and remote. She is my quiet one. Easy to imagine since both her parents are introverts.

Sarah, my daughter from my first marriage, nearly ten years older than Neala, is anything but quiet. She's always been outgoing and confident. As a high-achieving student, she regularly had friends at the house to work on projects and extracurricular activities. She also liked to sing and dance on stage. Once Neala came along, Sarah adapted to being a big sister quickly by learning to share and compromise.

Since Neala is the baby, and odds were good she'd remain the baby, she wouldn't need to adjust to sharing or cooperating. By sixth grade, her isolation aggravated me, so I sought a more stimulating environment for her.

We enrolled Neala in the expeditionary learning program through our school district. She didn't have to transfer, but she would get to know other kids from nearby towns who opted to relocate. She would benefit from a more active syllabus and mandatory participation in group functions.

We knew it would challenge her to find her passion, pique her curiosity, and teach her to think beyond textbooks. She'd also have to learn to deal with others. As her parents, we made a decision, and we signed her up.

Students entered the program in sixth grade and continued through the end of eighth grade. The program's success was based upon quality of work and critical thinking, rather than the standardized curriculum, which thus far, had bored Neala.

This educational program offered Neala the opportunity to work with other students and collaborate with them to achieve common goals. There were outdoor field trips—six to eight each year. Some were day trips, and some were weeklong camping and hiking experiences.

An eighth-grader, Neala would go to Yosemite. They would be going during the winter months to backpack and camp. In the snow. In tents.

Neala and Kane enjoyed shopping for her gear, and both of them had no problem reaching for high-end items. Although Neala liked the program, she resisted turning in her fieldwork and didn't keep her required journaling up-to-date. She could pass most tests without completing the homework, but each semester became more demanding.

At first, I felt happy when the report cards contained a few Cs, at least I knew her assignments challenged her. From K through fifth grade, she brought home As. I wanted middle school to push her. She started to complain that kids at school "annoyed" her. It became a daily gripe. She didn't want to do anything after school—not hang out with friends, nor go to parties—she even dropped out of sports and Girl Scouts.

As the Yosemite trip approached, Neala seemed both excited and nervous. This whole year had been arduous, I looked toward high school for the needed change. The day the kids set off for Yosemite, Kane and I brought Neala to school. Parent drivers—who I considered incredibly courageous—would chaperone the students by transporting and accompanying them on the expedition.

Kane and I were glad that one parent going with the kids was an RN. The teachers were trained in safety, and parents packed items for protection against the elements. I still remember a teacher telling us that cotton kills.

"If cotton gets wet, it won't hold in body heat." she'd said. "Polyester, wool, and fleece are good choices." I made sure Neala packed the right clothing. Not one fiber of cotton. I wanted my kid to come back. Alive.

Before leaving, the faculty, parents, and students participated in a ritual performed before each of the program's demanding trips. This one touched me. They started by lining all the kids into two rows, facing each other. One of the lead teachers read a Native American poem about passage from childhood to adulthood. Then they took a large vial of ashes from last year's trip and marked each of the student's foreheads. Following tradition, the empty vial would be refilled with this year's campfire ashes and brought back for the next eighth-grade class.

Each student stood tall, soot smeared across their face, as the teachers gave their final encouraging words. They spoke about the steps the kids would take on this journey, and how they would transform by the time they returned.

The eighth-graders learned about acceptance of themselves and others—ready to enter ninth grade as unique and authentic individuals.

I cried after the vehicles departed. I don't think Neala knew how much I cried when she left for her trips. When the students returned, and we got Neala home we reconnected her. She admitted she liked the trip, although she didn't elaborate.

NEALA

I can't believe my parents made me go. Yosemite in the snow. Dad took me to the outdoor shop and got me a sub-zero mummy sleeping bag. Didn't that tell him something?

The teachers and parents did a ceremony before we left, it excited me, but at the same time, it scared me a little. Just what did they mean we would be transformed? Didn't they think we would make it back alive? They said when we got back, it would be our turn to put good mojo ashes into the vial. I hope nothing wrong happens, and I am not the one to curse the ashes by being such a fraidy cat.

I don't enjoy these long trips so much anymore. Maybe I liked them in the beginning—I was out of the classroom and learning about nature. But now, the kids drive me crazy. Being packed in a car was bad enough, but the nonstop jabbering, punctuated only by them singing off-key to the radio, put me on edge. I tried to escape into sleep, but their garble kept me awake.

Part of this program involved teachers giving us solutions to problems, and we needed to figure out how they arrived at their conclusions. For example, before we left for Yosemite, we had to write a report about the Sierra Miwoks who had lived on the land. I chose to create a character and describe what daily life might have been like—recognizing plants, tracking animals, and living off the land—without modern tools and science. How did they survive without the sophisticated gear we have now?

Mom liked the story I made up. "Kaliskah of the Coyotes." I imagined being Kaliskah wandering in the Sierra's. How peaceful it would be to forage plants. The silence of the forest soothed my soul. As Kaliskah, I wasn't scared. My friends, the coyotes, protected me, and even alone in the woods, I wasn't frightened.

The reality was much different. Camping on a freezing mountain with a jumble of kids frightened me more than I thought. At first, I wondered how I would deal with so many kids always in my space. I also thought about what to do if I freak out again, but that didn't happen.

It turns out mountain climbing, setting up camp in the wilderness, and being far away from home is what really scared me. I couldn't wait to get back to the safety of my house. I missed Mom and Lady.

If my parents knew I loathed these trips, they'd be crushed. They seemed to think this kind of adventure would be right for me. I kept thinking about the world flipping at the beach and how out of control everything seemed.

Plus, I was getting pretty tired of being told how excellent my grades would be if I turned assignments in on time. The problem was, I worried too much about flunking. In the end, I would rather get a zero credit than an "F."

When it came time to set up our tents, only a few girls helped. The rest expected the boys to come over and set up for them. I called bullshit. First, I like to take care of myself and my own stuff. Depending on others to do your work is lame. Second, the whole point of pitching your tent was mastering skills. If the boys did all the work, how would those girls learn to survive?

On top of that, some girls started crushing on the popular boys. After three years of those guys in my face, they might as well be my brothers. Crushing on one would be gross.

The third night of the trip, my group found a fairly flat spot with just a small slope to pitch our tent. The icy ground made it hard to hammer in stakes. After a few solid swings with the mallet, I drove in two main stakes to secure the tent. I felt really proud of myself.

One boy, Jacob, is powerful, and he had a hard time cracking through the ice, but not me. Sure, go ahead and crush girls, but when it comes time to be warm, you'll all be coming to me.

I spent time alone on this trip. During the hikes, I lagged behind until we reached our destination. I couldn't tell if I became fed up with the classes, the teachers, or the kids. I wasn't feeling like myself. And the lingering fear of the world crashing down around me stalked me every step of the way. I thought a lot about it, but I felt embarrassed to say anything. I realized the worries bounced around in my head because I couldn't figure out a way to bring it up or talk to anyone about it.

By the time we came home, alive and well, I realized I had grown on that mountain. Carrying my own load, keeping calm when our food supply dwindled, and learning how strong I am, especially with those stakes, made me feel better about myself.

I learned to depend on my own resources, mostly because I was afraid to trust anyone during the trip. But the shadow of my obsession about losing control grew. Like a crashing avalanche, the fear roared in my head as it devoured everything in its path.

CLAIRE

When I met Kane, I was a single mom. Sarah was about six years old at the time. She and Kane became fast friends. Without her father around, Sarah welcomed Kane, who filled the void. Sarah was nearly ten years old when Neala arrived. It seems impossible how fast time has flown by. Kane and I are prepared for Sarah to move out of our home and into a house with her sorority sisters from Sonoma State. There would only be Neala and me to fill our days until Kane came home from work. On busy days, I'd fantasized about my future. In the next year, Neala would be off to high school and she would be driving herself to school. I'd finally have some time for me.

Or so I thought.

As eighth grade ended, Neala decided to attend her first dance. She had no interest in the Halloween Bash or the Winter Wonderland formals, but the Spring Fling grabbed her interest. Neala even asked for a new outfit. I got excited for her to find a dress. I'd not seen her in anything but jeans in a few years.

The outfit she picked made her look glamorous. A black dress, strapless, with maroon lace across its bodice—it was a beauty. And wow, her legs went on for miles, especially in her strappy high-heeled sandals. She moved with grace and confidence.

Kane and my decision to admit her into the middle-school outdoor program had been a success. She'd blossomed into a lovely flower.

Neala's interest in school went beyond standardized learning and testing, and therefore she was willing to look at other high school choices in Pleasant Hills. Besides Laughton High, our school district offered a technology high school, an art-based high school academy, and a charter school called Norden High School.

Tech High hosted an open house to present their curriculum. Neala asked if we could check it out. While there, she ran into a few older kids from her outdoor program. They filled her in on the new charter school, Norden, and they told her about the fun and challenging program, similar to the one she currently attended.

The next day, Neala and I researched Norden's website. The classes, which included blacksmithing and learning to speak Mandarin, sounded exciting to Neala. She mentioned each grade level participated in an outdoor adventure as well as local creek clean ups and community restoration. Neala filled out the application and submitted a 500-word essay to qualify.

Norden accepted Neala and she couldn't wait to tell her friends. Everyone was glad for her. Some of her classmates had been accepted there as well. Two weeks before school began, a parent meeting was set up to go over Norden's expectations from students and parents. They also discussed what families could expect from faculty and staff. That's when she learned the outdoor adventures were weeklong field trips.

At Norden, each class—from freshmen to seniors would attend a week-long outing which would challenge them and bond them. Each year was based on an element. The first year was earth (camping), then water (kayaking), air (redwood forest trapeze), and fire (a solo vision quest in nature.) With her experience and all her equipment she'd collected, Neala was a step ahead when it came to the outings.

Ready to start high school, I noticed Neala embraced the thought of becoming independent. Our Neala was on her way.

FRESHMAN YEAR

CHAPTER THREE

NEALA

I didn't want to go to Laughton High School. There were too many kids, and so many dumb rules that the place seemed like a prison. It was like I was preparing for a four-year jail sentence. My friend Joe suggested I check out Norden High. I did and decided it would be a good fit. I wrote an essay and was proud that it earned me a slot.

I got super excited.

Mom and Dad came to the parent meeting for freshmen. Mom worried that other parents would think she was "too mainstream" to have a kid at a remarkable school like Norden. But when she noticed a dessert table boasting a store-bought cake—not gluten-free, not organic, not homemade, not even special ordered—just a plain old supermarket cake, I think she felt better.

I recognized kids from grade and middle school, but I didn't know them too well. I saw Joe, who's a year ahead of me, but he wasn't there for the meeting. He and some other kids were the entertainment, and they also volunteered to set and clean up. Watching him and his friends jam was my favorite part. I knew he played guitar in middle school, but I was impressed with how good he was now. He and the other musicians gave an example of Norden's curriculum, showing alternative courses—like American Rock Music.

Cool.

I listened to components of the core curriculum, and it didn't sound too bad. I knew I could pass these courses and succeed. I watched other kids, some horsing around and some uneasy. I kind of felt in the middle. I was nervous about being at a new school, especially when faculty discussed field trips. It sounded like my middle school outdoor program, but Norden even had a vegetable garden on campus. I couldn't wait to get started.

When I thought about our upcoming camping trip, my stomach squeezed tight. It became so uncomfortable to think about that I had to remind myself to breathe. This coastal trip included the freshman class of thirty-two students and two lead teachers. The idea of this outing made me feel anxious, so, I pushed the field trip out of my mind.

One dark-haired girl caught my attention. I noticed how confident she seemed. She was hanging out with a boy—they looked like they were close, but not boyfriend/girlfriend close. Maybe her brother? I didn't know. As much as I wanted to meet her, the thought of introducing myself intimidated me. I didn't want to push my way into their friendship. But she looked like a fun person to know—not gabby and loud like a lot of the other girls.

By the end of the meeting, I'd learned about the four-year college prep program and was ready to begin. Dad got me a phone and a laptop—gifts for getting accepted into Norden. I could tell he was proud of me, but I felt sorry for him. Mom had signed Dad and me up to do some prep-work at school.

A brand-new charter school, Norden didn't have a yard maintenance guy yet, so faculty asked parents to pitch in for a work weekend to make the school grounds and quad area safe and clean for incoming students. And thanks to Mom, Dad and I were a part of that team.

A few days later, Dad and I arrived early for the school's first day of the work weekend. He brought a push broom, a Weed Wacker, and a wheelbarrow. A few other kids and parents showed up, one of them was the interesting girl from parent night. She came with her dad, too. She told me her name was Nola Stinson, and we shared a good laugh about our somewhat matching first names. We both have dark hair, too. She and her dad were friendly, and I liked how they made fun of each other, the playful way I do with Dad. She said she would look for me in class. I felt happy and ready to begin this new chapter in my life.

During a welcoming ceremony held the opening week of school, I got my first glimpse of upper-class students, teachers, and faculty. I stood near the flagpole in the quad and guessed who the secretary and other office staff were, and I figured out where my classes were located. Some upper-class students drew chalk lines from the entry of the school to the location of freshmen classes. At first, I thought they were sarcastic, but the chalk arrows made a difference for me. I wasn't late for my classes.

I got a school planner and filled it in with course assignments, projects, and report due dates, and I made notations of teachers' email addresses for each course. The first week was exactly how I expected high school to be. The kids, the teachers, the homework—everything. But the idea of the freshmen excursion still bummed me. When I thought about the trip, my stomach twisted. I tried to ignore how fast the day was approaching, but there it was, highlighted in my school planner for the third week of school. Each day brought me closer to the outing.

I wasn't sure if the uneasiness came because this was a new group of kids, or if I was just hesitant about going, period. I camped in this area along the coast with my old school, but besides camping, we would be hiking from campsite to campsite. We did that in Yosemite, I reminded myself. In the snow. Quit being such a baby. You lived, didn't you?

We were supposed to bring our gear in prior to the trip and have the teachers approve it. The camping excursion was set to begin in two weeks. From Monday through Friday. The Monday we left, freshmen needed to arrive early to load up parent vehicles for transportation to the coastal campsite. Whenever teachers talked about the trip in our classes, my hands seemed to open and close on their own, and my legs trembled. I never felt like this while sitting in a classroom before, or even when I presented oral reports. Then, the image of the Golden Gate Bridge swinging and the dark clouds consuming the sun flashed and I gulped.

CHAPTER FOUR

CLAIRE

"Mom," Neala gasped, "Stop the car!"

I jammed on the brakes, but there was nothing in the road. "What is it, honey?" I glanced at her.

"Can we please just go home?" Neala's long fingers gripped the door handle, and her body seemed rooted in the front passenger seat of the car. When I saw her face—white as clean sheets—my stomach dropped. Her breathing was ragged, and her eyes wide. Something was wrong.

Careful of students on bikes and skateboards, I approached Norden High School and found a slot to park the car. I looked at my daughter. Where was Neala's usual bubbly personality? My confident high-schooler from this morning had vanished. Instead, she looked like an eight-year-old child wallowing in fear. Perspiration glistened on her brow. A red patch bloomed from her throat and moved up toward her jaw. Was she ill? Did she have a fever?

"Do you hurt anywhere or feel sick?" I asked with a croaky voice. Suddenly, I couldn't swallow, I was cotton-mouthed from my quick-forming fears.

"I don't know," Neala pleaded. "I don't know, Mom. But I can't move my legs. They feel as heavy as cement. Please, just take me home." Her eyes pooled with fresh tears that threatened to ruin her carefully applied eyeliner.

Moments passed.

What on earth could be wrong with her legs? Possible diseases flew through my mind. Lime disease? Multiple Sclerosis? Chronic fatigue syndrome? Jesus! I delved into devastating thoughts. I searched the parking lot for teachers or parents, but it was empty; everyone was in their class by now. Seconds continued to tick away and alternating choices—to either run to the office or call Kane—consumed me. Neala's tears spilled over. I opened the console looking for tissues, found some stained coffee shop napkins, and offered them to Neala.

"Here, Cookie, wipe your eyes before you smear your make-up," I said, mustering a soothing voice. Calm down, I thought, I need to think about this.

Neala's emerald eyes narrowed as she snatched the paper napkins from me. She lowered the sun visor mirror to survey her make-up, then dabbed the corners of her eyes. "Just take me home. I can't move, I can't go in there." Neala pulled her hoody over her head.

That's when I changed from concerned to alpha parent. "Neala, you need to get out of the car, right now. Stop playing games. I need to get to work, and you're late for class." I yelled at her hoody.

That hoody move was Neala's way of shutting me out. Case closed. Not up for discussion. Neala scrunched so deep into her seat there was no way I could pry her out. I decided the best thing to do was to go home. I think we both felt relief when I started the car. I tried to think of what to say, "It will be better tomorrow." Or maybe, "When I went to high school, I was nervous, too." I wanted to comfort Neala, but comparatively, everything was trivial. I couldn't put my finger on what happened, so I said nothing.

Neala's tear-stained face looked pinker, but her eyebrows were furrowed. Clearly, she wasn't happy with her odd behavior either because she fidgeted with the zipper pull on her backpack and looked straight ahead for the drive home.

Lady greeted us at the door. I think the dog noticed the difference in our routine because she circled around Neala and wagged her tail until Neala acknowledged her. Ordinarily, Lady relentlessly begged for a treat when we got home.

Keeping my thoughts to myself, I went to the kitchen for a cup of coffee. Usually feeling shameful to use the one-cup-at-a-time machine I ignored the images of K-Cup mounds in the landfill, and I was grateful for my quick individual cup. Neala lingered in the hall. I wasn't sure if she wanted to talk about what just happened, so I asked if she'd like some cocoa, inviting her to join me.

"No," she whispered. "I'm so sorry, Mom, I don't know what happened." She came over to me and because she'd grown inches taller than me this past summer, rounded her shoulders and leaned in for a hug. I wrapped my arms around her and reached up to stroke her dark, wavy hair. Her height established she'd matured, but fear revealed her youth and vulnerability.

Patting her shoulder and rubbing her back, I let her fall into me and led her to the couch to sit. She broke into sobs. Her inhaled breaths racked her body, and her back and head trembled. Moans escape her mouth. She continued to bawl for a few minutes. I pushed stray strands of hair out of her wet face and continued to rub her back. Neala's cries became sniffs and whimpers. She felt heavy on my chest.

Minutes later, Neala lifted her head and wiped her nose on her sleeve. I laughed at her and groaned when I stretched over to the far end of the coffee table for the tissues.

"You are disgusting," I playfully scolded. I offered a weak smile and the tissue box.

Neala bashfully smiled, said she was too tired to talk and led Lady to her room for a nap. I microwaved my now-cold coffee and called Kane.

"You know, I sort of felt an attack like that once," Kane confided. "I was on the job with old man Whitaker. Pissed off at the crew, he got in his truck and left us there to figure it out. Everything became surreal—like I was underwater or something. Being young, I grabbed my smokes, sat on a sawhorse, and smoked a few minutes. I thought about what a bastard Whitaker was, then the wave passed. After that, I got back to work."

I waited for a beat. Kane often takes his time to spill his words. I imagined him, wearing his cap, furrowing his dark eyebrows, and his mustache twitching. He was strong from the physical work he did. In my mind's eye, I could see his rough hands draped across the steering wheel as he told me his story.

"Funny," he said. "I don't think I ever thought about it again. I know I never told anyone."

"So you think this is a one-time thing with Neala?" I asked, hating the sound of uncertainty in my voice.

"Hope so."

"Maybe you can talk to her, let her know about your experience?"

"Well, maybe, we should wait. See what happens before we make a thing of it. I know how you are."

"What's that supposed to mean?"

"Well, I know you." I heard a soft chuckle. "And I wouldn't change one thing about you. I'll see you tonight."

The conversation left me wondering if I was overreacting or overthinking Neala's behavior. Could I be the reason she was overwhelmed? After talking with Kane, I called the school for Neala's excused absence, and then I let work know Neala and I were taking a sick day. I poured the crappy coffee down the sink and headed outside to the backyard. I told myself to stop thinking about all the negative possibilities then decided to enjoy the bonus day at home. Outside, the crisp fall air felt good. I thought it best for Neala and me to leave today's business behind us.

CHAPTER FIVE

NEALA

We'd approached Norden, my eyesight tunneled, and dots floated by the windshield of the car. I tried to talk to Mom, but my throat constricted. The sensation of being choked slapped at me. Not caring the car still moved, I grabbed the door handle. Mom shot a look at me. When she saw my face, she turned stark white.

"It's okay," Mom had said when I tried to explain my inability to move.

Most kids were already in the quad, and parents were leaving the parking lot. Mom waited with me. For twenty minutes, she got in and out of the car.

"Just let me tell the office you're sick," She said. But I didn't want her to leave me alone. Eventually, I got her to turn the car around and go home.

During the drive, I felt like the car was closing in on me. I kept the darkness at bay, but I felt it push back. I persistently looked ahead while Mom drove. I felt guilt-ridden because Mom was worried about me, and she was running late for her job. This morning, the longer I sat in the car, the more she tried her mamma bear tactics. When Mom is scared, she rants.

"You need to think about others, you know. The world can't stop because you don't know why you can't get out of the car." She stared ahead, but I could tell she was glaring. "You are going to have to do it. Just move. There is nothing, nothing to be afraid of at school. I don't understand what's going on with you!"

I wanted to tell her to shut up, but I couldn't blame her. I was thinking the same thoughts. But I was just as scared.

I was relieved when we left school and finally turned onto our street. I wanted to get out of the car and away from Mom.

When the car stopped, I reached around the backseat for my books. That's when I noticed the camping gear for the freshman campout. Heaviness pressed my chest. My neck felt stiff, and it hurt to turn my head. I couldn't think about camping right now. All I wanted was to get to my room.

When we came through the door, the dog was the only happy one. I cried like a big baby, but Mom was cool. She comforted me even if we still didn't know what to do about my behavior this morning. My cheeks were hot from embarrassment, and my legs, though I could now move them, felt shaky as I climbed the stairs. I didn't want to talk to Mom and sure as heck didn't want to hear her talking to Dad about me.

I could tell she didn't know what to do. At first, I listened to her pace in the kitchen, then I heard the scrape of the kitchen chair sliding across the floor. It sounded like she was at her desk. I kept my mind occupied with Mom's actions, because I didn't want to feel my emotions.

My stomach hurt, and my head was dizzy, but at least my vision was returning. What if I'm not just scared, but what if something is wrong with me? What if I have brain cancer or some other weird thing? What if I am crazy or, God, I just don't want to know.

When I got upstairs, I flung myself on the bed and buried my head under a pillow. What had happened this morning? Mom attempted to act indifferent on the way home, but I could tell she was freaked out, too. I tried to be okay, but that terrible feeling kept clawing up my back. Like the eighth-grade outing to the Golden Gate Bridge—that same feeling of being out of control had returned after a year.

I got up, closed my shades, made my room as dark as I could, and curled up on my bed. Lady snuggled in close. I scratched her behind her ears, and I calmed down. Lady gives nose-nudges when you stop petting her, so she kept at me until we fell asleep.

CLAIRE

It happened again today. Neala couldn't get out of the car. Yesterday, I hoped it was a one-time thing, but a second time? Now, I couldn't be sure. I was shaking by the time I got home. I stood at the kitchen sink, fearing Neala's behavior could not easily be remedied. Wild birds dipped and pecked at the seed in the backyard.

Why can't I be a mama bird, shovel food into my young, and then push them out of the nest? Cruel as the thought was, after today, I would be okay with it. Hoping my breath would expel this growing pit in my chest, tears swelled. What was wrong with my daughter?

I recounted the past summer, to think of what might have led to her odd behavior. Neala passed a physical before starting school, a requirement along with an extensive health history for upcoming school activities. No red flags popped up from her doctor except she was behind on her tetanus shot. I vowed to have her vaccinated before she set off on various field trips.

My heart lurched—tetanus would affect her muscles! What had I done to my poor child? Shame felt like a sludge-filled wave hovering above me. My fault. All my fault. It was harder to breathe. Harder to think. Stop it, my inner voice commanded. I reached over the counter and snatched my phone. I called my office to let them know I would not be in. I needed another sick day.

I knew I had to get help for Neala. My health coverage information was in the car. Fumes of oil and paint thinner hit my nose when I went to the garage to get my purse. I dug the insurance card out of my wallet, and not sure where else to begin for help, I called Dr. Kessler, Neala's pediatrician.

Frustration threatened to get the best of me when the office manager told me they couldn't get Neala in for two days.

Two days wasn't good enough. Maybe I should go to urgent care or call 911? Apprehension crept up my spine. You are ridiculous, my inner voice jeered at me. Think. Neala isn't putting herself or others in danger. Calm down.

After tossing this morning's cold coffee, I put the kettle on. In the drawer, I found a pen and the backside of an envelope. Sacking the thought of making urgent calls, I kept Neala home for the rest of the day.

I called the school to excuse Neala, and they asked if I would bring in her camping gear. I hoped she would go on the camping trip and agreed to bring her equipment to school for inspection. With that done, I called the nurse to book a visit with Dr. Kessler. Watching the tea brew, I contemplated checking on Neala, but if she was awake, I wasn't sure what I'd say to her. I sat with my tea and lulled through another unplanned day at home.

CHAPTER SIX

NEALA

The panic kept coming, and even though I thought it was because of the camping trip, Mom and Dad forced me to go. I told them that I'd done enough hiking and camping in middle school. In what I thought was a brilliant idea, I offered to do the coursework without going on the trip. I realized I didn't have it in me to go on long expeditions with schoolmates anymore. The idea of twenty-four hours, times multiple days, had taken its toll on me. Maybe I wasn't cut out to be social for that length of time.

That's when I discovered that Mom had dropped my stuff off at school yesterday. She took it upon herself to move forward with the camping trip. Apparently, she didn't take my standpoint into consideration. I was furious!

The day of the field trip, my legs froze on the way to school. Fear hit me like a fast baseball, and I couldn't get out of the car. Uncertain why, I was afraid, really petrified to go. Mom practically made a scene when she went to the office to tell them I wouldn't get out of the car. Then some teachers came to talk to me. They agreed Mom could get me early from the trip if I needed to go home.

In the multi-use room at school, Mom and I huddled around my camping gear, while other kids and their parents gathered around theirs. When it was time to load our things into the attending parents' vehicles, I almost lost my shit and cried.

It isn't like I get homesick, which I'm sure is what everyone thought. It's simple. I don't like to be around people. One thing about this trip, which was good for me—I didn't really know anyone. Maybe they would leave me alone. It was decided that I would ride to the campsite with Mrs. Cutler, the lead female teacher. I then learned that two other girls would ride with her, too, at least I could feel a little less awkward riding with the teacher.

I made Mom promise—which she did—she would get me if I had the urge to leave. So I kissed her goodbye the way I always have in crowds—I lean the crown of my head toward her, and she kisses the top of my head. It's been our thing since middle school.

For two days, our class camped and hiked along dusty trails and sandy shores. We scribbled notes for our science class, and drew sketches of shells, birds, and small animals. I ate half-cooked noodles because the person in charge of our group's camp stove didn't bring enough propane. For the rest of the week, we begged for stove privileges from other groups.

During the day, I kept busy with my assignments, so I wasn't too wound up. But by the afternoon, I would be dying to have Mom get me. I challenged myself to see if I could hold out. Drained from emotions by the end of the day, I was glad to fall into my sleeping bag each night if only to check off another day.

By Wednesday, I was halfway through the ordeal. Good job. After lunch, we hiked from the beach to a meadow. I was the last hiker in line, but Nola fell back with me. As we hiked up a sand dune, she blurted out, "Fucking sand in my shoes!"

I watched a smile crack over her face.

"Fucking sand in my shoes, too."

We struggled a few paces upward at a time. By the time we reached its peak, Nola had shared that she wanted to work with the California Forestry Department when she graduated college. She wanted to be an environmentalist.

I'd wondered what I would do after graduation when she suddenly stopped in front of me. She turned, adjusting her backpack, and then placed a finger in her dimpled cheek, struck a coy pose and she asked, "You know who's hot?"

"From school?" I asked.

"The hottest ever," she coaxed.

"Jared Padelecki; Sam, from *Supernatural!*" We shouted simultaneously, then giggled and discussed all of our favorite episodes. We got along well. Having similar names and compatible interests made us natural friends. Other kids noticed our friendship, too, and I became immediately accepted by her group of friends from middle school. I was almost sad when Friday arrived.

After the trip, I hoped I would feel better about this whole getting-out-of-the-car thing. Meeting Nola made going to classes more comfortable, but I was still gripped with dread when Mom drove onto the campus.

Worried about me, Mom and Dad had me follow up with my doctor.

CHAPTER SEVEN

CLAIRE

When Sarah was a baby, she became ill. She was healthy one day and on the verge of death the next. After that frightening event, I learned health insurance was a must-have. Without health insurance, Sarah's heart virus could have killed her or bankrupted me, or both. Since then, I have been an advocate for medical well-care for children. Yes, I get overprotective, some might even say paranoid. Let them hear the words, "She has a fifty-percent chance to make it through the night," from a cardiologist and see how that changes their tune.

Images of Neala flitted through my mind. Her behavior mystified me. I tried to recall any specific trauma in her life but came up with nothing.

I emailed our insurance company and asked for detailed benefits for psychiatric care. After my divorce from Sarah's father, she'd had episodes of depression. I wanted to be sure Sarah didn't think she had any responsibility for our divorce. Kids do that.

Her father's rage led to spousal abuse, and it became healthier for Sarah and me to leave. We divorced, he stayed out of the picture, and I never looked back. Then, because of my single-parent status, I obtained group therapy at no cost and private sessions on a sliding scale. This time, married with insurance benefits from my job, I didn't know what the out-of-pocket fees would cost.

Viewing the website, my eyes widened with optimism when I saw a long list of providers. I called mental health professionals—those located closest to us first. After a few calls, tightness pulled from my belly to my chest, and I gripped my phone with frustration. As I waited on hold with office number four, my dissatisfaction turned to anger and then to fear. What if we couldn't find help? So far, none of the practitioners were taking new clients. Or they didn't accept adolescent patients. My long list shortened. Doctors' offices were getting further away.

After a few more unsuccessful calls, I made a connection. "Okay, that will work," I said to the receptionist, relief palpable in my voice. The constrictive bands squeezing my heart, loosened. "Yes, I will look for the email from your office," I said, wondering what kinds of forms I'd have to fill out before the appointment. I wasn't sure how to tell Kane we would be responsible for $50 co-pay fees for the visits, but at least we had a scheduled appointment to look forward to. The second step for Neala's consultation was to fill out the medical form with help from her pediatrician, Dr. Kessler.

A grueling forty-eight hours later, Neala and I were at Dr. Kessler's office. Neala asked me to come into the exam room with her. Dr. Kessler, with his curly white hair on the sides and thinning strands on top, wore wire-rimmed spectacles and a white coat. He sat on a swivel stool and smiled at Neala.

"How are you today?" He checked his notes from the assistant. "I see you can't walk onto your school campus, eh?"

Neala nodded and then looked down.

"Okay, let's take a good look at your health first." After warming the stethoscope on his sleeve, the doctor put it on Neala's chest.

Heart? Good. Lungs? Good.

Next, he checked her reflexes with the rubber hammer. Neala's toes kicked into the air with each tap below the knee, and Dr. Kessler confirmed nothing "organic" was related to the problem. "No issues moving your legs today, Neala?" he asked her.

She shook her head.

"I can't move my legs when I get to school. Mom drives me," Neala reported.

The doctor swiveled his chair and referred to his notes. "Well, anxiety happens to most of us at one time or another. I don't know why it is, Neala," Dr. Kessler said in his thick, foreign accent, "that the people who seem to care about everything so much have anxiety, and the weirdos who don't care about a thing, you know, they never have it." He chuckled and patted her on the shoulder. "You may be asking too much of yourself right now. Maybe you should take it easy for a while. I will give your mom referrals to a behavior therapist. How does that sound, huh?" Then he looked at me and asked, "You made an appointment with a psychiatrist, Mrs. Byrnes? Utilizing both types of treatment is the most effective."

"I did," I said. "We will meet with the psychiatrist in a couple of weeks. We're still looking for a behavioral therapist, so I'm glad you have a list of additional references for us."

Neala quizzically searched my face. I smiled to reassure her she would be okay. Then I addressed the doctor.

"Okay, Dr. Kessler, I will find a behavioral therapist soon. I don't want to put Neala on medication, but would you please prescribe something to calm her when we get to school? Something she can take to ward off anxiety when she feels it coming?"

What a hypocrite I am! Always saying I am against medicating kids. I felt ashamed for bringing medicine into the conversation. But watching her in pain was difficult, and I knew how my own happy pills helped me now and again.

"That isn't something I can do, Mrs. Byrnes," he said.

I was grateful he didn't have judgment in his voice.

He continued to address me, "A psychiatrist will be able to prescribe medications, which may help her condition. Neala should see her psychiatrist for medication, and her behavioral therapist to help her develop coping skills. As for my diagnosis, I think Neala should watch what she eats, exercise, and get enough sleep. All of those will contribute to better health overall, which helps reduce anxiety." Looking at Neala, he added, "Perhaps you can try to keep organized. That helps, too, eh?"

My eyebrows shot together with that remark. Other than clothes all over the bedroom floor, Neala was a neat freak.

Dr. Kessler's office gave a note excusing Neala from school for the morning. We both knew it was a waste of paper. There was no way she would get to class today. We went home, and I made calls for a behavior therapist. The average cost was $125 for a one-hour session, and effective therapy sessions were four times per month. The bad news—insurance did not cover this. Researching further, I found most drug rehabilitation programs are included in the plan, and I couldn't help but wonder—if the insurance companies provided preventive care for patients, perhaps they could divert future drug and alcohol dependency.

NEALA

Relief washed over me when we left the doctor. He's been good to me since I was a little kid, but I didn't like the weird smells nor sitting on paper. I was glad I didn't have to get undressed. My body is different, and my boobs are getting bigger. Thankfully, he listened to my heart and lungs under my shirt.

Mom was fidgety today. She kept talking, insisting I get medicine. Wasn't she against it? I didn't want to take pills, but I also didn't like the way my legs froze up when I got to school. Maybe it would be worth a try.

I'm glad Mom and I went home after my check-up. I didn't like going to class late; it is one more thing to fret about. Dr. Kessler said something which made sense, though; I do worry about stuff sometimes. I remember my 8th-grade teacher, Mr. Summer complaining to Mom once. "She turns her assignments in late. Look at this picture she drew for a field report," Mr. Summer said, handing the report to mom. "It is A+ work, but it is three weeks late. Being tardy on this assignment reduced the grade to a D."

Mom looked at me with sad eyes. She'd helped me with my project, and I'd told her I turned it in. Afraid I didn't do a good job, I kept it in my backpack for a few weeks. When Mr. Summer told the class he would be sending notes to parents because of incomplete work, I dug it out and handed it in. I'd wanted to turn my work in on time, but I wasn't confident it was good enough or know if it was right sometimes, so I'd procrastinate.

When we got home from the doctor, Lady was at the door. Used to this new routine, she didn't even go to the kitchen for a cookie right away. Pausing at the bottom of the stairs, Lady's tail was still, and her big brown eyes watched me. I could tell she was ready to charge up the steps and jump on my bed for a nap.

Because I didn't eat lunch yet, I went to the kitchen. The dog followed me, this time her tail wagged with excitement. She sat by the counter near her cookie jar. Her eyes darted back and forth between me and the cookies, drool on her lower lip.

"God, you are gross!" I said to her, but I figured she didn't care. Her tension mounted when I reached in to get a treat and jiggled the jar. She got up. "Sit," I commanded. She sat. I put the cookie on her nose. She sat steady until I said, "Treat." Tossing her head back, she tipped her nose up, snapped her mouth, caught the cookie as it flew from her nose. Her teeth clacked as she swallowed the treat without chewing.

For the rest of the day, Lady sat on the couch beside me, her muzzle sandwiched between my belly and my elbow. We watched TV until we both fell asleep, almost until dinner time.

CHAPTER EIGHT

CLAIRE

I noticed further occasions where Neala refused to get out of the car. At various parties, outings, or events, she held back. The mood swings had become stronger, and her behavior now showed up off school grounds. I attributed it to her shyness and at first, brushed it off. Then memories of other episodes surfaced. Especially incidents that had happened before she started eighth grade.

One time, Kane had wanted to take us to dinner. Neala was about eleven. When we'd arrived at the restaurant, she'd refused to get out of the car. Kane got physical with her, grabbing her by the arms, trying to pull her from the vehicle. I sat in the passenger seat, overwhelmed. What the hell was happening behind me?

Gasping for air, Neala sobbed. She pushed Kane's hands off of her, but he continued to grab at her. Kane lost his cool and tried to pry her from the car.

"Stop. Stop!" Neala screamed.

I saw him cringe as he attempted to minimize the scene. Her cries attracted attention. Passersby with looks of both shock and empathy left him no choice but to acquiesce. Without a word, he got back into the car, slammed the door, and drove home. Neala had leaped out of the car, banged it shut, and hurried into the house.

Kane and I'd returned to the restaurant, but we barely spoke during dinner. The scene with Neala had made my stomach queasy. Kane's violent behavior had turned my insides into jelly. I lost my appetite. Instead of ordering for myself, I ordered what Neala would like and asked for a doggie bag to take it home to her.

When we got back to the house, Neala was in her room. I could tell she'd been crying. She looked far away and lost.

"I don't know what happened, Mom, but Dad acted like such a jerk."

"I know, Cookie, but he's worried and unsure how to act. When you get into a panic, he feels out of control." I pushed her hair away from her face, but she put it back down.

I cringed at my shallow words and changed the subject. "I brought you a hamburger, the fries were getting cold, so I put them in the microwave for you. Dad's in our room, and the door is closed. Go downstairs and eat."

After that traumatic episode, Kane and I decided it was best to leave Neala at home if she felt the slightest hesitation.

Incidences like that ramped up, especially when we went to a restaurant with a full bar. Those nights, Kane wanted to go drinking more than have dinner. His conduct after a couple of drinks altered and he became moody or irritable. Neala would beg to stay home—I think she picked up on his behavior, too. Typically, Neala and I would be finished with dinner, but Kane would have another round, or two, or maybe three before we could leave.

My opinion? Neala's decision to stay home was a by-product of those full-bar dinners. She started to ask us to bring dinner back for her. When she was younger, she couldn't articulate her feelings, and she'd act out. A lot depended on the restaurant. Coffee shops weren't much of a battle, probably because they weren't that loud, nor did they serve cocktails.

The summer before Neala started high school, her incongruous behavior increased. She wouldn't go to parties she was invited to nor hang around when we threw a party at our house. I suspected the noise was a factor along with the uncontrollable feelings she got when people started drinking.

Her need for control carried into her freshman year culminating with Neala's legs not moving in the school's parking lot.

NEALA

The only thing I liked about going out to dinner with my parents was root beer. My favorite. Mom didn't keep it around the house—too sugary—but when we were at a restaurant, having a root beer was a different story. Other than that, I hated dining out. I used to think restaurants were scary, but it's mostly because Dad kept having "one more beer." Dad orders a beer when we get to restaurants with bars, during dinner, and afterward.

Mom and I would be ready to go, but Dad would order "one more beer." God, I hated that phrase. Mom and I would look at each other and hope that Dad would drink it fast so we could leave. I felt confused. I liked to be with my parents, but I also felt kind of afraid when they drank. Especially Dad. His behavior became unpredictable. He would get mad and pick on either Mom or me. I didn't like it.

When they went without me, I'd feel relieved. I'd get the house to myself. Lady and I hung out and played video games. Mom brought me dinners, which made me happy. But I saw the worry lines on her face. She'd linger and wouldn't leave me alone.

Mom tried to make sure I was pleased. And I was. But I didn't like going out. I enjoyed the food, but blaring noise upset me. Too many people talked at once. I felt backed into a corner and desperate to run. One night, Dad tried to pull me out of the car. It hurt my arm and my feelings. Restaurant dining with my parents became intimidating. I decided I'd rather be alone.

CHAPTER NINE

CLAIRE

One day, Neala's new friend stood at the curb and watched us pull up to school. Traffic had slowed, and the girl walked toward us. I pushed the electric window down on Neala's side.

"Good morning," I said to the young, dark-haired girl.

"Hi," she said with a smile and then looked at Neala. "You gonna get out of the car today, or what?" Obviously, the girl was aware of Neala's complexity with getting out of the car. The girls were in the same grade. Neala told me they had become close on their outdoor trip. The rare days Neala did make it into the classroom, she would come home talking about Nola.

I watched Neala press herself into the seat. "No," was all Neala said and stared at her backpack on the floor.

The girl leaned into the window, getting closer to Neala.

"Come on, I don't want to sit in there bored all by myself."

"Na-ah." Neala shook her head.

I wanted to say something to encourage her, but I waited for her friend to coax her. I guessed the girl sensed what I was thinking because she introduced herself to me. "Since Neala won't tell you who I am, I will. I am Nola." She waved her hand. Several silver rings decorated her fingers.

"Pleased to meet you," I said. "I'm Claire." I'd already known her name, and suspected she was Neala's new friend, but we'd never been introduced.

Nola got back to business with Neala. "Okay, then I am going to sit by Harvard without you. As in all by myself." Nola flashed her pretty smile at Neala then turned on her heel and headed toward campus.

Neala's face flushed, and her brows glistened. There was something about the way she held her mouth that showed me she was flustered.

"Harvard?" I asked.

"Mom, let's just go okay? Take me home," was all I got from her. It wasn't until after I came home from work that evening that Neala filled me in.

"There's a really cute boy, but he's kind of preppy, so we call him Harvard. I think Nola has a crush on him." By the sound of Neala's voice, I thought she might be crushing, too.

Having met Nola and hearing about Harvard, I hoped Neala would get along okay, yet, day after day, no amount of coaxing worked. Teachers and other students came to Neala's side of the car and tried to get her to join them, but Neala shrunk back into the seat, sometimes she even pulled her hoody over her head until they left. Then she would sob all the way home.

I wasn't sure how we ended up here or what to do next. For now, all we could do was be.

CHAPTER TEN

CLAIRE

While I was out walking Lady, a behavioral therapist returned my call. I was happy to be out in the fresh air. The bird calls settled my mind after being cooped up in my office. Thankfully, most of my work routine was flexible. I could juggle my workload and even work from home sometimes. The tricky parts incorporate getting to meetings on time. Luckily, my boss understood that things come up or the inability to control what life threw at you—especially when you have kids. One of my work duties involves making staff schedules. I made a note to maintain empathy for mix-ups and excuse the occasional tardy.

I noticed I spent a good portion of my day on the phone, including anticipating texts from Neala. I even brought my phone on my daily constitutional. I was pleased the call I got from the therapist was about Neala not from Neala.

"I have time to meet with you, Kane, and Neala next Tuesday at six p.m.," Alina Jenkin's said.

My gut twisted because sometimes Kane didn't get home until after six, but I agreed to the appointment. Alina said she worked with several families in the community from different social and economic demographics. She told me she would accept sliding scale fees, but we'd discuss it on Tuesday. Making an appointment with Alina felt like a good sign, and her office was only a 10-minute drive from home.

Two weeks after my initial call, the office of Dr. Marc Teller contacted me. Dr. Teller was a psychiatrist on our insurance plan. His office was a fifty-minute drive without commute traffic factored in. The receptionist let me know she'd email me a patient intake form that afternoon. Dr. Teller would review it and then see if he was willing to work with Neala.

That evening, after a simple dinner of vegetable stew and crusty whole-wheat sourdough, I took my laptop to the living room to search for his email. I read the short message from the nurse practitioner and noted the attachment. Clicking on the icon, I watched the eight pages download. Oh, boy! There are a lot of boxes for me to check with "No" or "Yes."

Scrolling down, I skimmed the questionnaire. Some of the more invasive questions provoked thoughts of catastrophic mental illness. The desire to pull back was intense. I began second-guessing the whole situation. Maybe there wasn't anything wrong with Neala after all.

• Is your child sexually active? I don't know, and I don't think I'm ready to know.

• Does your child ever feel like there is another person in their body? WTF?

• Does your child identify as a different gender? Her favorite movie is *Cars*, and she hates *Barbie* . . . Wait, what am I thinking here?

• Does your child hallucinate? That's kinda why we're here; she's afraid of something she can't see.

• Does your child abuse alcohol or drugs? Don't think so, We talk about drugs occasionally.

• Has your child ever been sexually abused? No. I would know, right? I mean really—I would know, right? She'd have told me. No, that has to be a "No."

• Does anyone in your child's household abuse alcohol or drugs? We drink, but only socially. I mean . . . I'd call it socially.

After that question, I headed toward the kitchen thinking how good a glass of wine would feel—I meant only enough to calm me—but realized the faux pas. A cup of hot chamomile tea would be better. I returned to the living room, sat back down on the couch, tucked my leg under my hips, and steadied my teacup.

Back to the questionnaire. The next set of questions continued:

• How was my pregnancy? Any complications, any surgeries or emergency room visits?

Then following up with eating, sleeping, and bathroom habits. Finally, the questions involved the family—our daily and weekly routines. What we did for relaxation.

As far as I could recall, Neala was a typical child with a normal childhood. Nothing traumatic had happened to her. The only time she went to the emergency room was when she stuck a Q-Tip too deeply into her ear.

Neither Kane nor I physically disciplined the girls though I guess one could say I was a nagger. But if they picked up after themselves and did what they were told—Kane, too—I wouldn't have to badger them so much.

Kane's voice could be tumultuous; the walls trembled when he yelled. It was even worse when he drank. Back to the alcohol question? Nope, still keeping the "No."

No abuse happened in our household. I thought about other places Neala went. She hated after-school care and going to a friend's house for the night. Neala didn't keep secrets, she talked about anything, so I concluded Neala would have told me if anyone was mean or weird to her.

Relieved to have completed the forms, I emailed them back to the doctor. I waited for the office to schedule an appointment. I thought it strange that doctors interviewed patients instead of the other way around. Perhaps this was the result of not having enough pediatric psychiatrists in the area? It took a full week to get a call back from Dr. Teller's office to schedule the appointment. I supposed after we met him, he would have the final say if he'd accepted us.

CHAPTER ELEVEN

CLAIRE

Kane, Neala, and I gathered in Dr. Teller's small office. The room was functional at best, with décor of oatmeal beige, chocolate brown, and Pepto Bismol pink. I first thought he had bad taste but realized I didn't know anything about "colors for crazies."

Sitting on the edge of the seat in the waiting room, I was grateful Kane went to the reception window to check in. Glad he paid the co-pay now; I would not have to think about the bill. I contemplated how we would pay them if we let the co-pays add up.

A few minutes later, Dr. Teller came into the waiting room to introduce himself. I immediately noticed his balding, egg-shaped head, and while I contained my composure, I smiled and shook his hand. Mesmerized by his dome, I only half heard what the doctor was saying. Kane was nodding, so I bobbed my chin up and down in agreement with him. Dr. Teller led Neala through the doorway to his office to speak with her privately.

"Man, that guy looks like a shrink, huh?" Kane whispered. "With that egg-head and all."

"Shush, they might hear you," I scolded, trying to contain my laughter.

"Just sayin'." Kane shrugged his shoulders. He reached over my lap and took a *Psychology Today* magazine from an end table. I watched Kane settle in and pulled my phone from my purse to check messages from the office.

I realized work was the only thing that made me feel practical. Maybe I should see the shrink. Perhaps the doctor would say that Neala's issue was typical high school jitters or a simple case of overreaction. Maybe it would be something she'd outgrow. Hoping Neala was comfortable and being truthful with Dr. Teller, I expected he would work with us. As long as Neala didn't downplay the severity of her problems, this would not be a waste of our time. Worst case—getting booted from Dr. Teller's patient list.

Thirty grueling minutes later, Dr. Teller appeared at the waiting room threshold and invited Kane and me to join them. I glanced at Kane. Dr. Teller seemed mechanical and very businesslike. Kane raised his eyebrows at my glance, then we followed the doctor. The room was a tight fit for the four of us, but Dr. Teller sat in his desk chair, and Neala stayed in a swivel chair near him. Dr. Teller offered us a seat on the small sofa against the office wall.

"Neala is a very bright and delightful young lady," began Dr. Teller. "I don't think there is much to be concerned about with the exception that Neala feels uncomfortable, even frightened in big crowds. Is that right, Neala?"

All eyes looked at Neala, and she nodded her head. I could feel Neala shirk.

Dr. Teller grinned and then continued. "I see this often in her age group. Sometimes in younger children as well. Some groups of people easily learn to modify moods and cope with anxiety. They reduce an event that may cause interference with their daily life. Some people come across this naturally, and others may need help with their behavior—creating safe routines with predictability.

Neala, though, says it's difficult to get out of the car when she arrives at school." He looked at his notes. "Neala, you get out of bed and ready for school, though, is that correct? You feel okay then, in that part of the morning?"

"Yeah," she said. "But sometimes, when I first wake up, I feel it start to come."

"Mm-hm, I see," Dr. Teller said and then wrote something on his notepad. "And when you get to campus, sometimes you can't get out of the car? You can make it to class on some days, but not without a sense of doom? Is this correct?"

"Uh-huh," Neala whispered. She looked down at her Converse shoes.

Dr. Teller pulled Neala's patient intake form from his file. He rechecked with me that Neala wasn't exposed to any obvious trauma. From my written information and chatting with Neala, the doctor proposed a diagnosis of generalized anxiety along with severe social anxiety and separation anxiety.

"She displays behavior of someone who suffers from PTSD, post-traumatic stress disorder, but there is no evidence of trauma," he said. "We may decide to investigate this more. Comparing this history with her symptoms mystifies me." He looked at Neala and gave her a gentle smile.

I recognized his smile as compassion toward Neala. I felt better about this doctor.

Addressing us, Dr. Teller said, "Feelings of floating, darkness, and inability to move as Neala describes are symptomatic of panic attacks. For now, I'll prescribe a mild sedative; this medication is usually used for high blood pressure." He turned to Neala once again. "It will help reduce your heartrate and keep your cheeks from flushing. You take this once a day."

Dr. Teller scribbled on a prescription pad. "I will also prescribe Ativan. Neala, you can take these pills when you feel a panic attack coming. This pill is not taken every day. It's only for acute panic attacks. Let's start with these and see how it goes."

Dr. Teller looked at me and said, "I would like you to make an appointment for Neala to see me in three months." He tore the page off the notepad and offered it to me. He looked at us as if to see if we had questions.

I spoke up. "That's it? A prescription?" I willfully accepted the little piece of paper with the doctor's cryptic scrawl.

"No digging around for skeletons in our family closet?" asked Kane.

"No, we won't need to do that quite yet, Mr. Byrnes," said Dr. Teller. "We won't take time figuring out what may or may not have happened. Let's see if Neala will feel better with these pills first. The brain is an amazing organ. But sometimes it needs a little help." The doctor flipped pages on his notepad and then closed it. "Neala said she visits a behavioral therapist once a week?"

I nodded. "She started with her last week," I said.

"Wonderful. Let's keep that up, shall we? Now, here is my email." he passed his card to me. "Each of you is welcome to email me if you have questions or concerns about these medications. You, too, Neala. You can email me anytime you want to. If you need to see me before the next appointment, call the office and set up an earlier one." Dr. Teller stood, and we followed his cue. He shook hands with Kane and gave he me a reassuring nod. He even reached over and patted Neala on her shoulder. I felt hopeful when we left.

That was that.

Appointment completed.

We were given a prescription, a diagnosis, and an explanation. We felt like we were on the right track and had a little breathing room. After a stop at the pharmacy, we called it a day. I was still unsure of the medications, but I didn't want Neala to self-medicate either.

NEALA

A few weeks later, we headed back to Dr. Teller's office for my follow-up visit. The appointment at 9:00 a.m. meant we'd be in a long morning commute. Dad drove an hour in the commuter lane, but traffic was still bumper to bumper. I slurped the last of my s'mores Frappuccino. The whipped cream caused my stomach to churn, and I burped marshmallow.

When we exited off the freeway, I sat up straight. Out of nowhere, a sensation of dread crept up my spine. Without realizing it, I'd held my breath. I felt compelled to listen to the wheels of the car, the revving of the engine. Mom's perfume choked me, and I gasped. My toes curled in my Converse shoes. I grabbed the door handle. As we turned into the doctor's driveway, white-sparkly spots flashed before my eyes. Dad parked the car. I heard him talking, but his words sounded like we were underwater.

Dad and Mom got out of their front seats. My stomach lurched, and my mouth got watery, like just before I throw up. I tried to shift my legs, too late.

"Come on, Neala. Let's go," Dad said when he opened the back door. I looked at him. "Hey." Dad kneeled down to my level. I could tell he wasn't sure if he should keep calm or yell. His fists were near his pockets, but his eyes looked soft. "Dr. Teller will only ask how you feel on your medication, nothing more." Dad extended his hand, but I couldn't reach out to him, I felt frozen.

Mom, already out of the car, paced behind Dad. Then she rocked back and forth. She put her purse under her arm, hoisted the strap over her shoulder, and looked at her watch. "Well, I'm going up to his office." She looked at me. "You know they will charge us whether we show up or not?"

She tried to guilt me, and said, to no one in particular, "I will at least let the doctor know we tried."

CLAIRE

I made my way to the office playing scenarios in my head. Neala doesn't feel well, she has anxiety. That's why you're here, silly. Neala is a stubborn kid who won't do as she is told. When I got to the reception desk, I came clean.

"Neala is having an anxiety attack, and she won't get out of the car."

The receptionist asked me to sign in, give the co-pay, and then she left her desk to tell Dr. Teller we were there. After a few minutes, the receptionist came back with Dr. Teller. Looking surprised, but reassuring, he greeted me and asked, "Neala is in the car?"

I explained to Dr. Teller what happened when we pulled in to park.

Removing his glasses and tucking them into his shirt pocket, he raised his eyebrows and said, "Then let's go see her, shall we?"

NEALA

Dad stood near my car door and did his best to bribe me out of the car. When we saw Mom and Dr. Teller, Dad stepped back and turned to shake his hand.

"Run!" the voice in my head screamed. I wanted to move my legs so bad right then. Crap . . . The doctor came to the car! God, that was so embarrassing. I hated Mom sometimes.

"Hi, Neala." Dr. Teller squatted down and looked me in the eye.

He was intense, so I shrunk back and looked up at the car's interior headliner. I pretended to be interested in its funky pattern.

"Do you know why I asked you to come here today?"

I tried ignoring him, but he kept talking.

"Because I wanted to see if your medicine was working. But you're in the car, so I suspect it hasn't. What do you think?"

"I don't know." These three words had become my mantra because I really couldn't describe how I felt or thought. I'd been seeing Alina, and we'd tried to come up with a wordlist to describe what this sense of immobility felt like. We looked for terms to name it, but I didn't know how to articulate it then and still don't. "I wish people would quit asking me!" I snapped.

"Are you feeling better at school?" the doctor asked.

I gave him credit for being persistent. I moved my eyes from the ceiling to my lap. This was so humiliating.

"Okay, I will talk to your mom and dad." Dr. Teller stood up. "You can talk to me if you want, or you can stay there." He offered a smile, but I thought it might be fake.

"It's still difficult for her to get out of the car for school?" the doctor asked.

"Yes," Mom replied. "The days she does get out of the car, she spends her time in the school's front office, not in class."

"All right. Let's have Neala continue to work with her therapist, and I'll write a new prescription for her." He took his pad out of his breast pocket. He looked at me. "This one is for anxiety. Stop your other pills and start this one right away. Keep the Ativan for panic attacks." Then back to Mom and Dad he said, "Sally, my nurse, will call this new one in. You will be able to pick it up on your way home. Let's get together in two weeks. If you have questions, email them."

Dr. Teller shook Dad's hand after he gave Mom a new prescription. Before he left, I heard Dr. Teller say, "This is a first. I guess I do make house calls." Then he walked away.

CHAPTER TWELVE

CLAIRE

The two-hour ordeal to drop Neala off at school drained me, but by the time I left her, Neala was sitting in the school office. "Well, there goes my workout. And forget cleaning the kitchen with last night's dishes," I said aloud to myself while I drove home.

When I pulled into the garage, I frowned when I saw the mound of laundry on the washer. I lived with a family that was different than I'd envisioned when I married Kane. My dreams of sunny days and smiling faces had faded away. I understood I was a part of a family with an illness. I stared at the laundry pile through blurry eyes and cursed the heap of dirty clothes—the random colors, shapes, textures, and odors. If I discarded one article, several others would remain. I could separate them all, but it would never be gone, just clothes spread out into multiple piles. They may be sorted, conquered individually, but until the entire pile was washed, folded, and put away, it would not be complete. And then, the dirty heap would start over.

I compared the laundry to my feelings about Neala. I'd lost hours. Chips of my life were gone. But while I contemplated what could have happened or caused Neala's angst, I wondered how I could stop beating myself up over it.

As suggested by Neala's counselor, I went to a National Alliance for Mental Illness (NAMI) meeting. The key-note speaker explained that mental or emotional illness is both organic and environmental. I let out a long sigh. How had I contributed to Neala's disorder? Did Neala have a predisposition to anxiety, because I wrestled with my own demons? What about how I dealt with worry?

I thought about my spiraling depression after Sarah's heart issues, my divorce, and how I'd handled Neala. How well did I handle my life?

I knew what brought my moods down, and I learned how to work through those feelings—to grow beyond my pain. After those events, I became a worrier.

But why was Neala suffering from this anxiety?

Environmental poisons might have been to blame. When I got that information, I vowed to watch what Neala ate. What chemicals had Neala been exposed to? What about family dynamics and occasional, yet volatile, displays of tension between me and Kane? And what about Sarah moving out to go to college—were these all contributors to Neala's condition? This was life, though, right? The overthinking caused my head to pound.

I wiped my eyes on my sweatshirt sleeve and sniffed. Just like that goddamn pile of laundry, I could pick at it piece by piece, but eventually, the cycle would repeat. I punched the pile of clothes.

The task at hand was to take a shower and head to work. I felt like I would crack any second. How would I get the staffing report done or get the schedules out?

I took a deep breath; remembered to keep it real and focused on one thing at a time. Shower. Coffee. Play relaxing music on the way to the office.

I climbed the stairs to the master suite, gave my unmade bed the finger, went into the bathroom, and turned the shower faucet to hot.

CHAPTER THIRTEEN

CLAIRE

Scrutinizing the company in my backyard, I walked through the French doors and immersed myself into the familial abyss. As usual, Neala would be a hot topic. Curiosity over her withdrawn behavior was a subject bordering on taboo.

I was armed with a medical diagnosis for Neala's ailment. But I didn't think it would mean much to a generation who pulled themselves up by the bootstraps, and "when things got tough, the tough got going." I struggled to defend my daughter when it came to old-school parenting. "If I hear one more time that I should slap her, ground her, or threaten her within an inch of her life—or that computers are the problem . . ." I said under my breath.

I looked across the yard to Kane. He manned the grill, tongs in one hand, beer bottle in the other. I envied his peace of mind. I watched him wave to Bill, his dad, to join him.

"Weather like we've had summons a barbeque," I heard Kane call to his dad.

Bill sauntered over to the grill and smiled at the new cement pad he and Kane had poured last summer. Kane and Bill had fixed a permanent place for the grill and smoker, which gave the appearance of an outdoor kitchen.

Bill and Pat—Kane's step-mom—lived a little over a mile away from us. They often came by to visit and to see the grandkids. Pat raised Kane and his sister, Julie, after Gayle, Kane's mom, deserted the family. All anyone said to me was that "it was the 60s." For them, that was enough, and that simple explanation justified Gayle's absence.

It haunted me, though. I couldn't imagine abandoning my children. How could a mother just leave? Especially, a generation raised during the Summer of Love?

Kane slid the prepared burgers onto the grill, and the smell of sizzling meat wafted through the air. My mouth watered. The guests must be getting hungry, too. Maybe the day will go smoothly. Everyone will eat and then go home. Hope depleted when I heard Pat call to Bill.

Bracing for Pat's litany of "what is wrong with this generation?" followed by Pat's summon: "Bill, get me another toddy, will you? The pitcher is on the bar over there." I watched Pat point toward the bar's makeshift countertop. I let the small defeat wash over me. Once Pat's liquid courage kicked in, there was no telling how fierce her wrath might be.

I watched Bill and heard him call back. "Sure thing, baby." To me he seemed oblivious of his codependency while he obeyed his wife. Bill's eyes moved from Pat to the fence gate where the bells jingled.

Sarah pushed through the gate while she balanced bags of ice which Kane had asked her to pick up on her way over.

"Hey, there's my girl!" Bill said, taking the ice from Sarah and giving her a one-armed hug. "I'm headed that way," he said motioning toward the ice chests.

Pat craned her neck to see her step-granddaughter. "Come sit by Grandma Pat," she coaxed, patting a cushioned lounge chair.

Sarah wiped water from the ice off her shorts and sat by her grandmother. "Hi Mom," she said smiling up at me.

I admired the ease between the two, and Pat used that commonality to display superiority. I am glad Sarah got along with Pat. Especially now with Neala's introversion. It would not surprise me to discover that Pat accused me of turning both of the girls against her.

I gave Pat credit for taking on the Byrnes family when they were left to fend for themselves. Pat tried to come off tough, but I suspected that deep down, she was vulnerable. Stepping in to raise Bill's children after Gayle split was the way into his heart. Plus, Bill provided her with financial security. Pat appeared content in her role, but once she was in deep with her toddies, she'd been known to spew nasty remarks. Recently the harsh comments were aimed at Neala, primarily because of Neala's unusual behavior. Bill, who used to be the grand patriarch since losing his own father to pancreatic cancer last year, told me life was much too short, and he planned on enjoying good times, even if it meant keeping Pat on a steady stream of her elixir.

Setting the patio table for dinner, I bundled cutlery and napkins for the meal. I wasn't far from Pat and Sarah and took the opportunity to eavesdrop.

"Tell me, Sarah, how is Neala doing in school? Better, I should hope." She tipped her glass toward Bill when he approached with the pitcher. Pat waited for her answer.

Sarah pulled at her shorts and shifted her hips in her seat. A tell she revealed when she was uncomfortable.

Offering appetizers, I changed the subject, "Would either of you care for some sausage-stuffed mushrooms? Neala made them earlier today. She's a wiz in the kitchen." I looked Pat in the eye while I offered the platter.

Sarah smiled with relief and mouthed a "thank you." She took some food and let Pat help herself.

I had prepared myself for this conversation since Pat accepted the barbeque invitation. Upon her arrival into the family, Pat deemed herself the authority on families and child-rearing. Kane was three years old when his mom walked out on them, which left the role of mother wide open for Pat.

Bill was in a helpless situation with two young children, and he often worked away from home. He gladly let Pat make bold decisions when it came to raising his offspring. According to Bill, Pat ran a tight ship.

Pat balanced a mushroom cap in her napkin. While her attention was diverted, Sarah said, "Gramma, Neala is okay, but she has anxiety, you know?" Then she carefully added, "I don't understand what happens at school for her, but I heard it is not uncommon for kids to have issues like that sometimes."

"I think she uses her nerves . . . anxiety is that what they call it now . . . to get out of doing things. I have been here for at least an hour, and she hasn't even come out to say hello to your grandfather nor me." Pat shot a glance toward me.

Avoiding confrontation, I looked down.

"But Gramma, she isn't trying to be insulting. I feel bad for her sometimes. She is incapable of being mean, but she comes off that way. Neala is the baby and gets away with some things. I get frustrated sometimes by that, but what she has is a real disease."

I felt proud of how Sarah stood up for Neala.

Pat waved her hand. "Pfft. Aunt Julie tried this nonsense with me when she was in high school, and I assure you, I didn't play into it. Then she'd tell Grandpa she wasn't feeling well so she could stay home, and he'd fall for it. Neala does the same thing. It's their crutch." Pat popped a mushroom in her mouth and washed it down with her drink. "Perhaps it's in the genes." She shrugged her shoulders in an I-don't-know-what-to-tell-you fashion.

My stomach clenched. Defending Neala and her emotional issues became my latest superpower with ignorant people. Was this old lady really going to go down this road? Armed with reality and facts, I stood straight, squared my shoulders, and said, "Pat, Neala does not dissuade me with phantom illness to get out of going to school."

I leaned back as if I waited for Pat to slap me. I realized how ridiculous that was, and I continued. "And I think Kane's sister, Julie, truly was sick. I know I went through my share of stomachaches in school. That's how my body let me know I was nervous. It's not unusual for kids to present emotional discomfort with physical ailments. In fact, if these kids did use actual crutches, then their disabilities would be seen. But they don't. Their issues are hidden inside. Their disabilities are invisible. God knows I still get butterflies in my stomach when I have to try something new." Like telling you how it is, for example, I thought.

I noticed Sarah shift in her chair and lean forward. Don't do it, Sarah, don't get sucked in. But it was too late.

"Mom, I think Neala does try to get out of doing chores around here, at least while I was still living at home, she did. She never sticks around to help you, and she also sleeps a lot."

"Sarah! Listen to yourself. Your sister takes a medicine that makes her very tired. She is still adjusting to it, and she does the best she can." I wasn't happy with Sarah's comment.

"Just because she is your baby," Sarah whined.

I crossed my arms in disbelief. "That is enough, young lady. You don't know enough to have a say in this."

"Ho-ho!" Pat chimed in. "I didn't say Neala is lying. Maybe she doesn't know what she is doing. Maybe she wants attention or something." Pat held her icy gaze on me; then she sipped her drink as if it were a period on her sentence. With a dramatic swallow, she continued, "So you know, I had Julie go to a doctor about her pains. He couldn't find anything wrong, but each appointment kept her out of school for the day."

I held Pat's stare, yet from the corner of my eye, I saw Sarah nod her head in agreement. I stepped closer to Pat who sat erect on the chaise lounge next to Sarah. I towered above my mother-in-law. Through clenched teeth, I said, "It is conflicting. I am not arguing that. However, Neala wants to go to school. She's an excellent student. Learning is not the problem—people are. Do you know she has trouble going to parties, too?" I shot a harsh look to Sarah, for Sarah had witnessed Neala's refusal to attend parties or to have them. I looked back at Pat. "It might take Neala twenty minutes to open the car door when we get to her best friend's house." I was ready to shake both my daughter and my mother-in-law.

I took a breath to compose myself then explained, "Neala goes to weekly therapy, yet she isn't able to go into a store and buy things." I glanced at Sarah. "Sarah, when Neala was a baby, you rode your bike to the market for milk and bread. You were only 10; Neala is 14, and she's only now building confidence to do that.

"Do you remember on Mother's Day when Neala wouldn't order her own food?" I directed this question to Pat. "Kane ordered her meal for her. God, she won't even order a sandwich at Subway. Maybe it sounds like Neala makes this up, by why would she? Neala isn't able to regulate how she feels, but she works hard on how she responds.

"That's why she sees Alina, her therapist. Neala does her best to modify her behavior." I threw my hands into the air. "Imagine how much work it takes keeping all your ducks in a row everywhere you go: at school, the store, home, a party. Keeping it together all day exhausts her. Damn it!" I slapped my hand down on the table, which trembled.

Pat's eyes blinked and opened wide; Sarah simply looked down at her shorts.

"Excuse me; I need to get the salad ready," I said and turned toward the house. Catching sight of Bill and Kane, who were coming my way, I gave a pleading look to Kane. Bill navigated over to Pat, and I suspected he'd been watching us talk. I think they were too far away to hear what was being said.

Bill sat down next to Pat. "What were you talking about?" I heard him ask. I pretended to fiddle with the door handle so I could eavesdrop. After Pat explained her version, Bill said, "You put your foot into it again, Pat."

"All I said is that I think Neala makes this . . . this . . . 'anxiety' up!" Pat raised her voice and looked at Sarah for support. "Bill, you used to always worry too much, remember? It wasn't anything a little drink couldn't fix. Why not give Neala a shot of booze to take the edge off and just get on with it? I mean, if she isn't faking."

Booze? That was it; I wasn't about to let that happen. I stepped away from the kitchen door, and I headed back over to Pat. "That's it, Pat. You and your generation got through tough times with a little snort here and there. Kane and I work with Neala and her therapists to keep her from drinking. Too many kids with her issues try to self-medicate with alcohol and drugs."

"Self- what? Who said anything about drugs?" Pat asked.

Bill's eyes shot to Pat. "Sneaking alcohol or taking drugs are ways to find relief from pressures. Especially at Neala's tender age. That is self-medicating. Christ, woman." He scolded her. "And, alcohol is a drug."

I was glad to see Neala come from the front yard where she'd been brushing Lady. With any luck, she didn't hear this outburst. Neala generally knew when conversations were about her—a smart kid, she understood those talks didn't bring out the best in people.

"Hi, Dad. Are the burgers done? Lady wants one," she said.

Kane walked back over to the grill. Peeking in, then lowering the barbeque lid he said, "Burgers will be ready soon." He winked at Neala.

Neala smiled at him and sent a small wave to her grandparents. Bill greeted her with a smile, but Pat turned to talk to Sarah.

I did my best to keep my emotions in check. I didn't bother to tell Sarah to back off or ask my in-laws to leave. Hurt as I was, I understood the subject was uncomfortable for them.

Traditional parenting went along with blaming yourself for the way your kids turned out. It must have been hard for earlier generations to swallow that much responsibility and then to add guilt over emotional problems to the list. It wasn't easy to confront Pat. She was old-school and believed the punishment should fit the crime.

I excused myself and headed to the kitchen. Kane followed me. I felt his eyes on me while I put slices of boiled egg on the potato salad. I relaxed when he slipped his hands around my waist.

He set his chin on my shoulder and said, "This looks amazing." With his sexy drawl, he continued. "And so does the salad." He folded me tight into his arms and hugged me. I sensed his smile. He was trying to soothe me.

"She can be so ignorant!" I pouted. "People are idiots and not only her. Sometimes Sarah thinks Neala is faking, too. Even teachers and friends. I get so frustrated, Kane."

"Confidentially?" Kane asked then turned me to face him. "Sometimes, I wonder about Pat's stability." He smiled, and I smiled back. "I'm glad you are Neala's mom. You're a good mom, a perfect mom, you know that, don't you?" Kane hugged me again, then released me. He searched my eyes. "Yes, babe, people are idiots, and if Sarah thinks Neala is making it up, then she's also an idiot. I am grateful for the smart woman you are. You are doing a great job with Neala—that you understand the social aspect of this for her too, you know?"

"I don't always know it," I said. I leaned into Kane's broad chest and sighed. "Sometimes, I feel like the worst mom. I don't have answers, I feel defensive, and I get pissed at people. I feel like they judge me and Neala. Christ, it doesn't end!"

Choking back a sob, I pulled myself together and turned toward the counter.

I shoved the last bits of egg onto the salad. "Let's go back out there and just move on. I don't want to upset Neala. She has a tough enough time at gatherings, so let's not let this become a bad day."

"Okay, let's get out there and 'party it up,'" Kane said. "I told Chuck to stop by.

I was glad to hear this. Chuck, Kane's high school friend, was always good at charming Pat. A few smooth lines, and Pat would be in a better mood. "Send a text and tell him to come earlier than later," I said.

Kane rubbed his thumb across my cheek then kissed me. "I love you; you know?" He pulled his phone from his pocket.

CHAPTER FOURTEEN

CLAIRE

I stopped by my desk to grab a notebook and pulled the scheduling spreadsheet from the printer. I plucked my favorite smooth-gliding pen from my "Make Today Count!" mug, which I used as a penholder. Rounding the hall corner to my manager's office, I felt my phone vibrate from inside my sweater's pocket. A text message. I tried not to use my personal phone at work, but I keep it near just in case. I wanted to be available for Neala. She might reach out to me throughout the day. When I lessened Neala's anxiety, it relieved my own.

Toward the end of the first quarter at Norden, Kane and I accepted the advice from Neala's therapist to allow Neala cell phone use during school hours. All agreed, even Norden, with its strict cell phone policy. Initially, it was a challenge for faculty, staff, and school administration to adhere to Neala's phone use. And some students questioned her privilege. In time, all parties concluded it was a useful tool, and other students didn't begrudge her. Most important, the phone deterred Neala's panic attacks. When she sent me a text, I was gratified. Neala acted responsibly with her cellphone. She avoided using it for anything more than to contact me.

I pulled my phone from my pocket and glanced to see the message was from Neala.

Neala: I'm freaking out and dying simultaneously

I was halfway to my manager,s office, but I stopped. I pursed my lips and let out a sigh. I'd wait until after the meeting to respond. By the time my manager, Larisa, and I finished, Neala may have worked through her issue.

The prearranged protocol let Neala text me without the expectation of an immediate response. However, if she urgently needed me, Neala could call from the school's office phone.

I was content with this decision because, during work hours, I couldn't always get to my phone, and, I confess, I wasn't always sure how to respond to Neala. The luxury of a few extra minutes gave me a chance to figure out the best reply. Often, Neala simply needed to reach out. A place to put her thoughts alleviated some of her stress. Texting me was a safe way to do it.

I continued to my manager's office, confident Neala's outreach could wait for twenty minutes, and I kept my stride.

Larisa looked up when I tapped on her door. She glanced at the clock and noted the time. "You have been running behind these days, Claire. Sometimes over an hour. At our last meeting, you mentioned trouble with dropping Neala at school." Larisa waited until I closed the office door behind me, then she asked, "Claire, is your punctuality slipping because of Neala?"

Most employees might be troubled with a frank comment from their boss, but I felt relief. I was grateful for the observation and the bluntness. It was one reason I liked working with Larisa—she made no excuses. Honest and compassionate, she didn't play favorites. I trusted her.

Seated in the chair in front of Larisa's desk, I admitted why I was late. "Yes. Sometimes Neala won't get out of the car. I sit there and wait. And wait. Sometimes there's a miracle, and she gets out without incident, but other times it takes up to two hours before she will resolve to relax and get out—but only to go to the school's office."

"I noticed the tardiness since high school started. You've worked here for ten years, and I believe you have always been on time. Early some days, too," Larisa commented.

Instead of a lecture which would have been appropriate, Larisa's voice softened. "How exhausting it must be for you, Claire. I don't know how you do it." Larisa smiled. "It must take a lot out of you."

I felt my jaw relax, but tears balanced on my lower lids. I controlled my voice as best I could—although it still cracked when I replied, "It breaks my heart to see Neala go to the office. I can see her little dark-haired head through the window, which confirms she's sitting on the sofa near the school secretary. I get another wave of sadness when I go to pick her up six hours later, and she's still there."

Larisa pushed a tissue box towards me. Taking a deep breath I said, "Over the past months, I have learned what will and won't work for Neala. One thing for sure—I do my best to follow through because I have to. I don't know what else to do. I am afraid of failing her." I brought the tissue to my mouth and audibly sobbed. "Neala must go to school—what else would she do? I guess I do what I think I am supposed to do at any given time." I dabbed the corner of my eyes, trying to keep myself from weeping. "My strategies may not always work, but I try."

I chuckled and blew my nose. "Maybe I should go into hostage negotiations; I'm getting good at bargaining and cutting deals." I sniffed, looked down, and wrung the damp tissue. I smoothed my skirt over my lap.

"Poor Neala! I'm sorry she is struggling," Larisa said. "She used to come here after school, what was she then, in second or third grade? She was such a happy kid—this must be so frustrating."

"Neala used to beg to come because she liked being with me and abhorred after-school care. She complained so much that when I worked short days, I would pick her up right after school. With full-day projects, I'd ask Sarah to drop her off here when she could. Otherwise, I go on late lunch break to pick her up myself and bring her here." I paused a moment to reflect on those hard days, realizing they had been exchanged for what was happening now.

"She's been to counseling, and her doctors agree that Neala is an amazing kid who puts too much weight on herself. They can't say why her anxiety physically manifests itself. When it comes on too fast, she freezes. It starts with her legs. They become like heavy logs. It stumps me. Oh! No pun intended," I laughed, then I added, "They don't really know if she'll get better. It could all boil down to how she is wired. We just learn to deal. Especially her. For now, our focus is not only about getting her better but also keeping her from getting worse. Her therapist mentioned she has traits for developing agoraphobia."

"Geez, Claire, I never knew all of this was happening at home. I thought it was mainly her hesitation to go to school in the morning." Larisa sat back in her chair and tapped her fingers on her desk calendar. "Let me think about this."

I imagined the wheels in Larisa's head turning. I could almost hear the cogs hum. I hoped the idea would be in my favor. Either way, Larisa was known for thinking outside the box, and I was willing to try something, anything, that might work.

Larisa looked over at her computer calendar to check the schedule. "How about this?" She leaned forward and folded her hands together on her desk. "Would it be easier to slide your hours back? Maybe come into work an hour later and then leave an hour later? Looking here, I see we can schedule meetings later in the day, and that will relieve pressure in the morning." Larisa leaned back in her chair and cheerfully added, "With some luck, we can reduce your tension—and Neala's." Larisa smiled and looked up at me. "What do you think?"

"I think that is a great idea, thank you for thinking of it." I tried to contain my excitement. This arrangement could affect Neala in a positive way. I felt my shoulders fall and the knot in my stomach loosen. My stress dissolved. It was true what Larisa said about my anxiety to get to work on time trickling to Neala. I hoped the new schedule would eliminate many rotten mornings.

"Thank you, Larisa. When do you think I will be able to start the new hours? Can I try tomorrow?" I asked. I hoped I didn't sound impatient.

"Sounds good to me, come in an hour later tomorrow. Let's try it for a while and see how it works before we make it official." Larisa smiled again. "As for today, show me those reports."

After the meeting, I checked my phone. No more messages from Neala. It might end up being a good day. I put my favorite pen back in its holder and felt at peace.

CHAPTER FIFTEEN

CLAIRE

For the last few weeks, I'd wake up close to 3:00 a.m. with my thoughts spinning. I'd get up and pace. I needed help.

After months of taking care of Neala, my headaches and sleepless nights were getting the best of me. Kane's indulgent drinking coupled with aggressive outbursts was a cry for help on his behalf, too. A new strain ebbed into our family. Sarah avoided visiting—especially family events. She wouldn't even answer texts until the next day, usually too late to participate or help with requests, like picking Neala up from school.

So I wouldn't wake Kane, I carried my tablet downstairs, sat at the kitchen desk, and leafed through some papers from work. I found a brochure Larisa had given to me. A benefit of working at Hill Haven Hospital was an anonymous employee service and intervention program, but I suspected evidence that someone in our department used the service would be apparent. Especially after the invoice was received. After all, Hill Haven was in a small community, and the hospital departments—administration, in particular, were even smaller.

I glanced at the clock. 4:15. An ungodly hour. I would consider this option in the light of day. I put the brochure back on the table. For me, the wee hours of the night magnified even the smallest problem, and I'd feel powerless knowing nothing could be done until morning.

I wrote myself a note to call the number on the brochure, and that quieted my thoughts. I went back to bed before my worries came back and then looped.

As if mocking me, the alarm blared at 6:00 a.m. I lowered my feet to the floor, stepped on bone and fur, and growled at the dog, "Move, Lady!"

Lady started the night in bed with Neala, and during the evening, ended up on the floor next to my side of the bed.

After a hot shower and a strong cup of coffee, even in the light of the day, I still felt burdened with worry. I feared my family would fall apart. After Neala was at school, I called employee services. It was time to take action.

I assured myself this was the best thing to do. According to the brochure, many employees obtained help resolving work, family, and personal issues. The least I could do was to honor Larisa's suggestion. The strain from home was collapsing in on me. I hoped it would be helpful, even feel good, to have someone listen to my problems and validate my pain.

"You're sure no one will know it was me?" I asked Stan, the service agent, when he answered the phone.

"One hundred percent. All the company will know is that the service was used. No name or employee information will be on the invoice. Completely private."

"Okay, I guess you can sign me up." I thought I sounded unsure, but Stan scheduled me to meet with psychoanalyst Dr. Felicia Morgan on Thursday morning. I specifically made the appointment for 10:00 a.m. giving me plenty of time to drop Neala at school first.

"Well, that's that," I said when I hung up. Then I called Larisa to arrange the time off.

Shortly, my appointment day arrived. My stomach felt queasy, and my heart raced with anticipation. All went well when it came time to drop Neala at school. She got out of the car, and I watched her go directly to the front office instead of her classroom. Though I was disappointed she didn't go to her class, I was glad she took her laptop today. An indication she'd attempt to work on her English assignment.

The office door swung closed, and once again, I could see her silhouette on the small sofa. My chest ached. My heartstrings, which were tethered to her, pulled at me. The pain—a soreness so deep it could not be soothed by word or touch was as ancient as life itself. This was the emotional bond between mother and child. As the cords between our hearts stretched, I practiced my breathing—with each inhale, I let the cord lengthen then thin until I was finally ready to let go.

The employee services office was located in unfamiliar territory, but I arrived fifteen minutes early. The distance to the building was a twenty-minute drive, and I felt confident I wouldn't run into any coworkers. I wasn't worried about an employee seeing me go to counseling; my discomfort revolved around the fear they'd think my issues were work related. I found sick humor that the parking area, landscaped with man-made waterfalls and palm trees, was designed to look like the entrance to paradise.

I walked in the lobby, found Suite C, and checked in with the receptionist, She handed me forms and I sat in the small waiting area. I realized the office kept the paradise theme with its white wicker furniture with pastel-print cushions, gorgeous silk floral arrangements, and lavish paintings of lush flowers that hung on the wall. It was almost like sitting far away in a tropical lanai.

Forms completed, I waited. Other than the receptionist, I sat alone in the waiting area. Minutes later, the door clicked open, and a plump woman wearing an ivory blouse and a pink skirt poked her head out.

"Hello, you must be Claire."

"Yes, hello," I said, following her gesture toward a narrow hall that led to an interior office.

Along the way, she introduced herself. "I'm Doctor Morgan."

I noticed her blouse had a pattern of miniature yellow roses tied with a billowy bow which fluffed up under her chin. I guessed Dr. Felicia Morgan was closer to sixty than fifty. Her hair was silvery blonde, and her roundness created soft lines around her cheeks and chin. She looked kind.

Her office was as floral as the waiting room and the doctor's blouse. When I plunked into the overstuffed armchair, I sank into the cushion and relaxed. Weird, but I could have sworn I smelled flowers.

For fifty minutes, I divulged my confusion about Neala. I wasn't sure how to support or reprimand her during times when trying to establish anxiety from acting obstinate. I spoke to Dr. Morgan about my worries; am I too soft? Too firm? Am I inattentive or overprotective?

"Sometimes I get so tired, I feel manipulated by Neala. I mean, am I gullible? Sometimes Kane thinks so. Several teachers at her school wouldn't permit her behavior either," I spewed.

Once I started, I couldn't stop and realized I should have asked for help earlier.

With each statement I made, Dr. Morgan wrote notes. Wondering what her scribbles meant, I felt a pang in my gut. Gullible woman? The kid needs a kick in the ass? Queen of codependency? Her husband seems wishy-washy?

I realized how much confidence had drained from my self-esteem, so I sucked it up and divulged everything.

When I started in about Kane and how indifferent he was to the daily trials, I thought I heard myself whine. I tossed in that I envied his detachment but that it also pissed me off. "Work is tough, and I recently discovered how stressed I am there," I said. "When Neala experiences her anxiety and needs my help, I am conflicted between motherhood and my income. I resent that I have to choose one or the other." I paused. The words spilled without a filter, and I must admit, it felt good. "Kane doesn't have these clashes because somehow, being a dad . . . It's a no-brainer. His job comes first."

I went on a tangent. "Perhaps Neala's behavior is a direct result of me working. Some days, if I stayed home with her, Neala would improve and feel better, even confident, and strong. My guilt about mothering overwhelms me. When those thoughts come, I feel like a failure because my daughter is in pain, and I can't fix it. It's evident that I should be home with my child. Yet, I have to work, especially now with the economy in the tank. My family needs my income. The guilt never ends."

Oh, God, I'd let the blame pile up on me! No wonder I felt crushed! My thoughts sucked me into a downward spiral, but I snapped back to the present when I noticed Dr. Morgan had stopped writing and was staring at me.

By the end of the session, I felt emptied and exhausted. Before the therapy session, I hadn't been aware of the size of the burden I'd been lugging around. For once, I explored and expressed how family dynamics affected my life. I'd been harboring overlapping feelings of fear and guilt and became aware of how angry I was. How could I get past this anger? I left Dr. Morgan's office with a clear sense that if I let my rage eat at me, I'd eventually have nothing to give.

"Come back next week. You have two sessions left, but we can surely add more if you want," Dr. Morgan said. "Let's explore more of your family dynamics and habits."

I paid close attention to my feelings, watched how they affected my actions, and noticed more when they did not. Seeking to understand myself, I became quieter than usual. Normally, when I'd see a 'train wreck' racing toward Neala, I'd try to head it off. Now, I held my tongue .

Controlling my outbursts was difficult at first, but I kept track of them by noting when I was tired, frustrated, or enabled. I'd head to my room to relax. practice being extra courteous at work, let complaints from upstairs roll of my shoulders, and not react when the staff popped off. I called on my daily Zen by searching for my honest and undistorted frame of mind and allowed myself peace. I practiced the art of being positive through actions like creating my thoughts before I let my internal chaos run wild. It was my new game.

By the end of the week, I had tapped into some buried frustrations. I looked forward to seeing Dr. Morgan again. I was grateful for the therapy and the safe place to expose my worries. I enjoyed the process and listened to myself. Letting it out was a relief.

Thursday morning, the day of my second appointment, my plan was to drop Neala off at school and drive to Dr. Morgan's office. Going over the topics I wanted to cover with the doctor, tucking memos in my mind from the past week, I forgot to factor in the dense cloud which had enveloped Neala that morning.

CHAPTER SIXTEEN

NEALA

I was still in bed. I looked at my phone, I had three minutes before we were supposed to leave for school. I let out a sigh and pulled the blanket over my head. I cloaked myself in darkness and tried to stop time. My scalp felt tight, and my shoulders ached. As if my feet were asleep, imaginary pins and needles twitched through my soles. Doing a quick emotional check, I validated I was in a mood. I predicted that I might be snippy—especially when I heard Mom in the kitchen. It sounded like she was stacking my lunch items on the counter.

Just because she was trying to help me, didn't make this easier. I'm already late, but that doesn't mean it will be a bad day—Alina always reminds me to remember this. Late or not, even going to class doesn't make the day bad or even a loss. I'm supposed to recall that in each moment—anything can change—and sometimes things can go from bad to good. I let the mantras float through my mind. Five minutes later, I rolled out of bed, brushed my teeth, and slipped on my Converse.

"There you are," Mom sort of said under her breath. I couldn't help but notice the lines around her eyes, and her eyebrows were closer together than usual. Poor Mom, she could sense a difficult day. Smoothing out the front of my black hoody—the hood already pulled over my head—I rounded my shoulders and dodged through the foyer past Mom. Best not to talk, I decided, as I gauged my mood.

"I can't see you with your bangs over your eyes," Mom called after me, her tone didn't hide her nagging.

Mom caught up to me, tried to pull the hoody off my head and pushed the hair away from my eyes.

"Stop!" I said.

She withdrew her hand then stepped toward me.

"Just stop." I held my hands out in front of me to block her. I knew my words stung, but at this moment, I didn't care. God, if she would just leave me alone!

I went to the kitchen, pulled a bag out from the drawer, and stuffed my sandwich, some fruit, and what looked like a leftover black bean brownie from last night into a bag. Blech! Cramming my lunch into my backpack, I saw Mom left her keys in the kitchen, so I snatched them.

"I'm starting the car," I yelled to her. She wasn't in the foyer, so I figured she went back upstairs. I hit the garage door button. The massive old design shook the whole house. Then the safety door slammed shut behind me. Lately, Dad has too much stuff in the garage to park the car in it, so I edged past his tools and materials to get out to the driveway. The morning was cold, and though there was no frost, dew covered the windshield.

I popped the car's locks open and put my backpack on the floor of the passenger side. Thoughts of driving a vehicle intimidated me, but I liked how it felt to sit in the driver's seat and switch on the motor. I turned the heater and the front seat butt-warmers to high. Cold air came from the vent and hit me in the face while I waited for it to warm up. Next, I used the lever on the steering wheel column to turn on the wipers. The first swipe was smooth, and little rivulets of water slid gracefully down its slanted glass. The next swipe screeched over the window, dragging the rubber wiper because it wasn't moist anymore.

Oh! I would get so reamed if anyone heard me say moist! Gym class, sweaty socks, and vaginas! God, Mom talking about moist cakes, if she only knew! The rubber wipers skipped across the glass. Enough of that. I turned the wipers off and flipped the sun visor down.

Mom said when she got nervous, she would look in the mirror. So far, she said, she could see her reflection and say, "Nope, I don't look like a nut job yet."

I stared at my reflection in the visor mirror. If I'm not a nut job, I must be close to being one.

Mom came into the garage, so I flipped her visor back up and got out to move to the passenger side. It was that instant I "got" that I'd started the car to go to school. It pushed me over the edge. My skin felt prickly, and sudden anger and meanness overtook me. I'd have to change that, or I would push myself into anxiety.

"Thanks for starting the car—oh! My seat is nice and warm!" Mom said. "Sorry, I had to grab my lunch and my purse." Then she looked at me.

I could tell she wanted to say something about the way I'd yelled at her when she'd tried to touch my hair but stopped herself. She did this thing where she'd opened her mouth and then she would purse it shut. Mom doesn't know how to cross her eyes, so this is her equivalent to making a funny face.

"Well, you didn't deserve me yelling at you, so I figured I could at least light a fire under your ass." I smiled at her.

"Good thing, because it's cold today." She smiled back as if knowing I meant I was sorry.

CLAIRE

I gauged Neala's temperament while I drove into the school parking lot. She appeared to press herself into the passenger seat. Her knees bopped from rocking the balls of her feet, and her hands had tightened into fists.

Not good.

"Here we are," I announced, trying to keep my tone neutral.

Neala pushed herself deeper into the seat and cast her eyes downward.

As some of her classmates passed by, they tried to catch Neala's eye. I appreciated their futile hope to connect with her and their willingness for her to join them. Other kids gawked or laughed as they strode by.

I felt a burst of empathy for Neala, but eager to proceed with my plans for the day, I stayed calm while I tried to coax her out of the car. "Come on, Neala, I have an appointment today. I'd really like to get there on time." I glanced at the dashboard clock for emphasis and noticed it was later than I thought.

My mood shifted from calm to mild irritation. Pressed by the sudden urgency to be on time for my appointment, I went from empathy to self-centeredness. I hated it when I turned Neala's uncontrollable events into my problems, yet, here I was. I played the victim card and implored her to think about me occasionally—the fact that her delay affected my day.

"Come on, Neala, I have to go." My voice was harsher compared to first attempts.

"I can't do it, Mom. My legs won't move." Neala dully responded from under her hoody.

Her body was rigid. I could see she was in physical pain—the anxiety of going to school consumed her.

This is not fair! I wanted to scream to the High Gods. I wished to lessen my daughter's pain, yet I wanted the kid to get the fuck out of the car. My inner voice screamed at Neala. Ruthless and non-compassionate, the voice shouted the command: "Get out. Make a choice, stand up, and get the fuck out of the car!"

With her immobility that wasn't going to happen. Not today. The only matter left was how long should we sit and wait. Ten more minutes? Thirty? I'd be late for my appointment. School or home? That was the choice I had to make, and soon. Minutes ticked by.

Torturous time passed as I sat quietly, not able to trust the words which might leak out. Neala's disappointment was written on her face. Yet she bravely tried to battle her demons using the square breathing exercises she'd learned. Breathing in for four seconds, holding her breath for four seconds, and then letting it out for four seconds.

After sitting there for one full hour, I knew I was close to missing my appointment. Internally I fretted, outwardly I sighed. Alternately looking at social media on my phone, I shoved it into my purse. Both of us were losing strength to carry on much longer. Suddenly, the silence was broken when Neala whispered.

It was a quiet voice, commanding attention. A vibration or tone, something I haven't heard from Neala in a long while, but it carried assurance. "Mom," Neala said, pulling her hoody from her head while searching my eyes. "If I go home, it wins. I. Can't. Let. It. Win. I have to try, but I can't move. I want to be in school. I want to go to class."

I guess I was holding my breath because I let it out with a long whoosh. Brushing my daughter's bangs out of her eyes, I smiled at her. "I know you are trying, Cookie." I felt a rush of pride. How did this kid get so strong? How is she so smart and brave?

I admired that Neala had chosen to fight this . . . this. . . monster. I can't let it win, a new mantra. Only moments before, I was ready to lose my cool over her stagnate behavior, and all the while, my courageous child was building a defense, a way to keep anxiety from consuming her. Fighting it to the end. Refusing to let the darkness prevail.

I wanted to praise Neala aloud but thought better of it and kept the mood light. "Do you want to stay in the car a bit longer?"

"Yeah."

Though I was happy for Neala's progress, I couldn't help being concerned for my day. A twenty-minute drive to my appointment. With traffic, it's thirty. I took another deep breath, counted to four, and slowly exhaled for four seconds.

I wasn't going to make it. But Neala was. I resolved to let my urgency to get to my appointment go. I would have to reschedule.

Another twenty minutes, and it was too late to make my appointment, Neala gathered her courage and finally unbuckled her seat belt. She popped open the door but did not let it swing wide. Shifting in her seat, still holding the door handle, she turned to me. "If I need to come home, will you pick me up?"

"Of course, I will." I always agreed I would come no matter what. And I would, I vowed, but I was guilty in knowing I might not be able to drop whatever I was in the middle of, although Neala didn't have to know that. Neala had to believe I wore a superhero cape, and that I could fly through the sky to be at her side the moment she couldn't cope. No matter what.

She lifted her backpack and with careful motions exited the car. I watched her head directly to the office to check in. I knew the office staff could view us through the window—we were excusably late. But Neala got her tardy pass so she could move along through her day.

Amazed at days when Neala could work past the anxiety, I felt confident Neala would battle the "big dragon," as she'd named her fear. One day, she would slay that monster, and hopefully, it would be gone forever. Satisfied Neala would be fine for the rest of the day, I reached for my cell phone to reschedule my appointment.

Dr. Morgan picked up on the first ring. "What do you mean, you are not coming?" Dr. Morgan took a tone with me.

"Well, my daughter, Neala, who I spoke about last week? She couldn't get out of the car, but she made a breakthrough so—" I started to explain.

"If I knew you were going to cancel, I would not have rushed all the way here from Clarion Heights. It's an hour away." Dr. Morgan scolded me.

Emotionally drained from the morning I'd endured, I cried. Hot tears welled in my eyes, and a thick knot formed in my stomach. I coiled in embarrassment and anger. I was not a person who cancelled appointments at the last minute. I'm reliable and true to my word. This was an extreme situation—the very reason I sought counseling. Rage boiled into my chest as Dr. Morgan continued complaining about her drive to work.

I stopped her short this time. "Hey! I just spent two hours in a car waiting for my daughter to gather herself together so she could get out of the goddamn—I wanted to curse at this woman—car. I did my best to keep this morning's appointment. Believe me, I would have called you if I knew how this day would be." I let my morning frustration spill out over the phone. I was livid. I wanted to shout at her.

Swiftly Dr. Morgan stopped moaning about her own problems. I think my outburst shocked her, but by now, I couldn't care less.

"Of course, after this morning's events, we can reschedule. I'll let you know if this appointment will be covered," she said, with a business-as-usual attitude.

"Seriously?" I was in awe. She could have hung up on me. Instead, her audacity to think she can get away with speaking to me with her shrill tone, and then dare to see if my company will be billed for her time? "You can take your appointment book and shove it," I snapped. "Let me be clear, I don't care if this is a confidential service. If this is how you handle things beyond your control, I don't see how you could ever help me. And another thing, Doc, I will inform my employer of your inadequate professionalism. I will suggest no payment for today."

I pressed the "end call" button on my phone extra hard. My chest heaved, and I trembled. I sobbed right in the school parking lot. I hoped the staff wasn't watching from the office. I looked at my phone again and searched the contact list for Larisa's personal number. I needed my own sick day. After notifying Larisa, who gave her blessing, I called it a day and headed for the shelter of my home.

Two hours later, Dr. Morgan telephoned. "I apologize for being unprofessional to you, Claire. No matter my day, it was not right to reflect it upon you. I have been in touch with employee services, and they agreed to pay for two more sessions; I will not charge them for the missed one. Would you like to set another time to come in?" she asked with a nonchalant attitude.

"No, thank you, I don't need more stressors in my life right now," I said and hung up on her again. After that, I checked the emails from work on my phone. Nothing pressing. I switched my phone to vibrate in case someone from the office needed me. I felt guilty for taking the day for myself, but I knew I needed to care for myself. I was worn out and imagined I was scattered around the edges. Like Pig-Pen from *Peanuts*, just a quivering outline of who I am. Wiping tears with the back of my hand, I knew I deserved a break. Today, I would let myself cave in, hang up my superhero cape, and pray Neala would not call or need me to get her.

I went to the kitchen counter to make myself a hot pot of my newly discovered tea, lavender lemonade, which was perfect with a generous plate of butter cookies. Placing the brewing tea and cookies on the coffee table, I found the remote control. Lady heard the TV switch on and wandered in to join me. She eyed the cookies, and I tossed her one. She and the TV were my companions for the day. Drained from the intense morning, I fell asleep on the couch. When I awoke, the tea was cold, Lady had eaten the cookies, and it was time to pick Neala up from school.

CHAPTER SEVENTEEN

NEALA

I sat on a bench outside of Mr. Tanner's art class. He didn't mind when I hung out by his classroom because he knew that bench got the morning sun. The warmth felt nurturing. I worked on my homework or read when I couldn't make it to my classes. While reading *The Great Gatsby*, I looked up from the book to see a young German shepherd.

"Hi boy," I said and reached down to scratch his ears.

"She's a girl dog, her name is Duchess," Mrs. Campbell, the horticulturist, said. "She likes to cruise around the quad looking for crumbs." It was late autumn, and Mrs. Campbell wore a turtleneck under her utility vest. Her red curls were pushed up into her straw hat and she held pieces of cornstalks, so it looked like she'd come from the garden. She often worked there in the morning, while the air was still crisp.

"I love dogs; I have a dog named Lady. She's a golden retriever. Together, we passed her Good Canine Citizenship last summer," I bragged.

Lady and I made a good team. We've taken agility classes on and off since I was in fifth grade. Sometimes, I got tired, and we would quit, but I would get Dad to sign us up again. I was the youngest student in the class, but with Lady, I did well.

Before Lady, Dad had said if we got a dog, the dog would be my responsibility. Mom fed her, walked her, and picked up the poop. But I trained her, and she became my companion. Looking at Duchess, I wished that Lady was by my side.

"Will you keep an eye on Duchess while I unload my pickup? I have some vegetable starters to bring to the school garden."

I was thrilled to watch her dog, and I thought Mrs. Campbell could tell because I felt the smile on my face widen. She must have seen it.

"Here's her leash," she said, pulling it from her fanny pack. "She should be okay until the next period. When the kids come out, leash her up, so she doesn't bother or scare anyone."

I scratched Duchess's head right behind her ears. The dog sat by me and looked up at my face. Her golden eyes searched mine. I wondered what she was thinking.

"Good girl," I said while nodding at Mrs. Campbell, so she'd know I understood her leash request.

I pet Duchess while I read about Daisy's parents forbidding her from seeing Jay leave for war. When I was done with the chapter, I put *Gatsby* in my backpack and then snapped the leash on Duchess.

"Let's go for a walk." I gave Duchess a slight tug, and we strolled to the school garden. I told Mrs. Campbell, we were going for a walk, and she instructed me to stay on campus and out of the parking lot. I walked Duchess around the edge of the school grounds. When the bell rang for students to switch classes, we avoided them by strolling near the backside of the playing field perimeter.

After Duchess did border patrol by sniffing along the fence and natural boundary of the campus, we walked back to the garden to find Mrs. Campbell. She stood under a pear tree donated and dedicated to the school when it first opened. Leaves on the tree looked ready to fall. She was talking to Karla, the school secretary.

"We're back," I said. "Is it okay for me to get Duchess some water? I think she must be thirsty."

Mrs. Campbell nodded toward a hose and bucket. "You can use them."

The next bell would be lunch, so Mrs. Campbell took Duchess home for the day. "The dog eats too many scraps and gets sick," she said. I didn't want to, but I handed the leash to her.

"Maybe I can help again, next time you come, I mean," I called as Mrs. Campbell left to load Duchess in her truck.

"You bet. She's friendly, but Duchess won't go with just anyone. I think you two made a connection." Mrs. Campbell shut the truck's passenger side door, and Duchess pushed her nose through a window opening.

I watched them drive away, and suddenly, I felt as if a part of me left with them. Strange I should feel this way. The last thing I wanted was to have anybody around. Especially at school.

The kids looked at me like I'm weird. Crap, I am weird, sometimes, but I can't change how I feel. Being on the campus with Duchess made a difference. I liked her company. Hoisting my backpack on my shoulder, I went back by the pear tree, sat down, alone, and ate my lunch. When the bell rang, it brought me out of my daydream of Duchess's next visit.

CLAIRE

I was pleased that after a few weeks, Neala created a routine at school—although not all of the teachers were happy with the arrangements. Those days when Neala got out of the car, she'd make her way to the main office to check in. Sometimes she sat on the small reception area's sofa, other times she hung out near the teacher's lounge. She did this when the reception area filled with other students, parents, or visitors.

Though the teacher's lounge accommodated Neala, it was bothersome for the teachers. Having her in their designated student-free territory limited their ability to relax between classes.

Though not perfect, this routine worked, almost long enough for me to gain hope. For those weeks, I noticed fewer refusal tactics from Neala to exit the car.

However, one afternoon, while in a finance meeting, I got a text from Neala. The magic spell of the teacher's lounge had broken, and once again, I was summoned to fetch her.

Karla sat at her desk in the school's office when I came in. "Hi Karla, I'm here for Neala." I clenched my teeth behind a grateful smile.

"Hey, Claire. Neala did really well until a little while ago. Particularly well when she was on campus with Mrs. Campbell's dog. You know, come to think of it, Neala is pretty comfortable when she's with Duchess—the dog," Karla said. "Hmmm."

"What are you thinking, Karla?"

"I wonder if it would help keep Neala calm if she brought her dog to school?"

"You mean, Lady? Here?" I asked in awe.

"Yes. After Mrs. Campbell took Duchess home, Neala came into the office. She carried on, nonstop about her dog, Lady. She told me about the training they did together, too," Karla said, a sparkle in her eyes. "It's the most I've heard Neala speak about any subject."

"That's something to think about." My imagination wandered. "What would we have to do to get Lady on campus?"

"Let me ask the principal and get back to you on that. Meanwhile, I'll get Neala." Karla left her desk and headed to the quad.

Thoughts of Lady on campus had me chuckle. Our beloved dog, a coveted golden retriever, was always the life of the party. How would that work? Lady's a rambunctious pup with an appetite. I could imagine students' school lunches being devoured. Lady ate everything, but she also won everyone over with her soulful puppy eyes. It was always a game with Lady and scolding her was unproductive.

My happy thoughts of our pup on campus vanished when Neala dragged herself into the office. Her head hung down, and her persona emitted sadness. A strap on her backpack was slung over one shoulder, but the other shoulder strap fell into the crook of her elbow, making her appearance catawampus.

Shuffling toward me, Neala placed her head on my shoulder.

"Not so good today?" I put my arm around my daughter.

"I couldn't get into the classrooms. I mostly sat outside. I ate lunch by myself in the vegetable garden, and now I am exhausted. I need to go home," Neala said.

CHAPTER EIGHTEEN

CLAIRE

When I was growing up, my mom made wholesome dinners. We gathered around the table, ready to discuss the day's trials and tribulations. Thirty years later, I was a working mom but still made the most of family time. Getting dinner together more than a few days a week presented a challenge—work schedules, school activities, and overall fatigue chipped away at our family meals and evenings. Although, when I felt a disconnection, I'd gather the family in the kitchen for dinner.

I wasn't sure if the value of hearty or homemade food came from my roots or if I liked the idea of cooking from scratch. Every so often, I demanded we sat at the table, used cloth napkins, and acted like the civilized family portrayed on our annual Christmas card.

I called for a family dinner meeting to discuss a plan to help Neala. I wanted to share Karla's idea about Neala having Lady at school. With a little luck, we'd solve some of Neala's social anxiety with Lady as her escort.

Lady, our golden retriever rescue, was a purebred with the superior lineage of the Pooh Bear variety—meaning she got mistaken for an Irish Setter because she was more red than golden. But she was a sweet, smart, and lovable dog. As with many Goldens, she commanded attention at every moment, which made her appear loyal. With an adorable face and big sad brown eyes, her charming personality contained a woe-is-me underdog appeal. She used her incredible "nose nudge" to solicit behind-the-ear scratches or under-the-chin rubs.

I couldn't think of one reason Lady couldn't accompany Neala to school. Well, maybe one—the dog had an unbelievable nose. A nose for food. One time, I caught her licking the oven door. When I looked inside, I found a piece of pepperoni, which had fallen off of a pizza. That's when I figured out not only how good her nose was, but also, how determined she was to get a morsel of food.

According to Karla, Principal Whitney looked up the district and state policies regarding having canine companions on campus. Because Neala didn't need a guide dog or a dog who could detect low blood sugar or other lifesaving skills, Lady would qualify with an Emotional Support Animal certification. Lady could be an Emotional Support Animal (ESA). The school would honor our request for Neala to have an ESA provided we met the criteria. I would discuss these measures and work out a plan over broiled chicken, roasted carrots, Brussel sprouts, and a tossed salad. I added quinoa to the menu, but I knew I was the only one who would eat it. My family was not quite used to this grain and called it "kin-o-a."

NEALA

"All we need is a current copy of Lady's rabies vaccine," I told Dad when we sat down to dinner. He actually stopped drinking his beer and listened to me. "Mom said she'd call the vet tomorrow. I already emailed the city for a copy of her license."

"Good job, Neala."

Not only did he grin; his eyes were smiling. As if my heartbeat was lighter, I felt a strange rush in my chest. It was weird, but a good weird.

Mom joined in. "I arranged an appointment with Dr. Kessler. He said he's familiar with prescriptions for support animals. He has two other patients who used them for therapy, and they are doing better in social situations. He thinks this is a great idea for Neala."

I was so excited. "We already have Lady's Canine Obedience and Good Citizenship certifications." I turned to Dad. "Don't say it, Dad," I warned when he started to tease me about how much food Lady steals. "You know Lady is good. You spoil her. She expects human food from you."

I was glad Mom and Dad enrolled Lady and me into dog training classes a couple years ago. How lucky was that? "I'm going to do some more research about Emotional Support Animals on the internet after dinner."

Dad chuckled and said, "Great news! I hope this works for you. I'll pick up a halter and new leash on my way home tomorrow. Any particular color I should avoid?" Dad had learned to ask what he shouldn't get; it was easier than choosing what he thought he should get. If I said red, he would get anything in the red spectrum, including pink. I hate pink. Better to say don't get pink, purple, or lavender. I learned to be specific.

"Thanks, Dad. The one she has now is worn and ratty. Especially for school. Avoid colors. Stick to neutrals like gray, black, silver. Even plain leather is good."

CHAPTER NINETEEN

CLAIRE

"Mom, it says here I can get Lady registered as an ESA, but it costs about a hundred bucks," said Neala. "We have to scan Dr. Kessler's prescription and a picture of Lady. I'll have to look for a good one of her. Then they'll send us her official tags in about a week, but I'm able to download a certification today when we pay. Can I use your credit card?"

I glanced over Neala's shoulder to the computer screen. She found a way to expedite registration for Lady to become an ESA once we got the paperwork in order. "Get my purse and credit card. You can fill all this online stuff out and submit those forms yourself," I said.

I felt elated. I looked forward to this adventure of Neala and Lady going to school together. Most of all, it pleased me to see Neala participate and actively engage in the process— to advocate and help herself. More often than not, Neala shut down when it came to talking about her anxiety or taking steps to reduce it.

Lady perked her ears. Hearing her name, she must have figured out this involved her. Although stretched out at Neala's feet, Lady's eyebrows twitched with anticipation. Neala reached down and rubbed Lady's belly. Lady was a trusting dog. She often laid on her back, stomach exposed, paws in the air, waiting for a belly scratch. I noticed some matting of fur on Lady's hindquarters and suggested Neala clean up Lady before taking her to school.

That night, I watched Neala bathe Lady. Pride washed through me. She used sweet-smelling dog shampoo. Trimmed

Lady's nails. Carefully brushed dreads off her pet's hindquarters—Lady seemed to get them every time she laid down. Then she grabbed Lady's mouth, pried the jaws wide open, shoved the doggie toothbrush in, and gave Lady's teeth a thorough cleaning. I turned my nose up at the bacon-flavored toothpaste, but Lady enjoyed it. After her pampering, Lady jumped up on Neala's bed, and both girl and dog went fast to sleep.

Before I went to bed, I peeked in on Neala. Neala often had a hard time falling asleep. That night, I witnessed a serene look on my sleeping daughter's face. Lady lazily opened one eye to acknowledge me. I patted Lady on the head.

Thanks for stepping up, little dog. You have a significant role at Neala's school tomorrow.

The next morning, Lady strutted around in her new harness. It wasn't her official ESA vest yet but would work until the authorized one arrived. Her black and silver leash would match the vest perfectly. Lady started her little prance, indicating she was excited. She was keen at sensing something good was going to happen—a ride to the beach, a slice of cheese from the fridge, and donning a new outfit. Neala took hold of the leash and headed to the garage; the dog could hardly contain herself.

I completed the school's paperwork authorizing Lady as an Emotional Support Animal and also signed an agreement that Neala would clean up after her dog throughout the day and dispose of the poop properly. I was glad Kane offered his full blessing for this experiment. We had our ducks in a row, it was time to take the ESA challenge. Lady would go to school with Neala for a couple of weeks as a trial run. If all went well, and Lady's presence lessened Neala's anxiety, the school would extend Lady's welcome.

I pulled into the parking lot. Neala calmly comforted Lady. "It will be fine, girl," Neala said softly while caressing the dog's ears. Lady, on the other hand, ate up the attention. Her tail wagged with anticipation.

"Mom look at that kid. He is so great on skateboards. Watch."

I took note of the slim teen do smooth gliding on what Neala explained was a longboard. Though he was agile and fluid on the board, my intuition clicked—there was more to this kid than Neala let on. Neala lit up while she watched him.

The boy tipped his head toward Neala, and she blushed.

"That's Landon from Evergreen. Remember him?"

I couldn't recognize any of the kids anymore. Their matured faces looked different from when they were in middle school. "Not really," I said. "Everyone is growing up."

Neala opened the back door and grabbed Lady's leash before the dog could get herself into trouble. My new car had a hatchback, and Lady was supposed to sit back there, but every time Neala, Kane, or myself asked Lady to "load up," she'd jump in the rear of the hatch and slink her way to the rear seat. From there, she placed her front paws on the console. If the sunroof were open, she would push her head through, ears and lips flapping in the wind.

I noticed the poop-bag container dangling from one of the harness's clips. So far, so good. Then I saw students heading our way. When Neala got out of the car with a bounding Lady at her side, kids came over to see what was going on.

"Whoa, this is your dog?" asked one teen with a skateboard under his arm.

"You got approved! You and Lady can sit by me in class today," a red-headed girl added.

Neala smiled but didn't say anything. They shot questions, one after the other, before Neala had a chance to answer even one. Could they pet her? Could they hold the leash? Was her dog actually going to classes? Attention was on the pup, not Neala. Several hands reached out to stroke or scratch Lady. The dog seemed to be in her glory as she stretched her chin to get as many scratches as possible.

"Neala, here are your papers. Take them to the office before you do anything else," I warned, handing her the folded sheets. God, the drop off was so easy this morning! I did my best not to show my excitement. Not one frozen body part to report! It was the first day with Lady, and it was good.

I got back into the car and watched Neala saunter toward the school. Lady, surrounded by kids, led the way. Smiling, I started the ignition.

Dear God! I watched as Lady turned around and struggled to get back to the safety of the back seat. Neala tugged on the leash and redirected the dog but Lady's eyes stayed locked on the car.

"Ah, shit," I said aloud, but then relaxed when Lady followed Neala. Wouldn't that be the end all? An ESA who needs an ESA.

I pulled out of the lot and drove home. Was Lady up to the task?

NEALA

After bringing Lady's papers to Karla, I introduced Lady to the administration staff. I stayed alert as I walked toward my first-period history class. She tugged on her leash to lead the way. A delay in the office made me the last person to enter the classroom. My history teacher not only welcomed me, he asked me to introduce Lady. My pup made her rounds, sniffing everyone as she went from desk to desk and adding a few nose-nudges for some petting. Then the commotion died down, as if it had all been planned, Lady settled in at my feet.

Lunch was an adventure. First, I tied Lady to a picnic table. The leash was long enough for her to jump up and sit on the table. Nola grabbed her lunch and moved it just before Lady stole a bite.

"Can't you control your dog?" a student I didn't know sneered as he walked by.

A flash of pain seared my heart.

"Yes!" defended Nola, "She can, can't you control yourself?"

I smiled at Nola. "He's been a jerk since kindergarten," Nola explained. "Don't let him bother you. He is probably jealous because his owner can't take him to work!"

"Ooh! Burn," I said, and we shared a giggle.

We finished our lunch and accepted compliments about Lady's beautiful coat. The kids discussed Lady's age in dog years and human years. Some kids stopped by to give Lady a scratch.

After lunch, Lady dragged me around the quad and lunch area while she inhaled crumbs, munched broken chips, and chewed any trace of food wrapper left on the ground.

Having Lady as my companion was cool. I'm not sure how to explain the difference. I could get out of the car at school. I focused on Lady and her behavior most of the time. Mom said she noticed I had less anxiety "creeping" through me when the dog was with me. I think she's right about our morning routine—the distractions of getting Lady ready and caring for her during the day alleviated tension. Plus, Lady was so funny. It was hard to be serious when Lady sucked in the crumbs and food scraps like a vacuum cleaner.

Most days were good. Having Lady with me helped me feel comfortable walking home after school. I didn't need Mom to pick me up early from class. My pup was a mascot of sorts. Most kids liked her, but some kids were mean. I could also tell which teachers had problems with a dog in their class and possibly even resented it.

Sometimes, I felt guilty. Alina said not to take on anyone's feeling but to pay attention to my own. But when teachers or parents, even some of my family thought I faked being scared, it was difficult. It made Mom mad when people didn't believe us. She told a resistant teacher that if I were blind or had another disability, the use of an animal wouldn't be questioned. Because they can't see my disability, it doesn't make it untrue. I struggled with it every day. Every single day.

Between my medicine and the effort to keep my shit together all day long, I got exhausted. Having Lady at school sometimes helped, but she also tired me out. She wanted to wander around the classroom, go outside, pull me to the lunch area, and beg for food. It was up to me to control her behavior. She listened to my commands, yet I felt sorry for her because it's natural for her to want to investigate all the smells. She's a curious being, no doubt about that.

After a few months, the routine between us stopped causing distraction. No longer interested in taking Lady to school, I often left her at home. But Lady continued to bounce around like an acrobat when I got my backpack but turned dour when I didn't grab and attach her halter vest. I felt terrible.

Lady had learned the routine pretty quickly, mainly because she got to "go for a ride," but I couldn't think about managing her all day anymore. It drained me. Mom got irritated because sometimes I called her to get Lady only minutes after she'd dropped us off.

I carried a certain amount of confusion inside. I understood why I should appreciate the effort my parents and the school made for me. Not everyone is allowed to take their pet to school. My mom was really patient. I felt safe knowing I could count on her. Some days, dealing with me must have taken a lot out of her.

The strangest part? Sometimes my heart wasn't in the right place. A dark space filled me up with worry, and it was difficult to let the good stuff in. Each day, I made a conscious effort to do my best, even though it might not have seemed like it to others. I could try my all-out best, but then I'd implode, fall inside myself, and drop into the darkness that swallowed me. It was tough to show my appreciation and gratefulness.

I felt ashamed of myself and my behavior, but really, I didn't do anything wrong. No one demanded anything or chased me except my demons, and they were relentless.

CHAPTER TWENTY

CLAIRE

Neala had a set appointment with her therapist, Alina, every Thursday at 7:00 p.m. Usually, between the fourth and fifth visit, Kane or I, or both of us, had our time with Alina. We'd check in, review our experiences, and gain insights. On my next visit, I would bring up the dog situation.

I disclosed the declining effect Lady had as Neala's ESA, and Alina explained that Lady was a temporary tool which, apparently, had served its purpose. Neala would need to move to another form of security.

"I understand your disappointment, but it's a good step," Alina told me. "If we don't help Neala get through these small steps, if she doesn't reach beyond these daily anxieties, it's possible she will develop full-blown agoraphobia," she explained. "We want to avoid her becoming housebound, which could debilitate her, hinder her quality of life, possibly for always." Then Alina added, "Don't give up. Though there were good days with Lady, she's not a permanent solution."

I think Alina could read despair on my face. I was at a loss for words because I looked at Neala's anxiety as a "high school" thing. I'd hoped she'd outgrow the anxiety before it damaged her ability to graduate and move on in life. Alina offered a thought I hadn't considered before. A lifelong disability like anxiety could delay not only her graduation but college, driving, getting a job, or possibly becoming a responsible and contributing adult member of society.

"It's okay, Claire. We are working with Neala to get through her panic attacks. You can help her. When you see her withdraw, remind her to take a slow breath." Alina told me to sit in the car for a moment when I dropped Neala off and for us to breathe together.

"She may take your lead and it will help calm her," Alina suggested.

At first, hearing how invasive her condition might become overwhelmed me. Yet it gave me a new depth of understanding. Knowing the painful anxiety Neala experienced daily and that this condition was at the core of her young mind, broke my heart. The fact she may never figure out what caused the anxiety or how to get rid of it brought me pain—like relentless stabs in my chest. Forced to conclude her disability was here and might never go away, I realized the best we could do was to accept it.

The second half of her freshman year, Neala's struggle to step out of the car continued to harass her. When she did go to school, she ended up spending much of her time sitting outside of the classroom, wandering around school grounds, or occasionally popping into creative classes like chorus or printmaking. Because those classes kept her from being confined to her desk, she felt like she could hide behind the commotion.

By the spring, a meeting with the school faculty was set up for an overview of the year. The discussion with Neala's teachers and school administrators proved to be both a blessing and a disappointment. Although Neala was out of the classroom much of the time, she completed enough of her assignments to get passing grades. She'd be promoted to tenth grade. What a relief. Before they adjourned the meeting, Principal Whitney suggested finding a tutor to help Neala keep on track and eliminate the stress of getting assignments turned in on time.

The last day of school arrived, and at the final bell, parents and students shared rides to the community pool for a party. Neala passed, so I treated her to a sundae instead. We talked about what we'd do with all our free time and what type of day trips we would take. We avoided the fact that summer, with its long break, would eventually sink into fall. Another semester was right around the corner.

CHAPTER TWENTY-ONE

CLAIRE

Sometimes, in the evening, Neala and I would make a quick grocery run, and on occasion, Neala used the debit card to complete the transaction.

"I like the card, Mom," Neala said. "You don't have to worry if you have enough money or counting it out. And even better, I can use the self-checkout and not talk to anyone."

I put a few food items in the bag and added the skateboarder magazine Neala wanted. "Actually, you do have to know what's in your account; the card could be declined," I told Neala.

As if she'd just realized there was no secure way to get around a money shortage, my daughter scrunched her nose.

"And sometimes, cash is better because you can't overspend. You have to stick to a budget." I smiled. "The trick is to round up the cost of each item as you put it in the cart. If I have twenty bucks, I round up to eighteen, getting the things I actually came to the store to purchase, then I check out. Safe every time." I winked at Neala.

I used as many opportunities to prepare Neala for events like shopping, restaurants, and parties—like the Fourth of July barbeque we were invited to. No doubt, there would be unguarded moments, and that was something we could plan for as well.

I practiced square breathing with Neala. The exercises felt silly when Neala didn't have anxiety, but I liked silliness. It took the edge off. Unfortunately, I forgot to calculate my own stressors from time to time, which gave the adverse effect.

I watched Kane pack our old green Coleman cooler with ice and beer. Summer offered a calm respite for our family. I minded Neala's behavior after school let out. Most days, Neala stayed home and watched movies or played video games. When Neala mentioned her online gaming friends, I wasn't sure if that counted as socializing, but it was definitely interactions with others. Once summer began, Neala's anxiety diminished.

"Neala, don't forget to pack your bathing suit," I called. "I know you said you don't want to swim but take it anyway. You might change your mind."

Getting ready to go anywhere became a battle. Whatever I suggested, Neala counter-suggested. When I'd give in to an argument, she'd change her mind. I resorted to the "diaper-bag theory" with my high-schooler. I had a bag containing things I thought she might need for the day. I put it in the car—ready for her to bemoan that she hadn't thought she'd want something when in fact she would. Chances were, if she left her bathing suit home, she would ask us to drive home and get it. She was unpredictable—I saw she wanted to participate in activities, but sometimes, her fears held her back.

When we left the house, Neala prepared for the worse, but I learned to prepare for the best. At the time, it never occurred to me that Neala would use excuses to avoid activities or prompt reasons to leave a gathering early.

I gained clarity of my tendency to micromanage Neala. Kane told me I babied her, and I guess it looked that way. I summed it up as preparedness. While I was hyper-organizing, she was major-manipulating. I am pretty sure that at the time, neither Neala nor I were aware of our behavior.

I loved going to Sophia's house, so I accepted the invite for the summer holiday without hesitation. She lived in a historic neighborhood that prompted me to remember that anything was possible. The old homes stood proudly as new occupants completed renovations. Time went by, the seasons of weather, war, and wealth. The highs and lows in life, and yet, these homes prevailed. The neighborhood reminded that life's moments passed quickly. Events fleeted to memories as we breathed. I was happy. The picnic would create fun memories of the Fourth of July celebration. I'd looked forward to the party for weeks.

Sophia asked me to bring my famous Nutella Ice Box Cake, a favorite with the crowd, especially Kane. For the holiday I added red, white, and blue star-shaped sprinkles on the whipped cream top. Smiling with delight I covered the cake in plastic wrap, careful not to get any of it on my clothes; white jeans with my red halter top for the party.

Kane said I was smokin' in that outfit, so I knew I could get away with anything my delicious dark side desired. I looked forward to cutting loose and tossing back some tequila. Mamma wanted to party! Besides, with any luck, Kane and I might have our own firework show later on.

The garage door rumbled and echoed throughout the house. Kane revved the classic Impala's engine then came in the kitchen, balanced my dessert, and put it in the car's roomy trunk. As he lifted the cooler of beer, he called for Neala. I pictured him in the driver's seat, the ancient A/C turned on, and waiting for us.

I touched up my lipstick in the entry hall mirror and then blew myself a kiss. Smiling at my reflection, I pushed my bangs out of my face, "Come on, Neala, Dad's in the car already."

Neala plodded down the stairs. She wore her typical black jeans, but I noticed she decided to get in the patriotic fun by wearing a Captain America t-shirt that dared to peek out from beneath her hoodie. Neala had applied make-up. She'd fixed up her eyes with trending colors and perfect brows. She looked pulled together for the party. Noting Neala took time to look festive spiked my anticipation for a fun day ahead.

On the jaunt to Sophia's house, I chatted nonstop. Kane gave obligatory nods, an indication that he was at least half-way listening to what I said. Kane pulled alongside Sophia's driveway.

"We can unload here, and then I'll find a spot to park," Kane said, stepping on the parking brake, then got out.

I climbed out of the car, my purse and light shawl in hand. The day was warm, but a crisp, clear evening was forecasted for the fireworks. Some younger kids ran through the sprinklers on the front lawn. I watched Kane head to the trunk, and I stole a glance at Neala.

"Hey, Neala," he called. "Grab Mom's dessert."

Neala sat in the back seat. She didn't acknowledge her dad, didn't unlatch her seatbelt, and didn't speak. Instead, she pushed herself into the seat cushion.

"Come on, Neala, let's go," I said, peering at her. I kept my voice calm with encouragement. "You don't have to play with the kids out here. And, you know how much Sophia loves you."

"Mom. Wait. I can't go," said Neala, then she smooshed her shoulders even further into the back seat.

I looked toward Kane and narrowed my eyes—a signal for help. He shrugged then hoisted the cooler over his shoulder. Closing the trunk with a free hand, he just stood there.

Undecided if I contained enough tactfulness to comfort my daughter or the gumption to throw a hissy fit, I blinked at Kane. The familiar knot in my stomach squeezed tight. In a snap, my fury cracked open. "God damn it, Neala! Come on," I growled like a rabid animal. "Don't start this now." I shot a piercing look at Kane. "And thanks for your help!"

It was in moments like this that I begrudged being the family's cheerleader. The past year, I'd been overcome with exhaustion keeping everyone on track. I resented Neala's anxiety and her behavior. Even on a day that promised fun and lightheartedness, her repeated bullshit ate at me. Feeling like a victim, I wondered if I would ever have another goddamn fun day.

As if my ego gave me an imaginary slap, I pulled from my pity and stepped away from the car. I thought of Alina's advice and remembered my job was to set an example for Neala. An outburst of fury wouldn't help the situation, but if I kept calm, it might.

I took a deep breath and dug my toes into the tips of my shoes for grounding. I let out my irritations with a long exhale. I shifted my weight, adjusted the shoulder strap of my purse, and said, "Okay. Here's what we are going to do, honey." I got into the rear seat with Neala. "Let me start again. I'm sorry I snapped at you. I had no excuse." I folded my wrap and laid it over my lap. "What can I do to help you?"

Neala put her hands in front of her mouth. "I just want to go home. I really don't want to go in there. I don't want to see anyone today."

"But Neala, it is the Fourth of July. Sophia made your favorite salad, and it's going to be a great day. You can even sit by me the whole time." I was annoyed with myself as soon as I said that.

Neala continued to sit silently.

"Okay, just have a root beer. Dad got the kind you like best—in the bottles. Then see how you feel," I coaxed.

Kane left Neala with me. The cooler looked heavy, so I guess he brought it to the backyard. When he came back for the dessert, he stopped to check in on us.

"What's going on?" Kane asked Neala. He bent down into the back seat, one hand on the roof to talk to her.

"Neala won't get out," I said.

Kane proffered his hand as I got out of the car. I closed the door so I could speak freely with Kane. "I just want to have one normal day, and now this—I know I'm being selfish but . . ."

Kane's calm logic often soothed me, and I waited to hear his advice. I knew I'd overreacted. Sometimes it was hard for me to let things unfold organically. Wanting instant gratification, I expected to see the full impact of results immediately.

Kane opened the door. "Neala, are you coming in or not?"

"Not," she said.

Kane closed the car door. "Look, I'll get her home. You go to the party, and I'll be right back. Obviously, this is hard for her, so let me take her where she'll be more comfortable."

"But it is the Fourth of Ju—"

"She doesn't care, Claire. She doesn't want to be here, so let's not make things worse for her. I'll be right back." He pulled his keys from his pocket then leaned over to kiss me. "Hey, I don't want to miss seeing you in that outfit for too long," he flirted, winking at me as he hopped into the driver's seat and drove off.

I watched Neala's face through the window when Kane told her he'd take her home. Through the tinted glass, I could see relief loosen Neala's body. She nodded in agreement, and her shoulders fell as if relaxed. I stood on the sidewalk and watched them round a corner. It was bittersweet—this was the first holiday Neala's anxiety had ruined for me. I felt sad when I thought of Neala sitting home alone for the afternoon. I remembered we had some fireworks though, so I vowed to return home early enough to let Neala set some off. Feeling a bit of resolve, I turned on my high heels and walked into the party.

Naturally, when everyone saw me, they asked where Kane and Neala were. I told them Neala didn't feel well. "Her anxiety grabbed ahold of her," I offered. "Kane's taking her home, and he'll be back soon."

"Wow, look at you!" Sophia said, approaching me from behind the built-in wet bar. "Take this, momma, you deserve it." She handed me a tall shot of my favorite Reposado tequila on ice with a slice of lime. "Bottoms up!" she cheered, and together we tossed the liquor down. Still feeling a little down, I set my shot glass on the bar.

I'd been waiting for weeks to cut loose and party, but now, while I waited for Kane, I felt deflated and sad. A plethora of moods rumbled through me: guilt for wanting to have a good time; anger at Neala's inability to cope—just for one goddamn stinking time. Was that too much to ask? Once again, I was disappointed in myself for having these thoughts.

Sophia poured me a second shot. I knew I should slow down before I became an emotional one-woman pity party. Doing my best to push away my sorrows, I began my familiar mantra: "Life won't be like this forever, keep the faith in myself as well as for Neala. Everything will turn out okay."

An abrupt raucous and loud jeering came from the garage. I could tell Kane, the life of the party, had returned. Calls of delight ricocheted through the house as the men gathered at the keg to greet him.

The hell with it, I thought. I was done overthinking this day. I swallowed the shot Sophia poured then grabbed the bottle of tequila from the bar and filled my glass to the brim. If there was a time to get drunk and fall into the abyss, this was it. Throwing caution to the wind, I headed toward the garage to indulge in some "party time" with my man. "Happy Freakin' Fourth of July!" I said aloud.

CHAPTER TWENTY-TWO

CLAIRE

July broiled into the hot, dry month of August and not-so-subtle hints of the new school year rapidly approached. The air was thick with heat, bodies were sticky with sweat, and nerves were maxed with trepidation. Seeing "back to school" banners in stores amplified disheartened feelings of the summer's end.

Kane and I sat with our coffee and Sunday newspaper—its inserts claiming the best deals on school items. "I always hated seeing these ads," Kane said. "When I was a kid, this was the worst."

"Me, too, honey," I sympathized. My depression intruded on my usually bright spirits as did my usual enthusiasm for school clothes shopping. Doing my best to cope included feigned advocacy for all black clothes and hoodies sold at the mall. Early on, Neala favored jeans and hoodies, but once she started Norden High, black became the preferred color for all her clothing.

At the end of the week, I dragged Neala to the mall. I looked around and Neala wasn't so oddly dressed. All the stores offered hoodies in their storefront windows; surf shops sported adorable turquoise with white piping assembled with fragile and feminine-looking fabric, and a Goth store displayed several superhero motif hoodies.

"Hi, Mrs. Byrnes." A cheerful voice arose from behind a stack of skinny jeans. Nola popped her head up.

"Hi, Nola. Getting some back to school shopping done?" I smiled warmly at Neala's friend.

"No, I've been working here all summer. My mom says I have to quit once school starts, though," Nola whined. "You know how she is. 'Education first.'" She mimicked her mom. "But I'd rather have store discounts and a paycheck." Nola laughed.

"Listen to your mom, she knows what she's talking about, believe me," I said to encourage her. "You have your whole life to work. By the way, have you seen Neala? She wanted to shop a little longer at *Hot Topic*. She said she'd meet me here."

Nola stood on her toes to peer over mounds of clothing on display. "I haven't seen her, but I just came off my break. I will keep an eye out for her. I want her to try on these pants." Nola waved her hand across a jeans display. Nola looked to the back of the shop. "Wait, there she is, at the clearance rack."

"She must have been ahead of me, and probably missed your return." Nola and I walked to the back of the store.

Nola had a magical way of charming Neala out of her shell and encouraging her to have fun.

Determined to find last winter's dark colors, Neala had gone straight to the sales rack in the back. I watched her stick her chin out, a look she made when she was deciding on an item. Surprisingly, she held a pair of black jean shorts with pre-made rips in them.

"Not today, young lady. No way those are for school," I said.

Neala put the shorts back and admired some heavy-weight hoodies. With Nola's help we searched through several articles of clothing before Neala settled on a pair of black skinny jeans and a dark charcoal-gray hoodie with a wolf on the back.

When we checked out, Nola told us that she'd get off work soon. I offered to drive her home, but the girls, crazy for their egg rolls, wanted to eat at the food court. Nola said her mom would drive them home later.

I was glad and gave Neala permission to stay for their dinner date and returned back to a couple of stores I liked. After making a few indulgent purchases, I headed home. It was hard to imagine that I was a few days away from driving Neala to school again. Though I tried to be optimistic by putting last year behind me, a sick feeling swirled in my stomach when I considered it.

I got home and deposited my new lipstick and silky socks on my bed. Next, I checked my email. Top of the list, in bold font, was a reminder about the first assembly and back to school pictures for students. Designated arrival times were determined by class. This year, Neala would be a sophomore; her time slot was eleven a.m. Neala's agenda would be to first go to the gym, get her picture taken for her school ID, and confirm her class schedule and electives.

I already asked Larisa to approve this day off in case Neala needed help. I was glad I'd asked Nola if she would be there. I couldn't put my finger on it, but Nola had a unique way of making Neala feel safe—sometimes by making Neala laugh at herself, giving Neala her space, or letting Neala find her way through complicated maneuvers.

I reflected on everyone's satisfaction when Neala earned enough course credits to pass freshman year and advance to becoming a sophomore. However, I procrastinated with the principal's recommendation about getting a tutor for Neala. I wasn't sure what area Neala would need help with, and the additional financial strain for the family would be challenging to pull off. It was tricky with Neala.

Though Neala didn't attend her classes, she completed the assignments. She fell behind when she didn't turn in the work or show up on test days. Considering how few hours she spent in the classroom, Neala seemed to absorb information and attain the knowledge quickly. When she did take the tests, she usually passed them, if barely. One theory was that Neala's lack of organization led to her anxiety and less than satisfactory grades. At this point, I wasn't sure a tutor could help with that.

I remembered that from kindergarten through fifth grade, Neala had complained that other kids at school annoyed her. Kane and I mistook her grumbles as boredom. When it came to remembering facts and filling out dittos, Neala was a straight-A student. But as her parents, we wanted her to learn to think rather than get through school by memorizing facts.

Comfortable with older kids, Neala often hung out with Sarah and her friends. We believed Neala also resented the juvenile rules because she held herself to high accountability.

Assessing last year's significant change in behavior revealed learning was not the issue. What was clear—Neala didn't like being confined to a classroom. When chaos hit, and the students misbehaved, additional stress flooded her.

Plus, it upset her to be held accountable for other kids' actions. When a student caused the entire class to be punished for being too loud or any other infraction, she detested being treated like one of them. She preferred calm, industrious, and safe learning atmospheres, not elementary school madness.

I heard the front door open and Neala call out, "Bye, Nola, see you tomorrow." She came upstairs and saw me sitting at the computer. "Hi, Mom."

"Hey, how was your shopping spree and dinner?" I asked.

Neala dropped some shopping bags on the floor. "Nola found a great pair of pants for me. I hope they fit after all the Chinese food I ate!" Neala laughed. Then, as assumed, she pulled out two black hoodies, one with a white skateboard logo on it, the other from Vans, and new shoes; her beloved Converse, but this year she chose a daring shade of red.

Getting ready to delve into sophomore year presented new challenges for both Neala and me. When Neala said she and Nola planned to take some classes together, I was grateful. The quick pace of high school meant it could be easy for her to fall behind. When the school year began, Nola took it upon herself to get assignments to Neala on days she couldn't get to school. When allowed, the two girls were study partners, and because Neala thought up good ideas but had a hard time getting them to the classroom, Nola typically occupied the lead, and together they did well.

Before going to bed that night, I felt both hopeful and uneasy. Many parents must get back-to-school jitters. But mine were demons, and they seemed so much more real.

CHAPTER TWENTY-THREE

NEALA

Mom dropped me in front of the school. After the hustle of kids getting out of their cars died down, I walked toward a mass group of sophomores. Heading to the gym for registration, I tasted a tang of barf at the back of my throat but told my body to chill . . . and it did. Kids from last year laughed and talked about summer or asked about classes. It looked like a sea of bothersome people waiting to hassle me.

Nola was at the end of one line. I walked up and punched her in the arm. "I found you," I said. Nola had dressed up for her class ID photo and looked pretty in her red outfit. Suddenly, I wished I'd worn something other than my hoodie. Maybe my green t-shirt underneath wasn't so bad. Definitely taking my hoodie off.

"Ouch, you ass!" Nola said. She rubbed her arm but flashed her famous smile. She let me get in line ahead of her. Nola was protective like that. I didn't know if she is aware of it. "Hey, did you see Harvard yet? His new haircut, oh, baby!" We nicknamed Charlie Bennet, who dressed like an 'Ivy Leaguer,' Harvard. It was our secret name for him at first, but now everyone called him that. Turns out, he didn't only dress preppy, but he had real brains, 4.4 GPA, and he was on the last year's student body.

"No, I didn't, where is he?" I looked in the direction of Nola's nod. Harvard was pretty cute. "What about GQ? Have you seen him?" I asked, referring to the cute boy in our oceanic biology class last year. He could get away with some odd fashions usually found in men's magazines. Most other boys would look ridiculous, but GQ always pulled it off.

"Not a sign." Nola pushed me along. "Keep it moving."

I shoved her back but shuffled a few steps forward. Before I knew it, I'd checked into every queue required for class enrollment for my sophomore year—including the headshot for my student ID. I decided to leave my hoodie on, after all. If anyone needed to ID me, I'd probably be wearing it.

Man, I desperately wanted to dye my hair electric turquoise blue, but mom told me not to do it until after class pictures. With my head covered, no one would suspect it wasn't blue before. I had argued with her. She didn't want me to draw negative attention to myself. I reminded her I already covered my head. So many kids dyed their hair, I would mix right in. She won the battle—I'd have to wait until after pictures—but I won the war. Now that I'd had my photo taken, I could use the bottle of dye waiting at home. Yes!

Nola asked me to go with her and some other kids to the sandwich shop across the street.

"No, not today," I said. "I can't wait to get home to the hair dye sitting on my bathroom counter." I ran fingers through my locks. Ten days until school started, and I wanted to look extra good on the first day. Nola understood and we went our separate ways.

CHAPTER TWENTY-FOUR

NEALA

Mom dragged me to her session with Alina one night because Dad had to work late. Since Dad couldn't make it, and Mom doesn't like being out at night by herself, I agreed. I pretended it was a pain, but in reality, when I'm with Mom, I feel better. Sometimes she annoys the shit out of me, but I can't argue that she doesn't care. Besides, with the first day of school approaching, we could both use some help. Mom's there for me. She doesn't always get me, but she tries.

Mom and I made our way up the steep steps. Alina's office was in an old Victorian-era house. Rooms had been converted into offices. The large space in the entry had been remodeled and now serves as a waiting room. The house was kinda cool because of the array of closets, cubbies, and nooks. I figured if I lived there, I would have Captain America action figures peeking out from most of them. Because the old house was used as an office building, especially for head-peepers, little decoration filled the walls or the halls. Part of me found the uncluttered décor in the common areas comfortable and soothing.

"Wow, I love your hair! You look ready for school to begin, Neala," Alina said after we settled down and finished the how-do-you-dos. I touched my blue streaks and glanced at Mom.

"Don't look at me." She smiled. "I only have to drive you. You and your hair," Mom said playfully; sometimes that worked to relax me, though it didn't always help.

"A big worry is that I will freeze when we get to school. I was doing better at the end of the year, but now I felt like I have to start all over again." I tried to sound neutral, but my voice cracked.

"Neala, you did great. You completed the last whole year of school, and you did it by yourself. Your mom and I are here to help you, but you are doing the work. We are proud of you," Alina said.

Mom looked like she was holding her breath. Like she was afraid to break the calming spell Alina had cast through the room.

"Actually, you won't be starting over. You will be picking up where you left off. That means you can get to your goals quicker. The rest of us: your parents, teachers, and me, are here to support you," Alina said. "So, have you thought about a practice run? You and Mom can drive to school a few mornings before school starts. Maybe go about the same time the school bell rings. Get out of the car and practice walking to a classroom."

"That's a good idea," Mom said, pressing her hands together.

I felt apprehensive about it but could tell that Mom was going to make me do it.

"It is a start," Alina said. "Also, I want you to be sure we keep your appointment the first week of school, so we can talk about anything that comes up."

"Perfect," Mom replied.

Before I knew it, Mom and I were walking down the steep staircase. "I don't want to practice. That sounds dumb."

"Tell you what," Mom replied. "We'll give it a try and see how you feel." Mom reached the last of the steps and opened the door to leave. "I don't want you to think about it or worry about it, okay? It will only be practice, and no one will be there. I promise."

She clutched my hand. I let her because it was dark outside now.

"Let's get some dessert to take home to Dad," she said, indicating the specialty market near our parked car.

I squeezed her hand and let go.

CHAPTER TWENTY-FIVE

CLAIRE

"Come on, Neala, I need to go to the store so I can get dinner started," I pled. I'd asked Neala to practice getting out of the car at the school two mornings in a row, and Neala had refused. Aggravated, I decided to get creative and planned to trick Neala. School started the day after next, and I figured it was time to play dirty.

"Can we get those fish crackers I like? I can put some in my lunch. Also, Lady needs more treats." Neala listed off additional items she wanted.

Feeling sneaky but justified, I drove to the store by way of a detour, toward the campus to do a practice run.

Alina suggested Neala work on her vehicle exit, then walk up to her first-period classroom, and touch the door. Neala only had to give it a try. I didn't care how lame Neala thought the exercise was, it was practice, and she was going to do it.

"Hey, why are we here?" Neala asked, her tone exaggerated her protest.

"It's the practice run. You wouldn't do it yesterday or this morning, so here we are." I stopped the car at the curb.

"I'm not doing that."

"You are, and you need to get out now." I wasn't about to pay for therapy and then ignore behavior-changing practices. I tried to make my voice louder, giving the impression I was a lot bigger. "Do it!"

"I'm not a mountain lion, Mom. You can't scare me by trying to look bigger like that. This is stupid. Besides, no one is here. The campus will be crowded when school starts."

Neala didn't get budge.

Exhausted, disappointed, and plain done, I drove us home.

The day before school, we went for the test run. This time Neala climbed out of the car without argument or hesitation. I watched her walk to her first-period class and slap her hand on the door. She continued to several other classrooms and did the same thing. She was demonstrating her frustration, but I didn't care. She'd done what we'd set out to do.

"See? Stupid." She got back in and slammed the door.

"Hey, watch it!" I scolded. I wasn't about to let her attitude into my car. "Maybe it is stupid to you, but the whole point is to note how empowered you feel about it and pull up that power when you are scared. So, how ya feel?"

"I feel stupid."

I knew there was no reasoning with her. She had the Byrnes' stubborn streak, but at least we had done the exercise, and with some good Irish luck, it would work its magic when needed.

SOPHOMORE YEAR

CHAPTER TWENTY-SIX

NEALA

I did my best to keep positive. The night before my first day of school, I'd gathered my back-to-school items and put them in my backpack. I arranged everything inside its handy pockets. When I slung the pack over my shoulder, I felt pressure from my pens and the pointed corner of a new sketchbook inside. I promised myself I'd relax if (when?) the anxiety-dragon crashed toward me. I'd gotten up early and applied heavy black eyeshadow. I didn't bother to comb out my hair; I liked the way strands showed off my blue hue when my hair was unkempt.

I found Mom's car keys, started the car, moved to the passenger seat, and waited for her. The drive was a mere five minutes, even when lights were red. I can do this. I snapped my seatbelt.

Aware of the floorboards vibrating through my new, red Converse, I held on to the sensation. As the quivering shook the blood in my calves, I imagined them waking from a long sleep. Pins and needles formed, pushed through blood vessels, pierced muscle, and poked my skin. Suddenly, my pants felt too tight on my thighs. Attempting to relieve painful, nabbing stings on my legs, I shook off the first fingers of fear by opening my hands wide then closed them into tight fists. The pointed tips of my faux nails dug impressions into my palms. Inside my head, a tornado brewed. Thoughts spun. NNNoooo, no, no, no, no! Mom, can't you see me? You just keep driving! Can't you tell how terrible I feel? How much I hurt right now! Silent screams filled the abyss of my terror.

As if thrown in a lake wearing weights, I suddenly felt pulled under. The heavy pressure of suffocation loomed, and my lungs burned. "Oh, my God, I can't breathe," I struggled to say. I clawed the armrest with my right hand, blindly searched for the down button, quickly lowered the window, and gasped for air.

"Christ, Neala!" Mom exhaled. She recognized my familiar blanched pallor and telltale sheen of sweat across my brow. She put her coffee in the built-in holder and used both hands for some tricky driving maneuvers. She pulled into the pre-school parking lot a block from Norden High, and parked the car.

"Mom, I'm sorry. I'm-so-sorry. I'm-so-sorry!" I cried. I pulled a tissue out of my backpack and wiped the tears from my eyes.

"Oh, honey, I am so sorry, too." Mom got out of the car and went around to the passenger door. At first, I wasn't going to unlock it, but Mom patiently waited. After a few heartbeats, I trusted Mom would not use intimidation to manipulate me. We'd already discussed how her idea for the sneaky trial run had made me feel.

I was precise. When I popped the lock, Mom opened the door and dropped down to my level. After unclicking my seatbelt, she tossed the backpack out of the way and wrapped her arms around me.

"It's okay. It's going to be okay," Mom purred into my blue mane.

I hugged Mom back. There was a preschool on the same block as the high school, so the view of little kids heading toward their classrooms made the conjoined parking lot feel surreal. I continued to hold on to Mom. I thought my hair was still damp from last night's shower, but I realized it was wet from Mom's tears.

The first day of classes, and I freaked out. Maybe I'd feel better on the second day. I kept thinking back to the day

Nola and I registered. That day wasn't so bad. But today, my stress overwhelmed me. I would do better, at least that was my plan.

The build-up that had surrounded the start of school was too much, and I cracked. Mom drove me home after my meltdown, and I slept until dinner. I was so exhausted from the ordeal; I didn't hear Mom leave home or return after work.

Lady cuddled with me most of the day. She's as moldable as Jell-O when she sleeps on my bed . . . rolling this way and that, keeping one paw near my face the whole time.

The next day, I prepared myself as we approached the campus. Mom didn't talk, but I knew she was concerned. She glanced at the clock. She'd been more relaxed over summer break without the worry about getting to work on time. That was part of my problem, I sometimes hoped Mom would quit her job. She seemed under pressure, and I worried about her.

We pulled into the parking lot. Go time! I took a deep breath—the way Alina had shown me. She'd said that when my mind raced, I'd forget to breathe. Then, with less oxygen, my brain went into a panic mode. Like yesterday. Alina explained it much better, but all I know is if I kept breathing, I would move through this anxiety. I would even live to see another day. Great.

I swooped my arm to the seat behind me, grabbed my backpack, and opened the door. "You'll pick me up right after school?" I asked Mom. She said she would. So, I scanned the area and noticed an open space that I could duck into before other students arrived. Nola texted last night and promised to stay close if I needed her. She didn't hurry over to me when she saw me. She understood how I felt about having my space.

"Bye, Mom." I closed the car door.

I didn't know who was more surprised when I got out, said goodbye, and walked toward the school. My teeth were clenched—but I did it!

Midway to my first-period class, I saw Nola with a cluster of kids in the quad. True to her word, when Nola caught my eye she didn't smile, wink, or otherwise indicate that she'd seen me. While other kids might think Nola was acting like a mean girl, to me, ignoring me was the greatest thing a trusted friend could do.

CHAPTER TWENTY-SEVEN

CLAIRE

I read troublesome comments on Neala's first quarter's progress report. I realized I couldn't hold off on a tutor any longer. Though more secure getting out of the car, Neala needed improvement getting into the classroom. To alleviate stress, I'd gotten Neala excused from the sophomore camping trip. Yet, according to comments on this report, Neala neither tried to collect course assignments nor turn them in.

Suspicious of her lengthy afternoon naps and mind-numbing hours of video games, I speculated Neala was not getting any work done. When I mentioned my thoughts to Kane, he said he could take her bedroom door off the hinges like he had in middle school, but together we decided it wasn't a good idea then and a worse idea now. However, the progress report alerted me that I needed to act.

Flipping through the file with Neala's doctors and other professional contacts, I found the tutor's number. Last spring, Principal Whitney had referred Jill Armstrong from the nearby university. Fortunately, I reached her. She was available on Tuesdays. Jill said she would consider a sliding scale. This was good news for our family budget.

In the beginning, I hesitated to hire a tutor. I knew my daughter was bright, so I didn't understand how a tutor could help. I brought the subject up with Alina. She went over the expending amount of energy Neala used to get to school and stay on campus, and therefore, there wasn't much drive left at the end of the day. Her liveliness was depleted, and homework, no matter how little, sucked what remained. Homework was a carryover for stressors. It wasn't so much because Neala couldn't understand or do the assignments, but it linked to her school anxiety. A tutor could possibly help get the work accomplished. Even though Neala would still have to battle her dragons.

After my discussion with Alina, I felt assured with my decision to hire Jill. Neala fell behind, and an action plan was imperative. With constant communication between Neala's teachers, the support offered, reduction of homework, minimization of reports, and waiving off-campus projects, it still wasn't enough to make up for the amount of work Neala couldn't bring herself to do.

Jill and I agreed to meet at the library for Neala's tutoring sessions. "It will benefit Neala if we can get her out of her home environment for tutoring. This way, home can remain a sanctuary from anything scholastic," Jill advised. "Also, the library will offer quiet space. It would be great if it became a place of respite and knowledge for her."

"Come on, Neala, time to meet Jill. Let's get in the car." The library was a ten-minute walk from the house, but I planned to drive to escape the barrage of complaints I'd have to endure from Neala about walking there.

"I don't need a tutor." Neala came down the stairs.

I knew Neala wouldn't win this argument after the mess she was in at school. The stomping I heard confirmed Neala would do as she was told, but it wouldn't be easy nor pleasant.

I parked at the library and got out of the car. I didn't hear Neala behind me, turned around, and went to the passenger side of the vehicle. Tapping the window with my knuckle, I said, "Well? Come on."

I could see my reflection; knitted eyebrows and a frown in the glass. Neala was sunk into the car's seat.

"Shit," I said. Tempted to give up, but determined to try, I went into the library without Neala. I hoped my daughter would eventually summon the courage to join me.

I walked by shelves of newly released volumes when a woman about mid-thirties with short hair and a pleasing smile approached me. The woman adjusted a satchel of books over her shoulder. "Are you Claire?"

I nodded

The woman extended her hand and added, "I'm Jill. Nice to meet you." As we shook hands, Jill looked past me. "Did Neala come? I thought I would get to meet her."

"Oh, she's here, but she won't get out of the car." I shrugged. "She's having one of her anxiety episodes. I am so sorry." I looked down. "It started at home, but I wanted to at least give this a try." I returned my focus to Jill. "Maybe we should try another day, I don't want to waste your afternoon. Of course, I'll pay you for your trouble."

Jill smiled at me and gave me an understanding nod. "Wow." She glanced at the entrance. "That's okay, it's all right." As if in thought, Jill paused momentarily. "Do you think it would be okay for me to go outside to meet her?"

Relieved with this idea, I felt like shouting, fabulous, but instead, I said, "Yes, I think it is a good idea," My deflation subsided upon Jill's acceptance of Neala's quirk. I dared to hope Jill would remain calm and nonjudgmental toward Neala.

"I left Neala in the car with the keys so she could play the radio," I explained while leading Jill back to the parking lot.

I tapped on the passenger window. Neala's head was bowed, she looked up and saw I wasn't alone. I watched the curiosity on Neala's face. I tapped the glass again. "Open up."

Neala switched the ignition on, then whirred the window down. A gloomy "Hi," came from Neala.

"Neala, this is Jill."

Jill bent down to peer in and acknowledge Neala. "Hi. Um, I know your mom wanted us to meet today," started Jill.

"She and your principal told me you might need some help with your classwork." Jill paused, but Neala remained quiet. Jill continued with a steady and upbeat conversation. "Would it be okay if I sat with you for a few minutes, maybe let you ask me some questions, get to know each other?"

"Uh, okay." Neala appeared unsure of what was happening, but she unlocked the doors.

I gave Jill a nod of approval when Jill looked my way. Then I stepped away from the car. Neala opened the door, and Jill placed her satchel on the ground, which left space between Neala and her.

Unsure what I should do, I retreated into the library. I drifted to the building's large front windows and noticed Jill squatting down, keeping her face level with Neala's. I watched Jill's face light up with laughter as they spoke. I'll be damned. Jill might just be the tutor we need. I walked to the back of spacious main floor and then to the entrance again, ridding myself of odd feelings. Jill had stood up.

Jill spotted me in the window and waved me out to the car. I approached the two of them, and Jill offered me a gracious smile.

"We are going to meet here on Tuesdays after school," Jill said.

"Yeah, Mom. Jill says she will help me with assignments and get them ready to turn in on time," Neala said with a tight smile. It was agreed the next time they met, Neala would come inside the library so they could work. Jill would email Neala's teachers to find out where to begin, but there would be no more car consultations.

Jill met with Neala once a week. I noticed folders of work ready for Neala to turn in. Jill also took it upon herself to stay in communication with teachers, which contributed to assignments being turned in on time and that subjects stipulated correct content. I was happy to have one less group of emails from school each week, and I looked forward to reports from Jill. Jill assured me that Neala was a great kid, definitely a bright student, and was a pleasure to work with.

CHAPTER TWENTY-EIGHT

CLAIRE

The next few weeks of school, I did my best to keep quiet on our morning drive. Neala meditated to her "safe place" along the way. Some mornings were rough, though they weren't as unbearable as the prior year. With Jill's tutoring support and the decision to continue Neala's counseling throughout the summer, I felt as though she was one step ahead.

I admired Neala's effort and her application of new behavior skills. Her intense work with Alina, which included sticking to daily and weekly routines, helped Neala and our family get through some tricky days. We looked at the calendar to note which days might require more groundwork. Days with assemblies were challenging, but Neala came up with her own preparations. She'd wait in the quad until everyone else entered the gym. Being the last student in allowed her to stand near the door instead of being crowded by the kids on the bleachers. Throughout Neala's shift in responsibility, I continued to harbor feelings of hope but was careful not to push her.

Each day brought slight but measurable improvements. I understood Neala used much of her day's vigor exiting the car and became weary as the hours ticked by. Neala's goals included staying at school for the full day, but she didn't always make it to her classes. She did, however, continue to hang out in the main office, the teachers' lounge, or nearby benches in the garden or quad. She was also allowed to text or call, which empowered her to reach out when she needed to.

Kane and I, along with school faculty, agreed that Neala's situation was not ideal, but it did encourage us. Plus, it was the best we could come up.

We arranged to meet when the second quarter ended to determine if Neala had kept her grades up. With the help of Neala's tutor, some grades improved, but not quite enough to catch up and pass courses. The principal and counselors set up the next steps which included notifying the faculty and staff to continue with Neala's progress. Kane and I would talk with Alina for advice.

In the meantime, I wasn't sure why, but I thought Neala might be on edge. The number of calls and texts from Neala throughout her school day increased. She'd ask me to get her early so she could go home and complained everyone suspected her anxiety was a fraud.

After the meeting, I returned to a growing mountain of documents on my desk. I didn't mind extra tasks and enjoyed my work. I treasured the relationships I had with my coworkers. They supported me and were genuinely interested in Neala's progress. Many of them had known Neala since she'd been in kindergarten.

I used to bring her to the office when my schedule allowed, especially when Neala refused to go to the after-school program. Even when she was little, she knew what she wanted and how to get her needs met. As she grew, I wondered why it was harder for her to define her requirements.

I dropped my notes in the IN box on my desk, and my phone vibrated. Pulling the phone out of my purse, I noted three missed calls and four text notifications. The texts were from Neala.

Neala: Can u get me?

Neala: Mom, I'm dying. I can't make it today. Can u get me?

Neala: Mr. Buckley makes me anxious. I'm in the quad, and he won't leave.

Neala: Can u get me at lunch?

Three missed calls, two from Neala. One from Kane—what should he pick up for dinner? Pleased with my game plan when it came to be responding to Neala, I'd connect by text first. Then I'd checked in with Kane.

Neala would probably text me while I talked to Kane, which gave me a chance to hold off answering her. I called it the "wait theory." The more I used it; the better life got. For example, if I gave someone—Neala or even Kane—enough time to figure out what they needed, they most likely would. The first rule: don't answer the phone, have them leave a message. The second rule: don't react to texts immediately. Wait. Chances were by the time I reached them; the issue would be solved. Job well done. Except when it came to dinner—sometimes Kane's menu choices were too elaborate for a weeknight!

Oh, third rule: I also prepared to respond to Neala's frustrations and accusations by getting into "cheerleader" mode. That's when I'd keep my tone and conversation positive, stable, and proactive. Neala hated it, but too bad, the goal was to keep her at school.

When I answered Neala's texts, I started with a quick question. Knowing what I was up against would determine the next move.

Me: Hi. Where r u now?

Neala: In Mahoney's.

I developed a strategy of using neutral words rather than commands, which bullied Neala to stay. I remained matter-of-fact. Often my texts to Neala were short questions which brought Neala into the present. I'd ask what she was doing, where she was, and with whom. This technique seemed to distract her from her anxiety. Looking for reasons to praise Neala, I asked what she'd accomplished so far.

Alina explained Neala most often felt "low" when she reached out. Helping her to stay in a calm, if not a positive place, supported Neala's efforts to make it through the day.

Me: What r u doing?

Neala: Sitting here.

Me: Did you go to any classes today?
Neala: No, just Mahoney.
Me: Ok, that's a good start.

To keep from jumping into the car to get Neala, I carefully worded my reasons why I couldn't. I kept the excuses impartial so it wouldn't sound like I was choosing work over her. My reasons for the delay sounded authentic. Though my excuses were legit, I reminded myself to look at the big to-do pile on my desk.

Neala: Will u get me?
Me: U only have 3 hours left in the day, one of them is for lunch. I will finish sorting my invoices by then. I bet u can make it.
Neala: No, dead.
Me: Sure, u can. Think about how great you'll feel when u get home—accomplished. You can do it!
Neala: Ok, I can try, but will u get me if I can't?
Me: Yes, of course.

I indulged in a bit of relief. I had feigned off leaving early to get Neala. To stay ahead, I needed to tackle the stack on my desk. Not only was this a busy time of the year because of internal audits, but upper management put additional demands on our department. I asked for more staff assistance because Larisa would be going away for a month. I'd be stepping in for her on some projects. My office needed me to be there.

A few moments passed without any further texts from Neala. She seemed to be handling her day. I'd coaxed Neala to pull herself together because anxiety or not, some obligations must come first. High school students attained greater responsibility and learned to manage greater stress. Neala was learning these lessons, which were as important as the classes she attended. Neala had her own set of life lessons to master. Even if they were going to be accomplished in her own sweet way.

CHAPTER TWENTY-NINE

NEALA

I walked into Alina's office. Although I'd visited many times before, today I felt relaxed enough to take in the space. The thoughtfully decorated room looked homey. Two different patchwork quilts gave colorful shades to the sofa. Folded on the seat of the overstuffed chair was a gorgeous crocheted blanket A big pillow on the floor invited both children and adults to play at a table with an array of toys and figures upon it. The lights weren't too bright, almost dim, making the room seem womblike—a safe place to retreat and contemplate.

Alina sat on her swivel chair, twisted a tea bag, and swirled it in the hot liquid. Smiling, she invited me in. "So how are you tonight, Neala?"

"I'm okay. My mom said to give you this." I pulled out a check and handed it to her.

"Tell your mom, 'thanks,'" she said and put the check in her desk drawer. "So, just okay? Tell me about your week?"

"Well, yeah, it's okay, but I'm kinda happy, too."

"Oh, good news! Tell me why." Alina took a tentative sip from her teacup.

"I got asked to homecoming, but I don't want to go."

"Hm. But this must be exciting for you," said Alina. "Let's think for a moment. If you decided to go, what part do you think would be most fun? Dressing up, seeing your friends out of regular school activities, hearing a DJ or a band?"

"Maybe being out at night. I don't know." I didn't want to answer incorrectly.

"So, you like to go out at night?"

"Yeah, because it's generally less crowded."

"What kinds of things do you do at night? Who do you hang out with?"

"Mom, mostly. Sometimes Dad and Lady. I like to go to the grocery store with Mom when everyone else is already home. Fewer people are in lines and parking is often better, too, so we can do our shopping fast."

Alina nodded. "That makes sense. You'd prefer to stay out of the dinner rush."

She remembers stuff about me all the time. I like that.

"We live really close to some tennis courts, so Mom and I walk Lady to the park when it's dark and let her run around inside the caged area. I really like the feel of the cold air, and when Dad comes, he brings the laser pointer. You should see Lady run around the park at night." I started to laugh, thinking about Lady chasing the red dot.

Alina smiled at me. She placed her cup on her desk and folded her hands in her lap. "So, who asked you to the dance?"

I kind of hesitated until Alina gave me another nudge.

"Was it someone from school?"

"No, a friend of a friend from school. He knows I don't like to do loud things, but he said we could sit there to see how I liked it, but we didn't have to dance."

"You told him how you feel about being in big crowds, and he's okay with that?"

"When I go to his house, we play video games and stuff. His mom is really nice. She likes to make us stuff to eat. And he has dogs. One is a Corgi named Bruce." I offered not ready to confide other details yet.

Alina leaned back and moved her hands to the armrest of her chair. "How was the rest of the week, what else happened? How was school?"

"The same, I feel scared sometimes, not just at school. I don't know how to explain it—let's say you watch a movie, you know, and you see a bad guy chasing someone with a gun. That feeling—being chased by a gunman—gets into my mind. I'm scared something awful will happen. I mean, in my head, I keep telling myself that everything will be okay, but then I worry, what if it isn't okay? What if everything is really wrong?

I thought Alina could tell I was getting worked up, because she leaned in close. "Okay, let's take a minute to discuss your feelings," Alina's voice calmed me.

God, I got crazy when she did this. I never liked to go into why I felt the way I did. First, I placed my head in my hands, my elbows on my knees, and kind of fidgeted. Alina moved forward, and I leaned back. I didn't know what to do, so I pulled my hands close to my face and pretended to look at them. My fingernails were chewed. I looked like a basket case. The thought got me more nervous, and I started picking at my cuticles.

"Remember the practice I taught you to use when you are worried?" Alina adjusted her shoulders. "Knowing when to create a bubble, remember? That bubble will protect you from everything around you. When the kids in the hall seem to come directly at you, or if you're in class and the noise level rises; you shield yourself. In those instances, you can protect yourself. We talked about how you are safe for real, but if something was unsafe, do you remember what we discussed? What you would do?"

I remembered this and felt a little at ease. I nodded.

"Tell me about what happened when you were in second grade—you were pretty small then. What did you do when you were in real danger? The time the big bully fell off his bike and broke his leg," Alina said.

I thought about that day. Me and the girl down the street were playing on the court near her house when one of the older kids toppled his bike.

"You found the courage to help. You got his mom. You were not only brave, but you also got him out of danger. How did it feel?"

"Good, I guess." I still picked at my hands, secretly glad to tell on that brat. He used to tease me for being small. Everyone thought I was so good for getting his mom. But in reality, I gained pleasure in telling her that he was doing daredevil tricks in the street. I wanted to say "ha, ha!" to him, but the blood on his pants changed my mind.

I ran to his house and told his mom about the accident, but I didn't leave out that he'd gotten hurt because he'd tried to make a tricky jump on his bike. No, I didn't like that he was bleeding that day, but I did like hearing his mom say, "I warned you."

He went to the doctor, and when he returned home, he sported a cast from toe to thigh. I was still mad at him for being a bully, so I never signed it.

"Right, so at a time when there really was an emergency, you thought clearly and did the right things."

I noticed Alina's voice catch a higher lilt.

"You have a natural ability to help, Neala; you are calm in an emergency and would be during real danger at school. What do you think would happen, I mean really happen?"

"I don't know." I squirmed, shifting my weight by uncrossing one leg and crossing the other. Probably shitty karma would happen to me. Feeling vulnerable, I adjusted my hoodie collar and placed my hands in the pockets.

"I think you do. Would you fall down fainting? Die right on the spot?" Alina asked. "You have told me this is the way your anxiety makes you feel. Is that going to happen? Seriously?"

"No, I won't faint, but my body feels like it will. I know to breathe, but when I worry, I forget. I know what you mean, though. If I feel scared, it's not like it's the for-sure future. It is only feelings. With practice, I can control my feelings," I recited.

Suddenly something clicked. Almost as if I'd heard these words for the first time. After repeating them for months, they finally made sense to me. I now realized that I wasn't necessarily foreseeing, and I secretly vowed I would remember this to beat my fears.

"The next time we visit I want to hear more of your plans for the dance and how we can get you ready for a fun night," Alina said. "For now, our time is up."

"Sure thing." I stood up from the chair. "I'll see you next week" I got up, hugged her and headed down the stairs. I felt good. I was happy to see Mom's car right outside.

CHAPTER THIRTY

CLAIRE

I wasn't sure why Neala put off shopping for a homecoming outfit. I was excited to look at beautiful gowns but was sure Neala would choose dressy pants. Her procrastination was revealed to me after dinner, when Neala announced that Nola was coming over.

Nola's mom dropped her off at the house with a half-gallon of mint-chip ice cream, a large can of whipped cream, a bottle of chocolate sauce, and two spoons. I welcomed Nola through the door and gave a wave to her mom as she drove off.

"Hi Mrs. Byrnes," Nola said. "Neala and I have a date with this luscious hunk tonight." She presented the frozen carton of ice cream. "And this one won't back out of a dance invitation." Nola raised her eyebrow.

I felt my heart skip with disappointment for Neala, but I loved the facial expressions Nola flashed at me. Neala would be in good hands.

"Can I put it in the freezer until we're ready?"

"Absolutely, right this way." I was glad Nola gave in to this challenge. After all, Neala called Nola, not me, to help her. Maybe this setback was typical high school stuff. At least, I hoped so.

The night of the homecoming dance came and went. Neala stayed home and played video games online with other gamers. She didn't mention what happened, nor did I bring it up. The night Nola came over, the girls rectified the pain. They ate ice cream, squirted whipped cream in each other's face, and girl talked. I was happy Neala had a best friend who soothed her first disappointment with the opposite sex. Once again, Nola's ability to understand impressed me. I was grateful for her friendship with Neala.

CHAPTER THIRTY-ONE

CLAIRE

I blew in with the breeze, it was almost time for winter break, and I felt the chill.

"Hi Claire, you're here for Neala's evaluation appointment," Karla said to me while she shoved her purse into the bottom desk drawer.

I noted Karla might be coming back from lunch. I would be spending my lunch hour in the principal's office. Exhaustion rode my shoulders. Plus, I didn't eat before the appointment, so I was hungry, too. Sometimes when I ate before a meeting, my nerves made my stomach churn. I concluded hunger would be easier to deal with than a twisting gut. Especially when I felt like my kid and I were in the hot seat.

Stop with that browbeating. You do a fine job. Kane, too. Just listen to what they say before you bang yourself. "Yes," I said to Karla, "Kane should be here soon. He's on his way. Do you want me to text Neala, or do you know if she is on her way?" Babble much? Sheesh.

Just then, more people came into the office. The psychologist, Merrill Jenkins; student advisor, Mr. Buckley; and Principal Whitney. None of them presented friendly faces.

"Hi Mrs. Byrnes, I am glad you could come in today," said the short, chubby school psychologist, Merrill Jenkins. Mr. Buckley came in behind Jenkins.

"Hi, Claire," said Mr. Buckley.

I nearly expected a sneer to smear across Buckley's lips. What a pompous jerk.

"Thank you for seeing us today. Kane will be here soon; he just texted that he is on his way," I said. Babble, babble—like I'm guilty, stop it. I imagined rolling my eyes.

Merrill nodded, "Please, follow me."

Neala came in, and we followed the small group into the conference room. We both chose to sit close to the door. I kind of smirked at that. Neala scrunched into the abyss of the chair and immediately fiddled with the ties on her hoodie. Hoods were restricted from the classroom and parent-teacher conferences. I noticed Neala had carefully wrapped her hoodie up high around her neck—technically, it was not on her head. I felt a surge of pride to see Neala attempting to push that rule as far as she could, especially to keep herself comfortable during this meeting.

Neala's composure was high-strung, but the casual placement of her backpack at her feet, and her artwork poking out of the unzipped top gave the appearance of a relaxed aura.

My mouth was dry. Where was Kane? Would Neala and I be left to handle this on our own? Just as I was about to pull out my phone, Kane walked in. I swallowed my concern and settled into my seat. After a round of introductions and greetings, the assemblage dove into the topic of Neala's progress.

Principal Whitney began the discussion with an overview of the first half of the school year as he passed out forms. "With the special circumstances Neala battles, the administration believes it would be in the best interest of our school, fellow students, and naturally, Neala, to discuss an Exemption Plan to help Neala complete coursework and thereby gain enough credits to advance to the next grade level," Principle Whitney said. "We will use this document to record our discussion and use it as a reference for future action." Paper rustled as everyone checked their form. "Today, we hope to create a list of exemptions which not only will support Neala's needs but will also keep her on track."

Mr. Whitney smiled at Neala when he made that statement, so I felt hopeful.

Mrs. Jenkins took the lead. "The Exemption Plan is a document used in our district, which allows us to address any modifications needed for a student at Norden, or any other school in the district."

I noticed all in the room nodded their heads at the comment.

"You see; our goal is for Neala to continue this year with as much assistance as we can offer." Mrs. Jenkins lifted an opened file and glanced at me. "You have submitted letters from her psychiatrist and her therapist as well as her regular physician, Claire?"

I craned my neck to see the documents in Neala's file. "Yes, those are from me."

Kane spoke up, "Does this mean that she qualifies for something like special needs?"

"In a way, yes," said Mr. Buckley. "We hope to set margins and make modifications for Neala. We'll focus on her needs at school and those outside of school, such as homework or off-campus learning—including field trips. Setting boundaries for her and her teachers will establish formal groundwork, so to speak. There will be adjustments. Maybe teachers won't call on her while she is in class. However, she'll be permitted to volunteer if she wants to."

Mr. Buckley paused to look at his handwritten notes on yellow legal pads. "I see here Neala has a tutor. Um, ah, yes. Hmm." He paused a moment. Peering at me over the top rim of his tortoiseshell glasses he verified, "She still has a tutor, is that correct? Grades were bordering below average last semester."

That I'm-in-high-school-again feeling made me want to shrink in the chair.

Kane looked at me and answered. "She does. Jill, uh— she was referred by Norden—sees her once a week." He nodded in my direction, and I gave him a faint smile. "I think it's helping, right?" Kane asked.

I nodded.

Mr. Buckley frowned.

I glanced over at Neala who let out an audible sigh. To me, Neala looked stuffy and bored. I heard her faint toe-tapping. I started to zone out watching her foot tap, tap, tap against the linoleum floor.

"When she turns her work in on time, most grades are high," Mrs. Jenkins said, referring to Neala's grades file. "Mr. and Mrs. Byrnes, Neala," she began. "Some students benefit from an Exemption Plan. The Plan, available for student progress, will allow Neala to have whatever resources—within reason, of course—she needs from the school or her teachers."

Neala's tapping sped up. It was difficult to ignore. I was pretty sure Mr. Buckley noticed as well.

Mrs. Jenkins carried on. "This Plan is modified from student to student, unlike the American Disabilities Act, which is followed on a federal level. The school district provided this plan for decades, and it allowed students with anxiety or other emotional, mental, or physical issues thrive." Mrs. Jenkins cast a slight glare toward Neala. It was apparent that everyone was focused on Neala's tapping.

The counselor sped up her monologue. "We like to think of it as a well-used tool that allows teachers, parents, faculty, and each student to create a set of guidelines to meet the student's challenges. The guidelines accommodate the needs of each individual student. Are you alright, dear?" Mrs. Jenkins looked directly at Neala.

Neala froze.

"Incredible. I've never seen anything like this," Mr. Buckley said. "It's as if something came over her body—it started at her feet. The tapping. And then her legs . . ."

Kane looked shocked. I know he'd seen his daughter refuse to get out to the car but had never seen the onslaught of nervous energy which delivered the fear and dread. As if her body was swiftly fueled with an invisible force, Kane watched his Neala transform. One minute she was composed, the next she lost control of her nerves. The tapping. The legs bouncing. She looked like a frightened rabbit ready to run.

I placed my hand on Neala's knee. I was glad she didn't push it off and allowed my touch to calm her.

Principal Whitney buzzed Karla and asked her to bring in a pitcher of water. Everyone was quiet while Karla poured the liquid into several glasses. Each person mumbled, "Thank you," when she passed them out.

"You know, recently, I heard a podcast," started Principal Whitney, breaking the silence. "And I probably wouldn't have listened to the full segment but for Neala and her anxiety. The speaker described how eating cheese and flying brought on anxiety attacks for him. He threw up cheese when he was on a plane or something of that nature, and since then he has had to battle his trauma." Principal Whitney looked over at Neala. "After listening to him, I realized you have a hard day ahead of you, every single day. I want this Exemption Plan to work in your favor, young lady."

For the first time, I felt like people believed us. This was not Neala getting away with irresponsibility, nor her playing games. This was real, and they had seen it happen. They believed us.

By the end of the conference, the plan determined Neala wouldn't be called upon in class, wouldn't be seated up front, or give presentations unless she wanted to. She would be allowed a desk nearest an exit and was granted permission to leave as needed. In the morning, she'd be permitted to sit on a bench closest to her classroom for the first period until she could work herself up to going inside. Homework was allowed to be turned in the next day if she could not make it to class.

"For safety's sake, I don't want her hanging out in the halls," Kane commented.

"When she can't stay in her classroom we'll grant her access to use her laptop at school, and she can work on assignments in the office when necessary. Naturally, we'd want her to check in with her teacher for each period," said Mr. Buckley. "I agree we don't want our students to be roaming around campus without supervision." He looked at Neala, "You do have a way of attracting other students to you, and then they become tardy." I immediately knew he was referring to Nola, but I kept listening. "With that said, we want to be sure the other students stay on track and attend their classes as well," Mr. Buckley finished.

I started to sense a thickness in the air, and my stomach rumbled, reminding me of how late it was getting.

Mrs. Jenkins spoke up. "Neala has great potential, Mr. and Mrs. Byrnes. We want to help her move forward the best way we can," she said with a smile. "We realize Neala likes to check in with you throughout the day, Mrs. Byrnes, I would like to propose Neala continues to have use of her cell phone during school, so she can reach out to you as needed."

"That would be great," I said, embarrassed because my voice cracked a little. "I know it is a stress release for her and for me, too." I patted Neala's knee. "I like knowing she can contact me when she needs to, but I also like when there are no text messages or calls. That indicates to me she is having a good day." I smiled at Neala.

Kane squirmed in his seat, and Mr. Buckley asked him if he wanted to add a comment or ask a question.

"Is it me, I mean, am I suddenly hearing about anxiety and all this 'school stress' because my kid has it?" Kane asked. "I don't remember anyone having issues like this when I was in high school."

"Unfortunately, you may not have heard of it because most students in our generation simply dropped out of school. They joined the armed forces or got jobs. Others stayed in school but turned to self-medicating with drugs or alcohol. I believe emotional and stressful problems have always existed, it's only now that we understand how to help. The first thing is to recognize it for what it is—an illness," Merrill Jenkins answered.

Principal Whitney and Mr. Buckley nodded their heads.

With that final comment, Mr. Whitney wrapped up the meeting. He reviewed the document once more and made sure nothing was left out for Neala's sake. The primary goal would still be to get her into the classroom and out of the front office. Everyone in the room signed the agreement, and they declared the conference a success.

I stood to leave, but Kane sat a moment longer. I noticed pain cross his brow. Then I remembered the kids we knew in school. Dropouts, or worse, kids who got killed in car wrecks because they were partying. Strange how we never questioned reasons why before, only accepted those kids' sad fate. Worried as we were about Neala, I was glad we were trying to help her.

"Well, then, I think we have all the topics covered for now. Just sign here." Merrill Jenkins offered a pen and indicated where to sign. I leaned over and made a scrawl.

Passing the form and pen to Kane, Mrs. Jenkins added, "We'll ensure the faculty knows of the plan when school reconvenes after the New Year. Please call with any questions."

I stuffed my copies of the Exemption Plan in my pocketbook and boasted, "I think that went well," to both Kane and Neala. Because school was out, and it was too late to go back to work, we voted on an early dinner.

"I could eat something," Kane said, giving Neala a sideways glance and a wink.

"Me, too," said Neala, slinging her backpack over her shoulder. "I'm gonna ride with Dad."

"I want ice cream for dessert," I added, remembering I'd skipped lunch.

"Me, too," said Neala with a hopeful look in her eyes.

Having witnessed an increased fear in my daughter's eyes lately, I was grateful to see some sparkle today.

"Okay, the usual then, Dee Dee's?" I asked.

"Yep, meet you there," Kane said.

I watched my husband and daughter drive away. Kane had looked relieved after the meeting. After all, compared to the trouble he got into in high school, this was a piece of cake. He was usually called into the office for instigating pranks. Hard to think because generally, he came off as a quiet kid. I thought about the two of us when we were Neala's age. We were both shy.

He was cool back then—usually followed the rules—but he would bend them enough times that eventually, he'd end up in hot water. Into building cars and hanging out with reckless and fast drivers, Kane was a popular ringleader. Me, on the other hand? I enjoyed drama class and journalism. Neither one of us were top athletes nor star musicians. Luckily, we enjoyed our close circle of friends.

Then my thoughts turned dark when I remembered the lost kids from high school. The hushed voices of parents talking when kids died in driving accidents, binge drinking, overdoses, or drug addictions. Parental judgments flew. Who was sleeping with whom and which kids were "loose" were well-known facts. It was no secret when girls were sent away to "secretly" have babies.

I can't change the past, I thought. I brushed my fearful memories away and turned toward a bright future. Neala was a part of the two of us, and that made her pretty darn special. Together, Kane and I would watch over her. A great kid, Neala carried the weight of all this, and it broke my heart. I wished I could find the magic words to help Neala get out of her own way. Perhaps if I were patient enough, the right words would come.

CHAPTER THIRTY-TWO

CLAIRE

"Get out of bed!" I yelled, stomping down the hallway toward Neala's room. Flinging the door open, I saw Lady and the cat, Beans, curled up on the bed next to Neala. An outdoor cat, Beans, was rarely seen, but he would sneak in during frosty mornings to share a bed—even with a dog sleeping on the other side.

Shoving Neala's thigh, I went on, "Get up. I am so tired of telling you to get up!"

"Stop!" Neala grumbled, stretching her arm above her head and then motioning to the pets. "Mom, I can't," she said, indicating the animals were pinning her down.

"I don't have time for this nonsense today, Neala, you need to start taking responsibility. Get your ass out of bed, now!"

I left the room and heard her continue to grumble. Part of my stress was that her tardiness made me run late. I headed back to my room to prepare for the day, and guilt snuck up on me. I felt terrible that I laid into Neala. I knew mornings were hard for her. Learning to get to school was a part of becoming an adult. Neala was aware of that, but she had unique issues. Unsure of how to deal with incapacity, I ended up exploding then felt like a heartless jackass.

I furiously brushed at my tangled curls. When I heard the shower, I seethed. I was furious and looked for a way to blame my obnoxious behavior on Kane. Venomous thoughts swirled in my brain; why couldn't he wake Neala and make sure she got out of bed once in a while? Faulting my predicament on him, I knew was petty, but I also was tired of doing this routine by myself.

CHAPTER THIRTY-THREE

CLAIRE

"Hey, want to come with me? I have to drop Neala at her friend's house during my break," I asked my co-worker, Sandy. Neala had arranged to go to Nola's for the afternoon. There was just enough time to pull the round trip off.

"I'm game. I brought my lunch, but maybe we can stop for coffee on the way back. I don't drink the stuff at work, too strong for me," Sandy said.

Sandy and I headed to the parking lot. The wind had stirred up, and the morning's drizzle had turned to rain.

"I can't believe you agreed to do this and on a day like today," said Sandy, "We only have 30 minutes for lunch. There better not be any slow pokes on the road."

"Yep, 30 minutes. As usual, I skipped my morning break, so if I hear any crap about being back five minutes late, I will probably blow a gasket." I put my car in drive. "You still want to come along? We might have to wait on the coffee."

"I do. Besides, I'm not going out in that downpour just to go back inside. We never get to catch up on stuff; this is a good opportunity. You know, for personal stuff," Sandy commented with a hearty giggle.

I rolled my eyes.

"Does Kane know this is how you spend your lunch break? Do you even get a break?" Sandy asked.

"Picking Neala up to drop her at Nola's was my idea. And to answer your questions, I don't know if he has a clue or not. He's busy with his own stuff," I said. "I'm glad you decided to join me for a ride—hold on!" I stepped on the gas when the light turned green.

"At winter break, it's important for Neala to interact with her peers," I continued. "I wish she'd think about getting her driver's license, but I can't rush that. Neala only does things when she is ready. That's about her only consistency. When she's set, she does things perfectly. Now that I think of it, she puts a lot of pressure on herself."

"Okay, sure, but does your husband know how you spend your lunch break? I want to know when you get a break?" Sandy asked. "Gee, it never ends for you, does it?"

I shrugged my shoulders but kept my eyes on the road.

"I mean, the pressure at work with the scheduling and financial budget," Sandy continued. "Then you have to run amuck taking your kid from place to place on your lunch break, then come right back—without taking time for yourself? I don't know how you do it. I bet you don't get much of a break at home—with Neala's appointments and all."

I smiled and shook my head. "I just do what needs to be done. Some days I don't have to go anywhere, and I stay at home and relax. I have to admit, sometimes I don't even answer my phone—it goes straight to voicemail. Especially if it's a friend calling to say hi. I'm afraid they'll want to get together, and I just need to collapse," I said. "Come to think of it, I have lost some friends because of my unavailability. I broke too many engagements, I guess."

"Wow. Well, too bad for them."

"I know, right? It used to make me feel like the world's worst friend. You know what? I spent a lot of time letting go of that guilt trip. By now, those who know and love me understand my social withdrawal. When I say I'll do something, I am committed to it. That's how I learned to keep my mouth shut and my phone off. It keeps me from making those commitments," I chuckled. "Right now, my obligation is to Neala. And Kane. My priorities include this job. The benefits help when your spouse is in the construction business and is self-employed."

"Jack and I both have benefits, we also contribute to retirement, which is finally building up. Maybe, when we are eighty-five, we can afford to live the life we dreamed," Sandy retorted. "With Kane self-employed, does he plan retirement at all?"

I winced. "If IRS bills count. His 'retirement plan' usually gets eaten up by interest, late-pay-fees, overdraft charges, and penalties when business is slowed. Especially when the income is delayed. Some years, it's one step forward, two steps back.

"No, I'm the sole contributor to retirement. I have invested in a canoe though, so when I can't work anymore, the girls can put me in it and ship me to Hawaii." I tried to sound light, but with bills piling up, I got serious. "Did, you know our health benefits don't have family therapist coverage?"

"No? I thought we have a good plan," Sandy said.

"Well, our benefits are fairly good, but the out-of-pocket expenses are high. There's no family or behavior therapist coverage. There is psychiatry coverage, with a four-times-a-year visit. That doc will prescribe meds. They ask for a fifty-dollar copay, not too bad. But make sure they prescribe generic meds. Some are really costly. The behavioral therapist runs a few hundred a month. She is not covered by our benefits."

"What?"

"You heard me. Believe me when I tell you, we are glad to have Alina in our life right now. Try finding a child therapist. No one is taking on new clients, and that creeps me out. I mean the fact that many kids have these kinds of issues. I knew I needed help for Neala. She's not eight years old anymore, so lifting her out and dropping her on the playground when she won't get out of the car is not an option." I smiled. "I am glad you accepted this ride with me. It helps to vent.

"There's the house. Will you use my phone to text Neala? She's waiting and knows to be ready." I prepared to pull alongside the curb and park.

Looking like a cheerful young lady, Neala bounded out of the garage and opened the passenger door.

"Nola said she got a new card game for us to play and—"

Neala stopped mid-sentence when she noticed someone in her seat. She gave me an accusatory glance.

"Hi kiddo, you remember Sandy from work?" I asked, breaking the awkward tension.

"Yeah, hi, Sandy." Neala flashed a shy smile, opened the rear door, and slid into the back seat.

Sandy bantered about the holidays. Neala politely answered but didn't elaborate. The rest of the ride was spent in uncomfortable silence because I didn't want to say the wrong thing and set Neala off. Some days, it was hard to read her. When Neala saw Sandy in the car, I'm sure it surprised her. Neala liked Sandy, but I understood that my daughter didn't like disruptions in her routine. She couldn't help it; her condition overrode her emotions sometimes. People might see her as being bratty or spoiled and self-centered. When I could, I tried to protect Neala by smoothing things over.

CHAPTER THIRTY-FOUR

NEALA

It was a tradition in the Byrnes family to host an annual tree-trimming party the week before Christmas. Family and close friends came to decorate an eight-foot-tall tree, which Dad boasted looked best in our home.

Dad and I were in charge of finding the perfect tree. Coveting time spent with Dad, I grew excited about the search and looked forward to it each winter. I preferred getting out of the house while Mom stayed home preparing the menu, which included dusting off Gram's Christmas cookie recipe. I liked to decorate cookies, but I was not a fan of mixing the dough or baking them. Therefore, this arrangement worked well.

Dad offered tasks, and I worked diligently to prove that just because I was a girl didn't mean I couldn't do just as well as a boy. I worried he wouldn't bring me along on "guy stuff," or maybe keep me from his job because of dangerous elements like power tools.

At least, that's what Mom's insinuated. Mom fussed too much. But Christmas tree hunting had been our father-daughter thing. Ever since I could walk, Dad gave Mom a holiday break and brought Sarah and me to look for a tree. Once Sarah got to high school, she opted out to be with her friends. I looked forward to our tree adventure, and it became our tradition—my one sacred holiday excursion.

"Should we stop for hot chocolate along the way?" Dad asked. He looked over at me and smiled. We wore jeans, boots, and hoodies. My hoodie stuck out of the back of my parka; Dad's peeked out from under his down vest. Mom would have made a comment if she noticed, but we wouldn't care. It didn't snow in this part of the state although the weather could dip to freezing temperatures. Hoodies were necessary gear.

"Yes, please!" I answered. I knew our routine; we would drive through the kiosk at the town center where they made delicious hot chocolate with a mound of whipped cream on top. Thinking about it, I licked my lips. Then we would be off to the Pine Forest Christmas Tree Farm—the same one we'd been going to since I was a little kid. Dad planned to take Lady with us on this trip. Mr. Duncan, the owner, said we could bring Lady anytime. My confidence strengthened with four-legged creatures, too. I liked that Dad asked Mr. Duncan about Lady and that Dad understood these things about me.

As we pulled up to the kiosk, I looked in the back of the pickup. We kept Lady's dog crate tethered to the side of the bed and close to the corner near the rear window. I knew Lady got excited when she rode in the truck. It usually meant a place more fun than home or school, and she happened to be right. Christmas tree hunting was a blast.

Another tradition for me and Dad involved a search for the perfect gift for Mom, and that meant a trip to the mall. She deserved something wonderful for helping me so much. I knew Lady wouldn't mind waiting in the crate while I picked out a gift. I'd become a quick shopper. The stores were too loud, especially this time of year.

Pine Forest was nestled in a valley surrounded by steep slopes of pine trees ranging from little saplings—reminding me of the humble tree in *Charlie Brown's Christmas*—to majestic pines reaching the heavens. I loved the quietness, even the squawking birds! In the woods, my mood became light and cheery. No matter how much stress I got when it came to seeing all my family during the holidays, my trip with Dad to Pine Forest made up for it. Every year.

Dad drove up the rocky dirt road and parked along a flat area cordoned off by logs. I hopped out, dropped the tailgate, and climbed up to unlatch the crate door. Lady could hardly contain herself, and she pounced, turned topsy-turvy, knocked me down, and landed on top of me in the bed of the truck. Lady's front paws stretched out on my chest. Dad came around the side of the pickup and laughed. He went back to the cab and grabbed the leash from behind the seat, handed the strap to me, and I snapped it onto Lady's collar.

We started out by walking in the grass near the parking lot so Lady could do her business. She enjoyed the vast number of toilets in the woods. Dad and I hiked up a hill. We were experienced tree hunters, but it took nearly forty-five minutes to track down the perfect Christmas tree. Ever since I saw the movie, *Christmas Vacation,* I called Dad, "Clark," when we did a tree hunt. Not only is it silly, but each year, like the character, he'd be on a mission to find a tree tall enough to tower the two-story-high entryway in our house.

"I think Mom will like that one, Clark. It should just about reach the ceiling, yet leave enough room for the star on top." I pointed toward a straight-trunked tree. I wrapped Lady's leash around my hand while Dad got the tree farm's saw out of the wagon. "Keep back, girl, Clark's got the saw!" I said, laughing.

"Think you're funny, huh?" Dad tried to frown, but his eyes smiled. He squatted to find the best place to make the first cut. Before he drew the blade across the bark, he looked up at me.

"You sure? If Mom doesn't like it, you'll have to take the blame." He laughed, and I relaxed into the rough sound of Dad's voice. He always threatened me with nonsense. He said things like he would "ground me for life" and he told me I'd have to "face the wrath of Mom" for our snafus. He made me happy. I loved our banter and the warm-fuzzy feeling that enveloped me when we spent special time together. I love Dad so much. I savor being with him because he makes life simple. Especially when he doesn't drink.

I imagine life must have been complicated, though, because Mom still freaked out about one thing or another.

Sometimes Dad remained my salvation. He didn't worry about too much. He let life unfold and then rolled with it.

"It's worth the risk, Clark." I gazed up the length of the tree and noticed gentle rustling in a few branches. Then the noise got louder. "Hey! This tree has a built-in squirrel's nest or something, look." I pointed up. Dad saw the nest. "Remember what Mom said about nests?"

"I recall her saying that nests were good luck or some mumbo-jumbo like that," he said. I smiled at him but was sure this tree wasn't for us. We would have to look a bit longer. We could take a tree with a nest but only if the nest was empty.

CHAPTER THIRTY-FIVE

CLAIRE

The night of the tree-trimming party, I couldn't find Neala to help with last-minute preparations. She was probably secluded in the back of the house. Earlier, Neala had mentioned she felt tired and needed to rest. I gave her a break. Over the years, I noticed Neala's reserve at parties had increased. I hoped when the guests arrived tonight, Neala would emerge.

The party was in full swing when I saw Neala at the bottom of the stairs talking to our next-door neighbor, Mr. Trainor. She looked graceful and sweet, and I swelled with pride. Even so, I knew from experience, Neala would eventually retreat to her room. Anguish swept through me. I felt sorry for my daughter, but sorry wouldn't help. As much as it crushed me, I understood that Neala preferred solitude.

NEALA

Mr. Trainor, was a pleasant old guy. He spoke softly and was nice to the neighborhood kids. He would yell at them when they drove too fast or played music too loud, but the tone of his voice expressed concern. He figured being an old guy with a cane, he might as well play the part of a cranky man. But he wasn't. He gave the best Halloween candy, and his flower garden boasted the prettiest flowers on the street. He even told Mom she could help herself to a bouquet any time.

Mr. Trainor has always been nice to me. When he watered his yard and noticed Mom and I were on a walk, he would stop Mom to tell her she was lucky to have such a good little girl. When Mom made banana bread, and when I became responsible to go outside by myself, she sent me over to give him a loaf.

"How is that dog of yours, Neala?" Mr. Trainor asked. "Heard she's going to school now?"

"Yeah, she—"

Suddenly Mr. Trainor's image dissolved. He became blurry around the edges. Everything near him looked like a soggy watercolor painting, everything muddled together. As if someone had filled the living room with water, noises became muffled. Hums and echoes filled my ears, and I couldn't make out the sounds anymore. Before I finished my sentence, my knees wobbled. Sharp dizziness pierced into me, and I grabbed the banister to keep my balance.

Afraid to look at Mr. Trainor, I turned away. The panic boomed in my head. I wanted to avoid causing a scene and positioned myself near the bottom step.

"I forgot something upstairs," I blurted and ran up the stairs to my room—my sanctuary.

I flung myself onto the bed, put my face in my pillow, and let out a small scream. Despair washed through me when I thought about the exhausting effort spent on my makeup and my carefully chosen outfit. Mom bought me a new shirt, just for tonight, and I wore it for fifteen minutes. I hated myself. I was so stupid! Why did our family have to have these stupid parties anyway?

Snot dripped from my nose, so I got a Kleenex and glimpsed myself in the mirror. My eye makeup was a loss, and my new "matte, non-smear" lipstick left a red streak across my right cheek. "You are such a loser," I said to my reflection.

I removed my new shirt and replaced it with my thick hoodie. After kicking my boots off, I put on my Mukluks. I pushed the pillows off my bed, turned down the covers, and got in. My iPhone charged on the windowsill near the bed, so I plugged in headphones and listened to *The Black Keys*. The music drowned out the party downstairs.

CLAIRE

Wearing his obnoxious light-up Christmas necktie, Kane reported that all was well in the bar area though he needed more napkins. I turned to summon Neala but noticed she'd left.

"Where is Neala headed off to in such a rush?" Pat asked, suddenly in front of me.

"Oh, yeah, and Pat's here," Kane said with a smirk.

Pat and I glared at him. Without moving my hand, I used a subtle slide of my finger and flipped him off behind his back when he headed to the kitchen to hunt down the napkins.

I squared my shoulders before engaging with Pat. "Looks like Neala needed a break."

Before Pat jumped into reprimand Neala's behavior, I added, "And no, I don't need to force her to come back down. She will figure it out."

Pat brought her hand to her heart and shot me a piercing look. "Merry Christmas to you, too, Claire," she said. She shrugged off her coat and handed it to me. "Where can a lady get a holiday toddy around here?" Then she made her way to the wet bar.

I wanted to slap Pat. How dare she provoke me? Simultaneously I became both mad and sad. I brooded about Pat. The woman wasn't graced with compassion, and it would be her loss. I opted to turn the other cheek. It was Christmastime, and I would not let Pat and her old-fashion ways ruin my night. "Merry Christmas, Ebenezer Scrooge." I laughed and reclaimed my holiday spirit.

I coveted family traditions that brought our families together for good times, bonding, and making cherished memories. Cousins, aunts, uncles, family friends, and neighbors filled our home. I enjoyed the moment and beamed with contentment.

Kane lit the fire, and Bill lifted the yule log, "Out with the old, in with the new." Bill tossed the wood into the flames. We cheered and toasted his affirmation.

Rich holiday foods and wine satiated everyone at the party. This Christmas tree trimming was one of the best parties our family had thrown. I felt gratified. A smile curved on my lips, but then a pang of regret flooded me when I thought of Neala, huddled in her room.

The hour arrived when we gathered around the tree to place treasured ornaments on tree boughs. Older folks told of Christmases past, and the younger children enthusiastically declared what they hoped for under their tree. Afterward, everyone gathered to sing jolly carols before leaving.

Within a few hours, the party wound down, and Neala remained in her room. I imagined her on her bed shutting out our intrusive sounds. She probably read a story or put on her headphones. Neala coped and celebrated life differently. My Christmas wish was to help Neala embrace these special days. I hoped next Christmas would be different.

CHAPTER THIRTY-SIX

CLAIRE

Kane poured me a second cup of coffee, which I relished in my comfy bed. He heated the leftover French toast casserole from New Year's breakfast. Our family enjoyed a good old-fashioned lollygag by sleeping in for the first time in weeks. When we did get up, Neala was dressed. She came romping into the living room and announced that she and Lady wanted to get out of the house.

"Can we all go to the beach today?" she asked.

On her cue, Kane made the day's plans to take a drive. Although stuffed from breakfast, he informed us that we would be stopping at The Dog House for hot dogs for lunch because it was Lady approved. I almost asked him what he meant by her approval, but remembering some of Lady's rancid belches, I thought better of it.

I checked the weather. The forecast was clear. "Living in sunny California sure graced us with its perks," I said. "A beach day in January? Why not take advantage of this crisp morning?" Next, I texted Sarah, who'd spent the last few days away with her friends, and said we'd be out for the day. She was at the age where time with her companions stole priority. I missed her company, but I recognized she was happy.

In an unspoken agreement, our family embraced this long holiday weekend one day at a time. No one mentioned the upcoming Monday that loomed over us after this winter break. No one wanted to bring it up, spoil our mood, or create tension. Lady jumped into her crate, and the rest of us piled into the truck. Kane drove us to a local coffee shop.

Since he'd slowed down on his drinking, his new habit was to stop for coffee when we set off on our adventures. Neala liked getting hot chocolate and a treat, often a doughnut or a pastry.

We stopped at Honey Badger, a coffee roaster that made honey lattes. They are like dessert in a cup. Honey was my favorite sweet because it implied healthy eating. With hot drinks in hands, we loaded back into the truck. Neala shoved her last bit of doughnut through the crate's metal grate to Lady before getting in the cab and buckling up. Kane and I sat up front while Neala sat it the half-back with her legs up sideways.

The ride to the beach—traveling over hills and through dells, we passed dairy farms and vineyards, and sighted baby lambs bouncing near their mammas—the drive was always breathtaking.

We didn't speak for most of the ride unless we saw a cow standing on the road. The sight brought on a stir of laughter. Road signs along the highway warned of them, but to see one was a rarity.

"Good reminder not to speed along these roads, Neala," Kane pointed out.

The closer we got to the beach, the more twisty the drive. Neala gave an occasional glance to the back of the truck. I figured she wanted to make sure Lady stayed secure. Sometimes our outings became commentaries on Lady's every move, but today Neala remained quiet.

Kane paid for an annual parking pass, and we pulled our truck into the lot. I got out and opened the door for Neala. A sharp, snap of wind sent a cold ocean breeze over us. I snuggled in my red down vest. Tightening my scarf, a Christmas gift from Neala, around my neck, I made a point not to mention it. But Kane did.

"Damn, it is cold out here!" he said. "Let me get my jacket."

Neala handed him his jacket, slid across the seat, and then got out of the truck.

I glared at Kane. Didn't he know by now to keep quiet about things that could discourage Neala? She might use the cold as an excuse to leave if she feels uncomfortable.

Neala let Lady out of the kennel. Lady wagged her tail enthusiastically. Nothing like sniffing beach smells. Golden retrievers are water dogs, and Lady stood true to the title. She immediately whined and pulled on her leash as she tried to navigate Neala toward the ocean's waves. I watched them run to the shore.

The moon was waning. The tide receded, leaving an expanse of sandy coast. "They should be safe," I absently said to Kane.

"Hey, we must be the first ones here. The beach is smooth and without footprints," Neala shouted over her shoulder.

It seemed like we were the only ones there, which was rare. What a treasure for my family.

Neala continued to run ahead with Lady, and Kane linked his arm through mine while we walked over the dunes and toward the water. He leaned in, kissed me on my neck, my cheek, and my lips. "Happy New Year, hon," he said.

I reached up and folded my arms around him. "I love you. Thanks for bringing us here today. It's going to be a Happy New Year, babe." Then I dropped my hand back to his—the warmth comforted me. I appreciated him.

Neala and Lady ran ahead to the water's edge. Lady jumped so much she reminded me of Tigger from *Winnie the Pooh*. I admired how Neala managed Lady. The dog obeyed every command as she followed at Neala's heels. Neala was a natural handler.

I beamed at Lady and Neala at the shore. Leaning against Kane, comforted by the sensation of my head resting just below his shoulder, I let out a happy sigh. I vowed to enjoy this sacred moment with my little family, especially on a day like this.

After Lady fetched the stick a zillion times, we loaded up and headed out for lunch. Kane started down the highway. I noticed my coffee had gone cold. I rolled down my window, and I tossed the liquid out. I did this just as Kane made a hairpin turn toward the right, and the cold coffee came back into the truck splashing on Neala. At first, I panicked—sure this would prompt Neala into a bad mood. I gave a sigh of relief when she good-naturedly laughed. For a moment, my old Neala revealed herself. I relaxed and enjoyed her giggles.

"Thanks for the caffeine perk, Mom!" she said, laughing and wiping the coffee off her hoodie. For once, black was a great color on her.

A sense of peace fell over our family, and I welcomed the calm. Too many days had been wrapped in commotion the past few years. Chaos, our family's theme, exhausted me. Discovering more triggers for Neala's anxiety and learning to deactivate them became my resolution for the new year. Tracking them helped since unpredictable factors brought them on. Some appeared obvious—like not mentioning the cold air today—but Kane had, and Neala showed no reaction. Same with the face full of coffee. Some days, I walked on eggshells. The surrounding tension might explode any minute, and the household would get as dark as her spirit.

I forced myself to stop focusing on the bitter and to concentrate on the sweet. Even so, a reminder looped in my mind: Monday was three days away. In 72 hours, I would be dealing with the crap. It wasn't Monday, it was Friday. We had no agenda, only freedom of choice. I made a conscious decision to let our day unfold the way the stars had deemed it. No one else brought up the looming doom, so neither would I.

CHAPTER THIRTY-SEVEN

CLAIRE

The cold was brittle the first Monday morning of the New Year. Only faint noises came from Neala's room, and I assumed she would resist getting out of bed until the last minute.

"We leave in thirty minutes," I belted from the bottom of the staircase.

The familiar thud of steps laden with lethargy sent my hopeful heart sinking. Neala plodded down the stairs.

At first glance, I noticed Neala wore no makeup, and she'd pulled the hood of her sweatshirt over her head. It's going to be one of those mornings. I poured a second cup of coffee, (a brief fantasy of splashing a drop of tequila into it crossed my mind), in anticipation of challenges ahead. I said, "Long breaks are the worst. But you got this."

I watched Neala stuff her lunch into her backpack. She snatched the keys from the countertop and said, "Let's go."

I grabbed my purse and followed Neala into the garage. She unlocked the doors, sat on the passenger seat, pushed the key into the ignition, and started the car. I slid into the driver's seat and buckled up; Neala turned on the radio. We drove in silence, but when our favorite oldie, "Own Sweet Way," came on, Neala turned it up.

"I remember that you like it," Neala said dryly without looking at me.

"Own Sweet Way" was my favorite song from high school. This morning we didn't sing along but remained quiet all the way to the campus.

"Park today, Mom," Neala requested.

I glanced at Neala and raised my eyebrow. I parked, and then settled into my seat. From the corner of my eye, I watched Neala pull her hood further over her head. She let out a sigh, closed her eyes, and sank into the seat.

Not good, but perhaps not bad. Keep quiet. Don't say anything, let her work through it. I noticed the school's new counselor, Blaze Johnson, walked toward us. I only heard about him from the write-up and picture in the school bulletin, and Neala had mentioned she liked him.

Blaze seemed to recognize Neala. He stopped by the car and tapped on her window.

Neala pushed the button, and the glass lowered.

NEALA

"Hey. How you doin' today, Neala?" Blaze's words dripped like thick honey. He was big, dark, and bald, but he oozed teddy-bear love and self-esteem. Me and the other students on campus detected genuine warmth. He attracted people to him and because he appeared so large; he made everyone feel safe in his presence. To me, he looked like a gentle giant.

I lowered my eyes and shrugged my shoulders.

"You gonna get outta this car for me today?" he coaxed, his grin showing white teeth under his black mustache.

I met Blaze earlier in the year when Ms. Jenkins introduced us. This was when the faculty put together my Exemption Plan. Blaze, who made himself available at National Alliance for Mental Illness (NAMI) meetings, was aware of my anxiety, and he had the idea to allow me to arrive a few minutes late to class. That way, I'd avoid the campus full of students before the first bell. Sometimes it worked.

I looked up at him from my seat. "No, I don't believe I can."

"How about if you try to get out, maybe put your feet on the ground?"

I sensed Mom's stress. She probably assumed this wouldn't work and had already given up. I recalled several attempts at this last year that ended in a disaster. I scrunched into the seat and withdrew from the conversation and assistance. I hated when I cried stupid, big tears. And there would never be tissue in the car for me to blow my nose or wipe eyeliner-streaked rivers from my cheeks. Please, God, I don't want that to happen today! Let my legs move a little. First, just open the door. Inhaling, I unfastened my seatbelt and simultaneously pushed open the door, then I exhaled. Blaze and Mom watched. After a few silent heartbeats, I said, "Okay, I can try."

Mom's eyes looked hopeful—I should at least try to lift one leg and then the other. As I let my right foot touch the ground, my left foot dragged, and it started tapping the floorboard. At first, I couldn't get it out of the car, but I put my hand on my leg and tried to stop the up and down motion of my foot. After a huge breath, I used my hands to raise my left leg, I inched in my seat. I wished to smile as I placed each foot, one at a time, on the pavement below but was afraid to relax just yet. I looked at my feet.

"Good job, girl. Do you think you can stand up for me?" Blaze coaxed.

I hoped to please him. He'd helped me a lot. But a weird sensation spread through me, and my hands and legs became numb. I managed to push my feet into the ground, but I was unable to detect the pressure—only the sensation of resistance.

Blaze looked over at Mom. She must have looked strained because he said, "Okay, for today. How about if you stand up. Come outside of the car for me? Just stand today."

"Okay," I agreed. I lifted my hips up out of the seat and stood between the door and the passenger seat. A thick apprehension seemed to surround Blaze, Mom, and me.

"All right," Blaze said, breaking the tension. "You did fine. I know we agreed you'd stand for today, but, I gotta ask ya, do you suppose you could move your legs to take any steps?"

"No, I can't move. It's like my legs are stuck." I trembled, not just my legs but my whole body. "I feel like I'm going to fall," I muttered in a shaky voice.

"Okay, how about if you climb back in? Are you able to move back to the seat?" Blaze asked.

I waited for a second to see if Mom would say something, but she kept silent. I got into the car without incident. Blaze glanced over at Mom who remained quiet. She seemed unsure of what to say, if anything.

Then Blaze asked, "Mom, can we speak a moment?" He darted his eyes toward the rear of the car. "Neala, you sit there, and let's see how you are in a bit," he directed.

Mom shrugged her shoulders at me and got out. She walked around to the back of the vehicle to meet Blaze. I looked back and saw them chatting. I rolled down the windows, in case I needed the extra air.

"I've never seen anxiety that paralyzed a person with fear," I heard Blaze tell Mom. He moved his hands while he talked and then dropped them to his side. "It's not just emotional or mental, but physical, too." He ran his hand over his head. "Wow."

Mom chimed in. "Well, I am glad you witnessed it. I mean, I'm not happy she's having a tough day, but the fact that you saw firsthand how anxiety affects her—that's a good thing."

When someone validated that we are not making this shit up, Mom got happy. Then she said, "Thanks for your help. I don't know if she would have gotten out at all without your encouragement." I expected Mom might be done, but she kept going, "It may sound silly, but for her, it's progress."

I'd heard enough and rolled the windows up.

After a few more minutes, Blaze came back around to my side. "Can you make it through the day?"

No way. "Can we just go home?"

Blaze told me to email him later, and he would get my assignments. "Come tomorrow, bring your completed homework, and meet me in the office," he said. "We will try some baby steps." He offered a sweet smile. "Especially after a long winter break."

The next day; another tough start. We made it to school—I wanted to push myself, so I got out of the car and walked to Blaze's office. He looked up and grinned when I came in.

"There she is!" said Blaze. "You got those legs to work today, huh?"

"Yeah," I said. I rolled my shoulders forward and looked down. "I have assignments from yesterday."

"Good work, girl. You gonna get to first period today?"

"No. My mom is waiting. I wanted to make it to the office today. Tomorrow, I'll try first period."

"I see, just a little more each day, huh?" He looked me straight in the eye.

My face got warm, and heat built in my core. I wanted to turn and get out of there as fast as possible. But instead, I sucked in a shallow breath then a bigger one. I reminded myself that Blaze was not Mr. Buckley. Blaze was there to help me. "Yes, a little more each day."

"Good for you! First, I want you to stop by here tomorrow, if you can, to check in. I will email you today's work. You have a good day now and take care of yourself." Blaze stood up and grabbed his coffee cup. "Tell your mom 'hey' for me."

I got back into the car and told Mom to take me home. Once settled in my seat, I seized a moment to congratulate myself. And, I had an adult at school who watched out for me.

"Blaze says 'hey' to you, Mom," I said.

"Well, 'hey' back." Mom smiled.

CHAPTER THIRTY-EIGHT

CLAIRE

"I'm dying," Neala moaned.

I cut her off, "You don't look like it."

"I know, Mom, but I can tell it's coming."

The familiar presence had taken over Neala's demeanor once again. I'd witnessed my daughter shrink into the front seat of the car and darkness overcome her repeatedly. Her hoodie had been pulled up tight around her neck, not quite up over forehead, but close. She avoided looking at me. Her shoulders curved forward, and her head hung low—my first clue trouble was brewing.

It's a hard thing to watch. Dread crawled over my daughter like restless scorpions, but the reason for the fear remained remote, unclear, and undefined. Sometimes, the pressure surged. Some days I questioned if the anxiety was made up—an excuse to get out of going to school.

Yet, she tried her best to make the most of her day. Some days no progress and other times success. I tried to pinpoint a trigger or a theory which might explain it away. The only thing I trusted was to keep my faith.

So much freaking faith. Faith in Neala, faith in the school, faith in the psychiatric system, and faith in my faith. I'm not a religious person, but I am a spiritual soul. I believed virtue would always conquer evil, the good guy won, and all things happened for a reason.

Letting go of the outcome became vital. The trouble? I couldn't control what was happening. If I figured out what to do, I would. I wasn't a patient person. In the end though, I understood how and why things turned out the way they did. Hindsight enables me to look at past events of my life, I found everything always came out alright. Not always how I wanted—I'd be a stay-at-home mom with an unending supply of cash, a clean house, a perfect figure, and I would spend my days planning trips with Kane (who would never be moody, by the way). I had to laugh, though.

Later, while on a Nautilus arm machine at the gym, I glanced at my feet. Geez, dog fur covered my pants, I still wore yesterday's dress socks, and my trainers were filthy. Even the threads on them wore out at the toe from floor work in the weight room. I looked like a disgrace. If I zoomed in and looked into the wall mirror I'd noticed the small coffee stain on my sweat jacket from where I dribbled coffee. My hair was a mess because I only had time to squeeze in one shower for the day, and it would be after the workout session. As the old shampoo commercial said, "Don't hate me because I am beautiful." I thought to my reflection in the wall-sized gym mirror. "Thank God, I'm trying." The words slipped out by accident.

But hey, I was working out. That's what it was all about, right? Welcome to this girl's reality. I scooted in to grab the bars, thrust the weights above my head, and my back muscles contracted with the lift. I did my best to keep in shape for several reasons. Working in the medical field, I learned that people who didn't exercise took longer to recover or survive illness and injury because they'd become weak. Those who bounced back and had less rehabilitation time had been in shape. They kept mobile. I observed that being in overall good health before a turn of events made a difference in recovery.

I also liked to look good in my clothes. My wardrobe had room for improvement, but I was glad I got away with the tattered and faded articles that hung in my closet. Besides that, I figured if I got out of shape, I would get depressed, and that would help no one, not Kane, Neala, nor me.

I held pride in cooking healthy meals with lots of vegetables for my family. I could understand how letting things slip like tidiness and home-cooking would compound the adverse effects of Neala's illness. I refused to go the junk food route for convenience though we'd indulge in them for fun now and again. I'd been tempted more often than not to pull into the driveway with a frozen pizza, a box of mac and cheese, even our favorite—Oreo cookies.

A sound person has a clear mind, and a clear mind meant proper nutrition and movement. I detested the word exercise because moving was key. That's where the gym fit in. We had a family membership, but Neala only came on occasion—at night when there were fewer members and we had the place to ourselves.

I finished my set. When I glanced at my ridiculous two-days-in-a-row socks again, I had to stifle a sob. I was exhausted. The constant strain of helping Neala, keeping her in school, meeting the demands at work, running the household . . . it's not like Kane didn't try to help, he just wasn't into it. But finding time to take care of me—rare. This was one of those infrequent times. I got headaches, which I never had before. I grew cranky, and my patience wore thin. I wanted to sleep more, but I fell asleep on the couch, and by bedtime, I would be wide-awake.

"I'm a mess," I'd said, and reached for my water bottle, a gift from Sophia. Written across the center were the words, This Might Be Vodka. I swallowed a long swig, inhaled, and let the air escape slowly. I warded off pressure, which threatened to trigger self-pity.

When I got too tired or overwhelmed, I'd throw myself a pity party. No one was invited except the self-loathing, shitty committee who held meetings in my head. First, they made me feel sorry for myself. Then they stabbed me with examples of how I might be stronger and do a better job. They harassed me for not being a good-enough mom, and they worked me into a tizzy. When they picked on me: You're not available enough for your daughter, you suck at being a wife, or you're a terrible employee, I'd fight my way through their bickering. I'd come to terms by repeating all the things I did right. I coveted being supermom.

So began the pep talk.

I'd rationalize that other mothers probably did as much or possibly less than I did, and their kids handled things just fine. I praised myself for being a good role model, having a job, and taking pride in what I do. Add balance of family and work. I sprinkled in playtime when I could, and I found humor in things.

When I needed to, I dug into my vast well, reached for words to inspire myself, and kept going. I dove deep for ways to survive because—God help me—I had begun thinking there might never be an end to this chapter of my life.

After several meek attempts to put in a decent workout, I stopped for the day. I gathered my towel and water bottle, headed toward the front desk, and noticed a hint of pep in my step. If my muscles didn't get a workout, at least my attitude was adjusted. I felt inspired to face the rest of my day.

When I got to my car, I put my phone on vibrate. Perhaps taking a little break from Neala—not ignoring her, but a short break—would help keep me in that vibrant mood.

CHAPTER THIRTY-NINE

CLAIRE

I woke to the sound of running water. Kane was in the shower. I'd have to wait my turn. I grabbed my iPhone from the nightstand and laid back in bed. It was a bad habit to go for the phone first thing in the morning to check my social media, but I ignored my conscience and waited for the screen to light up.

Productive days started with checking my calendar and planning my schedule as I sipped my first cup of coffee. Yet, I wasn't ready to get out of bed nor prepared to take on the day. I was tired and irritable, and it was 6:30 a.m. Besides, the iPhone tempted me: pick me up, check me out, and see what bullshit is going on in the world, so I caved. Icon Apps lit the screen, and I tapped the Facebook application. Scrolling through the posts, I came across one from Neala.

Neala posted an article about "How to Love Someone with Anxiety Disorders." Warmth spread through me. I was proud of her for posting about her anxiety. Then I had a flicker of uncertainty and wondered if the post was a plea for help. Skipping ahead, I found a section on dos and don'ts to support someone with anxiety.

The article suggested:
- Do notice stress
- Do help with appointments
- Do comfort when you can
- Do learn as much as you can about the disorder
- Don't presume you can fix it
- Don't get mad at the person or yourself

- Don't tell them to relax

And the list of suggestions continued.

So far, so good. This article validated I was doing the right things. I scrolled further down, and I noticed the word "doubt." I understood about not doubting Neala's anxiety, but this article said not to question when the person tries to make accomplishments.

I considered the times we went places as a family, and I would expect Neala to have a panic attack. Was this the doubt they meant? I was prepared, isn't that what the goal was? This was something for me to think about.

Perhaps the doubt I created manifested the expectation of Neala's anxiety to ruin events. I vowed to keep positive and to control my actions. My anxiety about Neala's behavior might be setting Neala up with expectations for failure. For upcoming events, I promised to keep my thoughts to myself and see if that helped. I'll stay cool for Sophia's next party. I'll follow Neala's lead and not push my fears on the kid; I'll step back. See what happens. Maybe it won't be like the Fourth of July barbeque or Valentine's candy making.

Last time we went to Sophia's, it was to make Valentine's candy. Just the three of us—Neala, Sophia and me. No big party like the barbeque. I assumed it was a fluke, but now I noticed a pattern. That specific day, Neala argued to stay home, and when we got there, she would not get out of the car. I figured she was acting out, not wanting to spend time with me

Since she was little, she had enjoyed going to Sophia's to make treats. Sophia, a closet foodie, enjoyed cooking and Neala loved to cook with her. It bummed me out that Neala's anxiety threatened our cooking excursions. Not getting out for a candy party disappointed everyone. Even if Neala's favorite part of the day included decorating and sampling. Plus, Neala and Sophia missed out on each other's companionship.

Sophia had been in Neala's life since birth. Sophia gave her gifts, talked to her at parties, and made sure she had fun.

Neala sought out Sophia for boo-boos when she was little, especially if I were MIA. Not making Valentine's Day treats included another day lost to anxiety. It robbed Neala of a good time and all of us of good memories.

After reading the rest of the Facebook post, relief and pride washed over me. Neala had been brave to post it. Sixteen "likes" from friends at school and her cousins confirmed my joy. I hoped the "likes" would help validate Neala to know she was not in this alone. I saw one comment in the feed, "Hang in there Neala, I am here for you." I didn't recognize the student's name. Curious, I clicked on their profile.

Cheri Jacobs. Cheri Jacobs was a senior, into superheroes, and the same alternative bands Neala liked. She appeared to be a friendly person, and her Facebook page boasted art and animals. It made me happy to see Neala attracted kindhearted and whimsical people to her life.

Scrolling further, I saw additional posts about anxiety. One click and dozens of them lined my feed. Despair moved through me; if there are hundreds of articles about anxiety, it meant this disorder grew with prevalence. How many people lived with this invisible disease?

The water shut off, and the shower door creaked open. Time to get a move on. I powered down the phone, grabbed my robe from the bed, and prepared for the unfolding of the day.

NEALA

I heard my parents down the hall as they woke up and got ready. I let my body sink into the mattress. I cuddled Beans and snuggled more comfortably into the covers. At the end of the bed, Lady stretched and sighed with a yawn. I had a sense that anxiety and panic might encroach on me later, but at the moment, I kept my dragons at bay. I nestled in and closed my eyes for a few more minutes of peace.

CHAPTER FORTY

NEALA

After the exercises with Blaze, I experienced a few panic-free days. But darkness soon flowed back to me like a restless sea. I attempted, but then I avoided, getting into the classroom. The walls seemed to close in on me, and my body locked up. The beast crept into my mind and hijacked my physical being. I tried calling Mom at work, but I got her voice mail. Mom said she would be in a meeting most of the morning.

While sitting in the quad, I considered how I might get myself to second period. I remembered the pills. Dr. Teller had given me Ativan to hold the panic at bay. I kept bottled water in my backpack and a small pill container in my makeup bag. The tiny tablets were hard to break, so I'd cut them in half with a knife at home. I pulled a half-tab from the lot, I put it in my mouth and gulped it with water. They have no taste. We agreed that I'd text Mom whenever I used one.

I reached around to my back pocket, found my phone, and sent a quick text:

Took half an Ativan.

The text would indicate the time, so I didn't bother typing it. While I waited for the pill to take effect, I slid the laptop from my backpack, opened it, and searched the web for information for my history report.

I felt eyes on me, so I adjusted the collar of my hoodie. I lifted it up to my ears and tightened the drawstring. I shifted my eyes toward the office. I noticed Mr. Buckley staring at me from the office door's threshold. He wore his typical condescending sneer, the one he gave many students. It was almost as if he'd perfected his grimace for me. He never believes me. Even after that meeting last semester. A wave of discomfort rose from the center of my belly to the back of my shoulder blades. I rubbed my hand on my neck to soothe the constriction. The vice-tighten around my throat, it limited my air supply. Then came a release with a cold shudder.

"Neala," Mr. Buckley called. "What are you doing?"

Prescribed drugs, I said in my head. I looked his way.

"Shouldn't you be in class right now?"

My chin quivered, and a snake of a chill slithered up my spine. I tried to hold myself together and convinced myself not to let him see my fear. Was Blaze here today? I wished I'd checked into the office.

I pointed to my laptop. "I emailed Mr. Kingly that I would be out here, I got special permission. I am working on the Sumerians and the Bronze Age for my history report." I sounded meek.

He shook his head. He turned as if he might to go back inside the office, but he pivoted toward me once again. "A call to your parents may be due. I'll call them and see about getting your Exemption Plan reevaluated."

I could swear I heard him snicker but decided it was a trick of my mind. That guy got off on being such a jerk. He was mean to all the kids, but I thought no one feared him as much as I did.

After spending the time wandering between the benches in the quad, the teacher's lounge, and the girls' bathroom, I struggled through lunch. The Ativan had made me sleepy, so I found a quiet spot near the vegetable garden to rest. I ate most of my meal throughout the morning, which left a piece of string cheese and sliced strawberries for lunch. I also pulled some fresh kale leaves from the garden to chew. Pupils passed by but didn't stop to talk. I wondered if the whole student body had knowledge of "the girl with anxiety."

I wanted to call Mom but made an extra effort to attend fourth and fifth period instead. Afternoon classes were calmer. Mom told me that by the end of the day, the kids got tired out and it acquired too much energy to be butt-heads. That made me laugh. I could kinda see how that might be true.

I assumed Mr. Lukan played loud music in his art class so people could get into the mood to paint. I also liked that the music drowned out our voices to keep him from hearing us. And Ms. Henry, the yoga teacher, had an especially natural way of keeping everyone relaxed in her classroom. Sometimes the yoga class meditations and the Ativan concocted the perfect mix for me to doze.

The sun was out, but not too hot with the spring breeze. Yet, the walk home was murder. I was worn out, and with each step, the soles of my feet burned when they hit the pavement. Mom told me to wear practical walking shoes, but my Converse were part of my identity. If the thin soles let each slap of the pavement burn my foot with each step, so be it. Once I got home, I would kick those shoes and socks off, put my feet up on the coffee table, play video games, and chill. That would soothe my soles and my soul. "Ha!" Me and my puns!

My mood turned with the memory of the earlier part of the day. What would Mr. Buckley say to Mom? "He is such a dick," I growled. He never gets me or my anxiety. Even though he saw it with his own eyes, he thinks I use it as an excuse. Why would I do that?

My fingers curled into fists. "Just once, I would like to see him have an anxiety episode. Experience how it physically controls a body." I practically cursed him. "All it takes is one bad spell, and even if it's not happening, the subtle build of trepidation is enough to warrant a full-blown attack."

I reminded myself of my support. Alina told me to recall people I could trust when I needed them, especially when I got overwhelmed by people like Mr. Buckley.

At least Blaze had witnessed how my anxiety manifested. He understood, for sure. Tears welled up; I would not let those jerks make me cry. Determined to overcome their scary presence, I committed to keep going to school.

I liked many things about school. Although I was diagnosed with social anxiety, I enjoyed the social aspect—meeting up with Nola and her friends, ripping on the teachers, and ogling Harvard, the cute college-bound boy. I often thought how cute he looked when he passed me in the halls. I did not hold back my flirtatiously long-lashed eye contact with that boy.

Sometimes being in a group seemed tougher than other times. If I could be invisible, I felt less pressure, but when all eyes, or even the feeling of all eyes, were on me, out the door I'd flee.

Fleeting feelings of worry and those of sheer panic coursed through me. I didn't always understand the triggers. Like when I pulled up with Mom to the front of the school. All I needed to do was get out of the car and get to class, but the fear built as if I were asked to jump out of an airplane. Every day. That terrified me. Buckley just didn't get it. Hell, I could hardly blame him, even I couldn't understand.

I pushed through sophomore year with plenty of struggles. I spent most of my time taking care of myself and coping with anxiety. My schoolwork, when I could do it, was stellar, but inconsistency remained a problem.

Blaze continued to support my family and me with information about mental and emotional challenges. The material explained much,, and theoretically, it made sense. But in the throws a panic attack, it helped as much as offering me a Tic Tac.

Continual work with Alina kept me focused and from plummeting further into anxiety, and I avoided depression. We also worked on staying comfortable enough to leave the house. Sometimes, I holed up in my room all day. At night, I would become restless, and Mom and I would walk the dog. Other times, we played fetch with Lady at the park in the dark. We shopped in the evening when stores were nearly empty. That concerned Alina, and she worked with me toward my overall ability go places.

At the end of the fourth quarter, it came as no surprise that the teachers recommended I retake my sophomore year. Though I accomplished much personal work, none of it applied toward advancement to junior year. On average, I was nine months younger than my fellow students.

For me to stay behind made sense, the faculty had decided, because I would be with peers my age and, hopefully, that would alleviate some of my stress. Principal Whitney also suggested I try to get my driver's permit—using the summer months to study and take the test. Perhaps that would build my confidence and keep me used to studying.

At the end of the school year, Mom, Dad, and I accepted the disappointment, yet we were also relieved. I'd get a second chance to be productive and allow my knowledge to grow next year. I would also gain the opportunity to strengthen my coping skills and another occasion to overcome my fears.

CHAPTER FORTY-ONE

NEALA

"Get it done today, Neala," Mom said before she left the house.

I heard the irritation in Mom's voice. Well into the third week of summer and she began to plan our family vacation. Mom wanted me to get my driver's permit checked off the list before we left.

"I will, Mom," I shouted to her.

As soon as Mom left for work, I logged onto the state's website to complete the last part of the driver's study guide before I took my test. Man, I found relief when I learned I could take the test online. Mom had tried to set up an in-person class, but Dad said he wasn't going to spend three hundred bucks to have me take a live course when there'd be no guarantee I'd get myself into the classroom.

Once I passed this segment online, I would be eligible to take the DMV test, and then practice behind the wheel skills. I had mixed feelings about driving. Alina and I had talked about it but driving meant responsibility. I liked the idea of going down the road by myself without Mom or Dad giving me twenty questions about my life, but I also didn't want to wreck the car or truck. How would I take on something that big?

Dad encouraged me and he bragged about my driving ability. He taught me how to drive a golf cart, a Sea-doo, his forklift, and his friend's ski-boat. Sometimes, he'd let me drive the pickup from the shop to the dumpster. The catch? I had to unload all sizes of sheetrock and wire.

To encourage me, he even brought me along to buy car parts and stuff, like when we changed the oil. I couldn't help it, but whenever I went to the auto parts store with him, there'd be an aisle of glass cleaner, and I swear, each time I saw it, I had to make a video from my phone and send it to him. When you walked in, the first thing you saw was a shelf lined with canisters with glass cleaner wipes. From the angle you walk down the aisle, the labels appeared to say, "Ass Wipes." Oh, my God! It cracked me up. I send him videos from my phone every time he texted me to do a chore.

I told Alina that Dad said driving wouldn't be hard for me, but I had to pass the tests. And pay for insurance and gas. "Do it right," he'd say. "Be safe."

Sarah told me if I didn't know how to drive a stick, I didn't know how to drive. She promised to teach me, so I wouldn't ever be stuck somewhere without being able to drive one. "Be safe," she said.

Study the rules of driving. Be safe.

The following week I practiced with an online permit test, passed it the first time, and my official certificate was in the mail. Everyone could chill out now.

CHAPTER FORTY-TWO

CLAIRE

Work and friends ate up most of Sarah's time, and I missed her. My family foursome had dwindled to a threesome. Sarah would be home for summer break, and I wanted to take advantage of that. Typically, I encouraged my family to try new things. In hopes to bring us all together, I planned a vacation

Kane once told me about a place he used to go with his family. They went somewhere near Granite Lake, and they would spend two weeks camping. Granite Lake was a few hours from where we lived. With the idea of fresh air and new sites, I concluded, the time arrived for the next Byrnes generation to carry on the camping tradition.

I asked Kane for reservation information, but unable to recall the name of the campground, he suggested I call Pat. I tossed the hot potato back to Kane. I longed for adventure, but a disaster like Pat, no thanks.

"Seriously, Kane? Granite Lake Campgrounds? You couldn't remember that?" I laughed at him. We spent a few minutes chuckling that "old age" must be settling in. We both forgot the easiest of real-life specifics, yet we had the ability to recall trivial aspects of episodes on TV.

Once I confirmed our reservations for two weeks in July, I sent Kane to purchase a tent and other camping items we might need.

"I got this ten-man tent." Kane showed me the picture on the box. "I figured we'd need the extra space with three women, and all the suitcases that come with 'em," he said.

I shook my head but secretly agreed.

Kane added, "Plus, I will be able to stand up inside the 84-inch tent, and there's a dividing wall. Neala and Sarah can have their privacy."

Radiance melted my heart.

From the beginning, Kane claimed Sarah as his own but didn't always show it. He embraced their stepfather-stepdaughter relationship but tended it more as a friendship. He'd kept a parental distance from Sarah, and he allowed me primary authority.

As far as this camping trip, knowing he took into account Neala's feelings meant a lot, too. He caught on by moving slowly with her. Sometimes he was selfish, and he expected everyone to appreciate all he did even if he hadn't considered their needs. Seeing him grow as a dad impressed me.

Our camping trip plans were underway. Like a prepared Girl Scout, I made an appointment for the car to get a safety check, restocked the first aid kit, and planned the safest route. I made sure I included landmarks and sightseeing stops along the way. I also used my GPS to locate coffee shops and diners for pit stops. When I learned of more places to visit near the campground, I got excited and looked forward to our family's chance for adventure.

I found Kane in the shed; he'd spent the afternoon organizing the fishing gear. I wanted to share my list of stops with him.

"I remember spending time at the lake with Dad. I am considering taking Neala fishing," Kane said.

Again, my heart warmed.

"This one place, a secluded fishing hole, may be good for Neala."

I understood that he might be processing his thoughts after another long year of Neala battling anxiety. It was good to see him excited about his idea, and he looked damn cute sitting in the middle of a bunch of fishing flies and tangled line. I smiled a smug smile. I'd gotten everyone to agree to get away from the daily grind and out of the hustle of suburban life. Time to let nature take its course, and perhaps, help us all unwind.

Ten days before the trip, Sarah announced that she wouldn't be joining us. "Mom, I need to cover for a co-worker, and I can use the extra money," Sarah said.

I frowned at this news, but I got it. I was young once.

"Plus, I am going to take extra time to enroll in my final classes so I can graduate early," Sarah added.

Though disappointed to hear she wouldn't join us, I looked on the bright side. Kane and I would have some bonus time with Neala, even have a chance to spoil her. It also meant I' be able to lavish more time on Sarah before she left for school with no guilty-mom hang-ups.

NEALA

Looking forward to the family camping trip, I poured my toiletries into tiny bottles. I found that activity pleasing. I liked the challenge of packing light. It was much different than packing for school trips. My ultimate goal: leave room for my devices, to stow as many as I was able. My laptop and cell phone topped my packing list. Imagining hours of uninterrupted screen time gave me decadent pleasure.

I heard Mom talk about getting firewood and jugs of water from the hardware store on the way, but I was more interested in aux cords and battery life. I should have gotten a portable battery-charging device online. Second to electronics, I considered a new bathing suit, Teva sandals, and some boy's board shorts to wear with the bathing suit. I should have been aware that Mom had other plans.

"But I want to take the laptop, Mom!" I said.

As our voices rose, Dad came into the kitchen.

"We will be camping, you know, swimming, hiking, fishing, lazing around? Making s'mores, telling ghost stories. Remember what camping is?" Mom rebutted. "That means there won't be time for any electronics. Besides, I bet they won't even work in the mountains. Also, Lady will want to go for walks."

"Everything is ready to be packed," Dad said. "I emptied out the truck, so we can pack now, and head out first thing in the morning."

Mom looked at Dad. Was he purposely avoiding eye contact?

"If we leave at sunup, we should be able to arrive in the early afternoon. I don't want to be pitching the huge tent in the dark, ladies."

I think he was trying to change the subject.

"I'm just about ready. I've been sorting all the food we'll take. Neala already packed the dry goods into boxes, and I have the coolers ready. I'll pack food from the fridge in the morning," said Mom.

Aware that they avoided my argument for electronics, I spoke up. "Mom said no laptop on the trip. I'm bringing my cell phone. We might have service at least halfway there. I have my headphones to listen to my own music on the way. I don't want to be subjected to your radio stations until the last minute."

"What is wrong with our music, missy?" Dad asked.

"More like what is right with it, Dad," I said, hoping to push his buttons. I actually enjoyed some of Dad's music. I liked 70s Rock, but I wanted my gear.

"Okay for the phone, smarty pants, but if you bring the laptop, you will have to be responsible for it and chances are you won't be able to get Wi-Fi in the mountains," Dad said. "I have to agree with your mom on this one, kid, it will be a waste."

"Mom, Dad, I never ask for much. I don't even want to go on this trip, but I am doing my best to keep it together. Please let me take the laptop, just in case there is Wi-Fi, please?" I begged; my eyes focused on Dad.

Dad looked at Mom and then back to me.

"We'll talk about it and get back to you in the morning."

Mom gave him a knowing glance, confirming they would discuss it without me in the room.

"Okay, but I am charging them for luck," I said.

I connected my laptop to its charger and set them on my dresser. I couldn't lose touch with the outside world for two weeks. "Are they insane?" I mumbled. "What kind of tomfoolery is that?"

Typically, I enjoyed the day trips we experienced, seeking adventure at the coast, or the rivers nearby. But, honestly, I wasn't sure how I felt about being out of touch. Two weeks! Impossible as it seemed to my parents, I was not a total loner. I'd accumulated a network of online friends. I had connections through websites, social media, and emails.

"If no one hears from me in a week, they'll think I died," I groaned while I plugged the charger to the wall outlet. "After a week or two, they'll forget I even existed!" I moved my duffle bag from the bed to the floor. I waved my hand over the empty space reserved for my devices. "I hope and pray they let you stay," I said.

I flicked my fingers and imagined my wish cast to my parents' subconscious minds. I supposed I did all I could do to get my way. The last thing I did was settle into my comfortable bed to wait.

CLAIRE

In the seclusion of our bedroom, Kane and I discussed Neala's plea to take her electronics on the trip.

"I say we let her take them," Kane said. "They probably won't work up there anyway, so moot point." He sighed and slid into the covers on his side of the bed. "Nevertheless, she'll have to give in, and she'll be forced to be entertained by nature. Even if there is Wi-Fi, there won't be that many power outlets and the devices will run out of charge. Poor kid may actually succumb to the beauty and peace of the great outdoors." He smiled at me.

"I hope you are right, Kane," I said and climbed into bed next to him. "Sleep well, we may be laying on rocks tomorrow night," I added, then I kissed him on the cheek.

Neala may not be too excited about the trip but having her "security blankets" would help alleviate her stress. We made the best choice. I settled down. Within minutes, I fell asleep to the gentle sound of Kane's snores.

CHAPTER FORTY-THREE

CLAIRE

The drive took five hours. Stops included a landmark diner, which served huge, country-style breakfasts, two roadside mini walks for Lady to stretch and pee, and a visit to a rock shop. We arrived at the Granite Lake Campgrounds turnoff, and Kane drove up a bumpy and twisty dirt road.

From the highway, we could see thick trees on the mountain, but first, it was essential we prevail through a meadow of wildflowers, then thickening shrubs. The roadway darkened, and we drove along a mile of scenic forest, dense with sword ferns. We caught glimpses of squirrels and several species of birds before we reached the ranger's shack. I handed the printed email confirmation to Kane, and he gave it to the guy with his driver's license.

The ranger scanned the confirmation. "Welcome to Granite Lake Campgrounds. You're in campsite 26." He circled the site on a map. "Over near the community campfire. Restrooms are up to the left and a small hike to the amphitheater, here." He smiled at Kane, then me. "Oh, and if you need any assistance, there's a pay phone at the little diner—burgers and dogs mostly—just a stone's throw from the campfire pit. And, uh, campfires are allowed in the designated pits only, it's been a dry winter, but plenty of water in the lake."

He glanced at Lady and said, "Dogs must stay on leashes at all times, but are welcome to swim in the lake. It's all in this brochure. Enjoy your stay." The ranger tipped his hat at

Neala. "There's Wi-Fi near the clubhouse for all the folks who can't leave the phones behind."

We thanked the ranger. Kane put the truck in gear, and I looked at Neala whose grin seemed hard to contain. I also smiled knowing Kane and I were determined to make Neala have a good vacation even if we couldn't totally "unplug" her.

CHAPTER FORTY-FOUR

NEALA

We located our spot , camp 26, nestled between two other sites, both already filled with campers. The campsite facing us included a family with two teen girls who spent too much time "cupcaking" around in their bathing suits. It was apparent they vied for attention—especially from the campers in the site behind ours. The site boasted four outdoorsmen, probably on college summer break, who seemed to spend their nature gazing "vay-cay" playing beer pong on the site's picnic table. They were all so stupid, I felt like a monkey in the middle.

Soon, I arranged my routine for this vacation. I missed Sarah though, she usually cheered me up by making funny remarks about people around us. She ran commentaries (without being mean) that put me at ease. Other people were no different than us. I spent mornings staking out the scene to see if anyone interesting had come to the campground. Mom hated it, but I stayed hidden inside my hoodie on most days. I did my best to chill by hanging out with Mom and Dad, sipping hot cocoa while evaluating the surrounding people.

At lunch, I'd leash Lady and schlep over to the diner. Located in the woods, I was surprised to find the place offered a great selection of ice cream. I treated myself to cotton-candy flavor and got Lady a vanilla "pup-cup." The best part about this lame place was that I could get on the web by the diner. I tried to be inconspicuous behind my sunglasses—didn't want Mom to find out that I maintained my internet presence. She actually thought I might be doing summer reading. Please!

When dinnertime arrived, I moseyed to the family's site to help prep dinner. Mom and Dad stayed at the lakeshore until the sun went down or their cooler was empty. I would walk around the lake trail, and Lady and I could see everyone boating and canoeing. I used to like kayaking, but not so much anymore. It got too crowded. I only kayaked when Dad took me to the river in the late fall. Most people had gone back to work by then.

I liked to do the meal prep because being at the campsite without Mom and Dad offered total freedom of culinary choice. I rummaged through the food and chose what to serve for dinner. Dad made me go fishing one morning, but it was a loss.

"Get the net," he yelled when he thought he had dinner on the line. Turned out he caught an old coffee can with a big warty toad inside. Yuck! We decided to stick to burgers, so we didn't go back. I did enjoy that quiet time with him, though. My old self emerged when I hung out with him.

I cast my eyes on a redwood tree trunk, and I gazed upward. I remembered Alina saying just how insignificant our little planet was in the vast universe. My tiny presence in the scope of the world kept me in perspective, not so important, and even hidden. Calmness caressed my body when I looked into the treetops. My breathe flowed with ease, and the dappled sun, which I usually hated, kinda felt like warm kisses on my shoulders. Being in nature validated that I was being held by the earth, and that felt okay.

The tranquility broke when my parents returned. Bustling with activities, choking on Kingsford until Dad got the meat on the barbeque, finding enough forks—we always had too many spoons—and settling at the crooked picnic table to eat brought on a commotion. They had to talk to all the neighboring campsites, commenting on the day, the fish, the troublemakers in site #32 with loud music, and so on. Then they bugged me about what I did all day. More often than not, I didn't like the after-dinner activities, like bingo or sing-a-longs, and the movies they showed were for seven-year-old babies, but I did enjoy s'mores night at the community campfire.

About the third night, I was done. I got my sleeping bag and declared I hated sleeping in the tent because Dad snored, and Lady farted. Turned out Netflix streamed on my laptop! Thank God, even the hillbillies got Netflix out there. I was glad Dad parked close enough to receive Wi-Fi. From there on, I found evening solace with Stan Lee films until I'd fall asleep in the car. Maybe this wasn't the ideal vacation Mom and Dad envisioned, but at least I found ways to make the best of it.

CLAIRE

With Neala's withdrawal and Sarah's absence from family trips, I used the vacation time to practice an empty-nest experiment. I savored the private time with Kane. During our camp adventure, I was pleased to discover our romance was still alive and breathing. We engaged in long walks beside the creek that fed into the lake; picked blackberries and dreamed of homemade pies; drank margaritas on ice at the lakeside; and held hands by firelight—I was delighted when I pictured our future together.

Taking time to be a couple also shook off the guilt which built up when we reminded one another how Neala found contentment doing "Neala" things. I got that it wasn't necessary for us to experience happiness from the same escapades. Letting go, easing into the next stage was innovative, not uncomfortable.

Kane and I agreed the trip helped Neala come into her own being. She was chatty and didn't seem as tired as usual. As far as we were concerned, in her own way, Neala showed contentment.

After two weeks outdoors in the sun, the morning arrived for us to pack up and go home. Neala was the first to shove her clothes into her duffle bag and hop into the car.

"What are you doing? I asked you to scrape the ashes from the fire pit before we leave," Kane said to Neala.

I kept an eye on Neala as she dragged herself out and searched the back of the vehicle for the whisk broom and dustpan. Standing over the cooled fire pit, she drew the dustpan through the ashes and made sure there were no hot embers or smoldering coals. Only fine dust whirled. She scraped the fire pit clean and dumped the ash in a paper bag. I watched my daughter do this task, a simple lesson in leaving things as you found them.

"Okay, it looks safe to throw that bag in the ash barrel at the end of the campground. How about you walk it over, and I will put these away," I said. I held out my hand for the whisk broom and dustpan from Neala. I loaded the items and other belongings, and we affirmed that the weeks away provided what was needed, but, like Neala, I couldn't wait to get home.

Once home, we fell back into our routine. Kane and I returned to work, and Neala drifted through the days. One evening, after dinner, Neala came downstairs with the laptop. She gathered us around the computer to share the "camp montage" she'd made.

During the two weeks, she'd taken pictures of our family and many beautiful nature settings. She'd set the photos to music to create a slideshow. We laughed when we heard the song she chose. "Own Sweet Way" by Renunciation.

There were pictures of Kane and me holding hands, sitting by the fire, and fishing by the lake, I could see Neala felt a sense of profuse happiness. I winked at her, and I reveled in delight that Neala indulged in extra time to make the montage.

Neala laughed when Kane and I sang (way off key).

There comes a day,
You can't go away.
But you can have your say.
You'll do it your way, your way.
Your own sweet way

Gathered together, sharing memories of our trip, we acted like a typical family, if only for a little while. No one mentioned school started in three weeks.

SOPHOMORE YEAR (AGAIN)

CHAPTER FORTY-FIVE

CLAIRE

I watched from my car while Sophia pulled into the parking lot in her sporty white Lexus. Sometimes I envied my friend's life. Sophia did whatever she wanted. Single, no kids, and she worked harder than anyone I'd ever met. She spent time and money on herself and her glamorous home without worry. She lived in our favorite neighborhood. When we were kids, we used to call it "Uppity Avenue" but now, my dear friend lived right on the corner lot in the very mini-mansion we had dreamed of living in one day.

I'd looked forward to meeting Sophia for lunch. I made sure not to schedule any tasks and arranged the afternoon off. I hadn't seen Sophia for weeks, and I wanted to make the most of it.

Neala planned to meet with her school counselor, and I anticipated a text-free lunch. School started two weeks ago, and for the most part, Neala used the same coping skills as last year. Her breathing meditations got her out of the car and sometimes to class.

The first week, Neala seemed down. Yes, she met new kids this year, but she also had to explain to her old classmates why she wasn't with them. Only Nola sought to meet her at lunch break. I assured Neala the other kids weren't ignoring her; they didn't how to talk to her about being held back. They would come around on their own, and meanwhile, she should try to ignore it.

Headed toward the restaurant entrance, I called out, "Hey!"

I caught Sophia's attention. She turned and threw her arms up. When she reached me, we greeted one another with flamboyant hugs, kisses, and "you-look-amazing" remarks. After all the fuss and flattery, we mentioned to the maître d' that the weather offered a gorgeous day, and that we'd like to sit outside.

"And enjoy our food alfresco," Sophia said with a smile.

We perused the menu and gave our order to a stylish waiter—two fancy salads with pomegranate seeds and chilled glasses of sparkling waters with lime.

"You don't have to go back to work, shall we up the order to Prosecco?" Sophia said with a devilish grin. "As for me, well, some days, I work better with Prosecco! *Garçon, s'il vous plaît*, be a dear and change the drinks to Proseccos."

"*Oui*, a fine choice."

"*Merci*." Sophia snapped her napkin open and dropped it onto her lap with flair. "I am so glad I learned French in high school," she joked. "At least my good manners show."

Amazed that Sophia had kept in shape after all these years, I glimpsed at my own pouch of a belly. Sophia dressed casually in stunning clothes, and her hair looked covered in gloss. A few gentlemen stole glances at her.

A stab pushed through me. For a fleeting moment, my heart jabbed with jealousy that Sophia was wealthy, elegant, attractive, and the best cook I'd ever met. But we were best friends, and she loved me, no matter what. Quit comparing.

The waiter returned with our beverages. I lifted my glass.

"To finally getting together." I clinked my glass with Sophia's. "Lunch with you alfresco is so much more pleasant than my meals *al desko*!"

"Yes!" Sophia laughed at my toast. "You mentioned you've been quite busy at work. Plus, the time you spend with Neala. Tell me about it; how's work? Kane and Sarah? Christ, even tell me about your dog. But first, how is Neala getting along?"

"Well, she's doing much better. She gets herself going most of the time, makes her own lunch these days, too. Oh!

She warms up the car. I suspect she secretly anticipates driving soon. But sometimes, when I take her to school in the morning, boom! She still freezes up when we get to the campus. Some days, we return home." Again, I sipped from my drink.

Sophia moved her silverware out of the way when our salads arrived.

"I'm glad to hear that. It saddened me when we missed our Valentine's candy making day," she said. "Have you tried anything new to help her?"

"Mostly I stick to what has worked. And I've learned what not to do when she's anxious in the car: Don't coax her, point out the rational, and don't mention teachers, homework, or students." I counted on each finger as I spoke. "Don't sound too upbeat; don't sound sad. Don't be a cheerleader—It's okay for me to show my fear and disappointment. But, most importantly, I can't hint that the clock is ticking, and I have to get to work. That's the kicker. The minute I stress out, her anxiety doubles."

"So, what happens?" Sophia gingerly examined her salad, lifting the greens and poking at the croutons.

"I push my shoulders back into place and wait. I browse through the apps on my phone until Neala musters the courage to exit the damn car." I had a forkful of my salad. "Sometimes I pop a Xanax."

"Really?" Sophia seemed astonished.

I shook my head, "No, of course not, but I do keep my prescription bottle filled." I changed the subject. "Good dressing, huh? I tried to copy it, what a fiasco! Ha!" Then I put my fork down. "Sophia, I hate to say this, but I'm going to. I realize how much you love Neala. But, are you sure I don't bore you with her stuff?"

"Stop that. You and your family do not bore me. Tell me more about Neala's therapy. How does that help?" Sophia nibbled a bite of food.

"Knowing Neala has a place to sort stuff out helps," I said. Neala's troubles hovered near the front of my brain. I told Sophia about the resources at school, including Neala's tutor, her therapist, Alina, and her medications. "Her psychiatrist is retiring soon, which sucks because we'll have to search for another one. Oh my God, finding him was exhausting—one doctor wanted to diagnose her as a boy trapped in a girl's body, and another told her to organize her backpack.

"Hey, some good news, the school psychologist says Neala is a particularly interesting case because she is super smart." I smiled with pride. "She said that typically, students with poor learning skills, emotional problems, or physical limitation fall behind. Their learning shuts down or stunts. That could be the cause of their generalized anxiety. Apparently not for Neala, but she still is at risk."

Sophia continued to chew.

"Her psychiatrist categorized her anxiety conditions as generalized severe social and separation anxieties. The difference between anxiety and severe anxiety—a person can basically function with anxiety, but they cannot with severe anxiety. That is when it becomes a disorder. Such as Neala's inability to get out of the car."

Sophia set her fork down and sipped from her drink.

"When she was diagnosed, my first concern was her that her therapy would be on record. Was it a good idea to give her meds? I wanted to avoid the 'anxiety-problem-child' label or allow it to become her identity. That's not happened, of course. Alina broke down her weekly stressors and taught Neala how to put a vocabulary together. Neala can now state precisely how she suffers. She named the overwhelming anxiety 'the dragon.' She can speak freely, in a safe place, without feeling judged. I can tell it is helping her because I see my old Neala reemerge from a very dark place."

"The dragon? Wow, that is a good name for anxiety. I get a better understanding of how she feels." Sophia said. "Do you worry about her getting depressed? Don't anxiety and depression go hand in hand?"

"I used to be concerned about depression. Suicide is not farfetched, for someone with mental illness. Unfortunately, a young man in Neala's class died. Fellow students heard rumors that he might try to harm himself, but by the time his parents were informed, it was too late. I can't imagine living without Neala in my life." I kept quiet for a moment, respecting the sacredness of life.

"Gosh, that is so sad." Sophia said. "Does her therapist think she will outgrow her anxiety?"

"Neala may never be completely rid of anxiety, but the overall goal is for her to learn cope with it." I considered a metaphor Alina had used. "Like adjusting to living in a wheelchair. It's not impossible, but there are necessary alterations to live life to the fullest."

"Wow, Claire, this situation with Neala is complex. Remember that I'm here for you and Neala as much as you need." She pushed her plate away, reached for my hand, and gave it a squeeze. Then she raised her glass and took another sip.

I smiled at my friend. I knew she would always have my back.

The rest of the meal flew by with funny stories of Sophia's latest dating escapades and travels. I slipped into the fantasy of a fun and less complicated life. By the end of our lunch, the furrow in my forehead relaxed. I congratulated myself for taking this time. I needed that break.

CHAPTER FORTY-SIX

CLAIRE

The first semester of sophomore year, part two, remained the same for Neala. She got out of the car nearly every day, and although most days she made it to class—her attendance remained inconsistent. Jill met with her every week and did her best to keep Neala on top of her work.

I followed up with faculty to ensure Neala remained on track. Weekly visits with Alina focused on keeping Neala in school. I heard Neala mention driving, dating, and the possibility of getting a job. I kept my fingers crossed.

Neala's withdrawal and snippy attitude when I brought up these subjects made it clear that she didn't want to talk about any of those things with me. However, Neala agreed that her main goal for the next couple of years was to get her high school diploma.

I addressed the recent incomplete mark on her report card. "If you don't have a diploma, you will be throwing in the towel before you even get a chance to start your life, Neala," I said. "I promise you, my sweet, there is life after Norden."

"But I can take the equivalency test next year. I already passed the exit exam," Neala moaned. "This is stupid."

"I understand your frustration—"

"Mom. Mom, stop. Okay?" Neala demanded.

"No, I won't stop. If you want to get anywhere in life, you'll need a diploma and a driver's license." My voice rose above hers. "You say you hate school and other crowded places, but your condition may not last forever, or be as bad, at least. If you succumb to it now, you might have regrets that you can never go back to change."

I stared at Neala, who immediately backed down.

My voice softened. "Let's see what you get done over the break. I'll call Jill and see how she can help." I tried to put my arm around Neala, but she ducked under me and headed toward the stairs. I wanted to assure myself I'd said the right things to her. I wanted nothing more, not one thing more than for Neala to get her diploma. Then she would be able to accomplish whatever the universe willed for her.

I contacted Blaze before the winter break. Neala fell behind on a few assignments, and he got some due dates extended until after the break. We'd already discussed how Neala might earn extra credit. We scheduled an appointment for us to meet before the end of the second semester I remained confident she'd make progress this year. Being proactive was stressful for Neala, but we hoped the results would be worth it.

Blaze invited us to join him in his office. He sat down at his desk and fired up his computer. "So, just like last time, Neala. I want you to come and see me on your first day back from winter break. Then the next day, try to get to first period. The day after that, second period, and so on. You got that?" Blaze paused, then said, "I emailed the teachers with our plan." He smiled at Neala, and that's when I noticed he wore a burgundy shirt and a white tie—he was just the Santa Claus Neala needed.

"And you want me to bring in the work I did over the break, so it won't be late," Neala confirmed.

"That's right, girl. Now, you know you can come for the full day any time before that, right?" Blaze made the comment comfortable by teasing her, but I could tell he harbored best intentions for Neala. "You got any questions, Mom?"

"Nope, I got it." I smiled and winked at Neala. "Thank you for helping us, Blaze, I presumed you would come up with a plan. This is the hardest comeback she has all year."

"Hey, don't I know it! I'm looking forward to a long winter nap. Ha-ha!" Blaze slapped his knee, then stood up. "Merry Christmas, Neala, and Merry Christmas to you, too, Mrs. Byrnes." He started to shake my hand but gave us both a big hug before we left.

After the meeting, I calmed down knowing I'd turned over some responsibility. For the first time, we'd initiated a plan to help get Neala off to a good start for the second half of the year. That would be her roughest haul. Self-assured all would go well, I indulged in thoughts of a Merrier Merry Christmas.

The two-week break flew quickly, and Neala seemed calmer than she had in the past. I deduced having a plan with Blaze must have been the reason.

The week after the break, I had a terrible cold and left work early. On the drive home, the promise of hot tea and TV comforted me. In my mind, I reviewed Neala's baby steps to school and acknowledged satisfaction with the progress we'd made. The plan stated that this day, Neala would stay until fifth period. I took it as a good sign that hadn't texted me.

Once home, I'd have the house to myself.

I pulled onto our street and saw Kane's truck in the driveway. There goes my alone time with this cold. When I came through the garage door and into the kitchen, I saw Neala sitting on the couch eating the lunch packed for her that morning.

"Hey, what are you doing home?" I asked.

"I couldn't make it today, Mom," Neala said as Kane came in the room.

"Hi babe, you're home early," Kane said. "You okay?"

"It's this head cold—what happened to the plan about school today?" I asked, waving my arm in Neala's direction.

"She couldn't get out of the truck today, so I told her to stay home with me. No big deal," Kane explained.

Anger slammed through me as I realized Neala's forward progress had taken an enormous backslide. I tossed my handbag on the couch and turned to Kane. "Are you kidding me, Kane? After the improvements she'd made this week, you let her stay home?" My anger now bordered on rage. I wasn't sure if I was feverish or going to explode.

"I drove her to school, and she couldn't do it today, so I told her it was okay, and that I'd do some work at home. We ran a few errands and we came here. I made the decision, Claire, not her," Kane rebutted.

"Oh, you made the decision, did you? Kane, you got played." Livid, I threw my arms up. "Un-fucking-believable!" The couch was the closest thing to slap. "She tells me she can't go to school nearly every goddamn day, every hellish and crappy week, and I go through the whole rigmarole just to get her ass out of bed. I watch her put on her black attire, every day, then we put her ass in the car. I drive to the school, watch her cry—black makeup running down her face—hear her sobbing and telling me she doesn't know what to do.

"I tell her to get out of the goddamn car because that is what she's supposed to do. She doesn't have to know 'what to do,' it's what you do that makes the difference. Goddamn it, Kane." Taking a breath, I turned away. "And you know better, Neala. What did you think, you'd get away with this?" I dragged Neala into the conversation.

"I don't know," Neala answered meekly.

"I don't know," I mimicked Neala and gave her a bitter scowl.

I immediately felt awful.

Kane retorted, "I am done talking about this. How would Chuck handle this if his kids acted like Neala? He would kick their asses. You tell me to be sensitive, then you tell me to be firm. They wouldn't put up with this!"

I noticed Kane's tactical attempt to turn the conversation against me. "Yeah, and his kids would probably suffer, Kane. A kick in the ass isn't always the answer. That is not what I am asking for. Some kids do need it, but not kids like Neala.

She needs us to be committed to consistency and predictability."

Kane turned his back on me.

He loved me even when I got fired up. Even though he was aware that I was right about this. I hoped it might occur to him he may have done something wrong today, but damned if he'd talk about it now.

Kane headed toward the garage without looking back at me.

Typical. Kane leaves instead of dealing with a problem.

Turning to Neala, I told her to go to her room. I didn't want to take my anger out on her.

My body trembled as I mentally listed the struggles I'd endured the last couple of days, how I vowed to get Neala back into her school routine. Grabbing the ingredients for dinner from the cupboard, I slammed the cabinets shut. Monday, we saw Blaze, just a quick pop into the office to say hi, drop off her assignments, and then go home. Tuesday, Neala made it to her counselor's office where they confirmed the plan for the rest of the week. Wednesday, Neala made it half a day. And Neala was supposed to stay until fifth period. Friday until sixth.

"Jackass!" I said to no one. "He blew it all away—and goddamn—the work I did to set this up just flushed down the toilet. Thanks, Kane. No skin off your teeth. You didn't do any of the work even though you were made aware of the plan. Don't you ever think things through?"

The door to the garage opened then slammed. I braced for his attack.

Kane stormed into the kitchen. "Neala was emotional today. She started crying. She couldn't move. I didn't know what else to do but to come home."

I'll just bet. I figured Neala had filled with guilt because she copped out and did not stick to her strategy. Everyone understood the importance of this week and goddamn it . . . I was pissed, frustrated, and beyond belief.

"Christ, Claire, you're not her only parent," Kane said.

"Oh, I know. Since she does have two parents, I guess it is time you take the lead for a while."

I refused to look at him, filled a pot with water, ignored his babbling, and pulled vegetables from the fridge. Finally, I'd heard enough.

"You know what? Forget it. Forget dinner." I turned off the stove. "There are two adults in the house, and there's about to be one. You cook dinner."

I marched off to our room to get my gym bag. A sauna might be just what my achy muscles needed; a hot sauna would cool me off. Once again, defeated and taken advantage of. I was tired of being a fool and frustrated with aggravation that amplified my worries and stressors. Tonight, Kane could stay home with the shards of a family he conceived.

CHAPTER FORTY-SEVEN

NEALA

Mom drove up to the curb, and I got into the car. I saw Mom smirk when she noticed the smile plastered across my face. I promised myself I would downplay my exciting news, but it was too late. Mom seemed to sense something different—that something good was about to happen.

"So how was your day?" she asked.

I was too elated to hold back. "Mom, it was great. First period sucked, as usual. I spend most of the morning gathering courage just to get into the classroom, and it didn't happen, but I got my assignments."

"Well, that's okay. What else?" Mom asked.

She pulled out of the school's parking lot and onto the street.

"Second period wasn't horrible, but after lunch, the day got totally cool." I tormented her by taking my time. I felt a little powerful and liked it. Usually, she drives me crazy. Funny, part of me didn't want to tell her anything, but Mom and I were best friends, so I was bursting to share.

"Do tell."

"Well, you know Nola, of course, and Chris from biology, right? Well, they told me one of the guys in our lab wants to meet me. He told Nola that I'm 'hot.'"

"Hot, huh?" Mom looked over at me when she pulled away from the stoplight.

Mom wore her dark sunglasses, and the lenses hid her eyes and what they might imply. "Does this guy who thinks you're hot have a name?"

"Yeah, Mom. Slater Green. So, anyway, Nola invited him to meet us right after class, and he did. He said he wants to take me out, Mom!"

Not sure how to bring up the topic of dating, I blushed. Too nervous to ask if I would be allowed to date, I rehearsed that I should be a junior, so I am old enough. I prepared to mention she lets me watch *Breaking Bad* and *Walking Dead* with her.

"Slater Green? A sophomore or junior?"

Mom began with the whole age/grade thing. Darn it. I figured I would slip in his grade. "He has blond hair, sun-streaked, really. He is in Nola's sister's class, and he works at DeeDee's Diner on weekends. He told Nola he saw you, me, and Dad at DeeDee's. And that he liked my eyes. Like who remembers eyes? God, I hope Dad didn't act like a dork that day." Thinking I would break it to her gently, I added, "He's also on the varsity baseball team this year. He plays shortstop or something like that. He wants me to watch him on Thursday. Can I go?"

"That's up to you. Besides homework, you need to consider transportation. Dad and I have a meeting to go to. Grade, age?" She cornered me in our driveway.

"A senior, seventeen, I guess."

"Oh." Was all Mom said, but I recognized the "well crap" all over her face. Once again, I was grateful for her dark glasses.

"And he drives." I squeaked in. "A Mustang. So, he and Dad will have car stuff to talk about."

"Let's talk to Dad about it when he gets home; see what he has to say about all of this." Mom had just ducked behind the Dad shield.

"Just so long as he doesn't go Heisenberg on the guy," I said. I got out of the car and headed straight to my room. For the first time in a long time, I bounded up the stairs bursting with happiness.

CHAPTER FORTY-EIGHT

CLAIRE

I made my list, grabbed my wallet, counted my cash, dropped the wallet in my purse, and was ready to go grocery shopping.

Kane came to the front door to see me out.

"What do I owe this lovely opportunity to?" I asked. "You forking up extra cash for the groceries?"

His face fell and he looked as if at a loss for words, so I gave him a moment to collect himself. He pulled out his wallet and handed me two twenties.

Shame crept through me. My fly-off-the-handle responses last night must have made it hard for him to bring up touchy subjects today—including the budget. I offered him a kind smile and said, "I'll put cookies and milk on the list."

He stood there but said nothing.

"So, what's up?"

"I spoke with Neala," he started. "She asked me for money to go out with this Slater kid. Says he is her boyfriend. I only met the kid a couple of times, and I get that they date, but I'm not sure what 'boyfriend' means these days. But one thing I do know. I'm not dating him and won't hand money over to her so she can buy a boy popcorn at the movies. Boys treat girls on dates."

"Things are different these days, Kane," I started. "When kids date today, they split the cost of stuff. I like it— the girls don't expect to 'owe' the guy anything if you know what I mean." I raised my eyebrows." However, I do agree we need to talk to her about money."

I knew we needed to communicate with Neala about money. Sarah accepted a job when she was a freshman, but Neala had never worked. Sarah babysat the neighbor kids when she was twelve, Neala only did occasional dog-sitting—those gigs came few and far between, too. Since Neala did little of anything, she never needed an allowance.

"We'll need to talk to her about a budget," Kane said, shoving his wallet back into his pocket.

"I agree, Kane, but with Neala, it's unusual. Other kids go to school, have jobs, and even get sports or volunteer hours in. Babysitting is not an option for her. She doesn't want to be alone, and she worries she might have a panic attack while she's in charge," I said. Then, I remembered something.

"I did speak to her about volunteering, I suggested it would be a good introduction to getting a job; she could even help at my office."

"That's not what I mean. I have no problem taking care of her needs," Kane said. "Money for her is one thing, needing my money to buy stuff for a boy is another. I can't support that behavior, Claire, it's just not right. She needs to come up with the money herself or find a way to figure this out.

"I get it, I do. There is a variance, and you have a good point. Giving her a few bucks won't lead to her living here with her boyfriend while they raise their six kids though." I tried to take the conversation down a notch.

"Not funny," Kane said. "But, that's just it, where do we draw the line?"

"I guess that is the line. We don't give money for 'boyfriend things,' but I want to take care of her activities, like going out for yogurt when Nola offers. Otherwise, I agree, she has to find the motivation to earn some cash somewhere, this could be the catalyst."

"God, I hope so. Besides, I want my money spent on you, honey." Kane smiled.

My heart did the little flip-flop, which happened when he looked at me in his special way. Even through all the darkness, he was a beacon of light for me.

"Come here," he said and held my hand. He guided me to the overstuffed chair in the living room, sat down, and pulled me onto his lap. I placed my arms around his neck and kissed him on the cheek.

My feet dangled above the floor, and I felt small, protected, and safe. I liked Kane's height, even when he sat. Secure, I collapsed into a tender moment and leaned in for a second kiss.

Kane's kiss was gentle. He wrapped his arms around my waist and drew me even closer.

Letting my body fall into his, I snuggled against him.

He let out a heavy sigh. "I wanna move this upstairs, but I have work to do. Especially since there is a boyfriend to impress now." He chuckled and released me from his embrace.

"Yeah, lover boy. I have groceries to buy. We can't afford takeout on our budget," I said. I stood, straightened my skirt, and smoothed my blouse. "I'll meet you upstairs later."

Kane hugged me before I walked toward the front door. Slinging my purse over my shoulder, I paused, looked back at Kane, and winked.

CHAPTER FORTY-NINE

CLAIRE

I was about to wipe down the refrigerator when I saw it. The bright pink piece of paper Neala had received in the mail for completing her online driver's course. It stuck out among mementos posted on the fridge. The driver's license conversation had begun last year, but Neala only seemed interested in the having the license part. She showed no interest in taking the course, getting a permit, or passing her license test. That is until her principal had suggested it as her summer goal.

Neala's feelings must be changing. Did putting the notice on the fridge indicate she was ready to take her written exam? Ready to get her permit? I shook my head. Nope. Grease spots confirmed the course completion certificate had been clinging to the fridge for four and a half months.

Past experience alerted me to Neala's difficulty with her completing goals. Visions of the dust-covered sewing machine and the unfinished embroidery on the coffee table popped into my head. I hoped driving would not be one of those discarded objectives. Don't go there, she'll learn to drive. And there are the driving lessons. I groaned. I tried to ignore my hopelessness. Having learned to keep my worries to myself and not let them spill over onto Neala, I kept cleaning the fridge.

I mopped the kitchen thinking since Neala had completed the online driver's class and passed the test, her confidence had improved. I wanted to support my daughter—keep the momentum; lift her over every hurdle—until she obtained her driver's license.

I wasn't sure of Kane's perception about this. He liked being the dad who provided registration fees and sports gear. And accepted car and insurance premium increases. Sure, he taught Sarah the practical aspects of driving, such as how to change the oil and a flat tire. I suspected there would be no problem there. Neala loved to hang out with Kane when he worked on the cars.

The disparity was that Sarah couldn't wait to drive. Getting through the process wasn't much of a chore, even if it terrified me. Contemplating all of the things that I fussed over distressed me to death. "Drive safely, and don't land in a ditch," I'd warn Sarah whenever she left the house.

Each time Sarah came home, she'd call out, "I never saw the ditch, Mom." Somehow that little banter became our ritual for safe travels.

When it came to Neala driving, some days I couldn't even broach the subject with her. More sensitive than Sarah, Neala's angst overshadowed simple conversations, which may start pleasantly but end in tears, frustration, and occasional slammed doors.

The strange thing was this time, I kept encouraging the driving, not fighting it. Funny how life kept me on my toes.

CHAPTER FIFTY

NEALA

After calling the Department of Motor Vehicles, Mom found out we needed to make the appointment online, so she asked me to do it. We were able to set the date for three weeks out; Mom said she was glad. She asked for time off work to accompany me. All I needed was to pass the written test, and I could learn to drive. I talked to Alina, and she assured me the rush I experienced was excitement, which differed from anxiety.

When the day arrived, just before lunch, Mom drove me to the DMV. Butterflies darted in my stomach, so we agreed we would celebrate with a late lunch after the test.

"Ready for this?" Mom asked as she pulled the car into the Department of Motor Vehicles parking lot.

"I just completed an online practice test on the way here, and I aced it," I said, which explained my obsession with my phone on the drive to the appointment. I'd noticed Mom's eyes on me.

"Whoa! Good for you! Good idea, Cookie," Mom said. "I'm sure you'll do fine with the real test, too. Then we can get this done and move to behind the wheel training. After that, you can practice with Dad." She added a laugh that sounded pretty nervous to me.

"Yeah, it will be cool, but I don't really want to drive. Especially your big car."

"We'll see about that, kiddo. Once you have your license, you'll be in control and have more freedom to come and go as you please. When I was a kid, our family attended a funeral. My mom and dad met there, so there were two cars. After the funeral, the reception was at some weird house. My brother and I didn't want to stay, so we kept asking when we could leave. My dad tossed me the keys to his pickup and said, 'now.' That was the best feeling! Whew! I could escape. Besides, do you really want me chauffeuring you everywhere for the rest of your life?"

"No! You are creeping me out, Mom, so no."

"That's what I thought. So, get in there, and get your permit," Mom said like a get-up-and-go cheerleader.

Even though we had an appointment, the long line spilled out of the door. We checked in and registration began. I presented my birth certificate and the online test certificate, but we didn't have my social security number.

Mom started to freak, muttering things like, " We'll miss your appointment time if we need to go home." "This is all I need." "Can't things ever go smoothly?"

"When you get back, come to the front of the line," the clerk said.

"Okay, let's make this fast," Mom said.

"Not too fast, Mom, you don't need a speeding ticket the day I get my permit."

"Right!" she said and slowed the car.

We chose the back roads, so we'd avoid freeway traffic. We made good time, except Mom forgot one little thing. The new commuter railway was up and running. As we approached the crossing, the red lights flashed, the caution arms went down, and the train whistle blew.

Mom said, "Shit. Forgot about this."

"You know the train whistle is saying 'Screeeww yooouuu, Clairrrrre!'" I said.

Mom put her hand on her chest and laughed.

"Thank you, Neala. You're right," Mom said through her belly laughs. "I gotta calm down. We have plenty of time."

We pulled into the driveway. I stayed in the car while Mom ran up to her office to get my social security card. Then we turned around and headed back.

"Pray we miss the train, will ya?" Mom said.

"Yoouuu beeeettt, Clairrrre!" I said.

We both laughed as we sped away.

When we got back to the DMV, we headed to the front of the line. Mom clutched her purse to her stomach; I think she was nervous. She told me that even though she had been driving for over twenty years—with a perfect driving record to boot—she wouldn't want to be evaluated by written or driving performance. What's the exact distance you had to turn on the blinker? She didn't know. She said she clicked it on "when it felt right."

I handed over all of my documents. "Mom, you need to sign."

Mom signed the form, and I headed to the little booth to take the test. Mom told me there would be a mile-long sheet with a list of important driving and safety questions, so imagine my surprise to see the booth accommodated a small computer screen and a stylus. That totally made me chill. "I can do this, I'm comfortable with computers. Screw anxiety."

It took about twenty minutes to finish. The lady behind the reviewer's desk had fuzzy hair barely contained by a crazy scarf wrapped and tied like a headband. Her look created a sense of comfort within me. All my life, I'd heard DMV jokes and comments about the horrible lines and service. Now I was part of a new group. Okay, the jokes were right, but there were plenty of odd people to look at.

"Great job sweetie, you passed, only one missed." Fuzzy Hair said. "Stand over here and let's take your picture."

I could feel Mom watching me from the chairs. I turned to look at her, and I raised my arm in victory. She hurried over.

"I passed. I only missed one. I guess I just got nervous because I missed one that I knew the right answer to."

The excitement came rushing through me. My mood lightened. I didn't realize how much this had weighed on me. I was glad it was over. The lady handed me my temporary permit, and my chest swelled with pride.

"Well, all right," Mom cheered. "This is terrific! Wanna call Dad and tell him?"

CLAIRE

Neala flashed me a brief, quiet smile, but her eyes sparkled. Her cheeks were pink when she handed me the test results. I've come to recognize this look of personal pride, although the times I'd seen it were rare. Neala had acted cool about the test, but in reality, she must have been terrified. Even so, she'd sucked it up, kept herself together. She'd gone through the motions and ended up with a learner's permit. I was proud of her.

While she called her dad, I became flooded with emotions. Joy filled my heart. I wanted to hold my baby, to cherish this moment. An overwhelming sensation to shield her from the world shot through me. She'd grown up right before my eyes. Happy for her, I held back my tears. I knew it was silly. I coveted this day—this milestone for Neala, but a tiny part of me hated the independence that would come along with it.

"Yeah, okay. Me, too, thanks, Dad" Neala clicked off her cell. "He's really happy, Mom," she said with a smile.

"Me, too, very proud. You want to celebrate at your favorite deli?"

"10-4."

My stomach had unknotted. "I'm glad we waited for lunch afterward, I don't think I could have eaten before."

"Yeah, me, too. I'm hungry now. Mom, I am really proud of myself."

I reached for her hand. "I'm really proud of you, too, sweetheart." She let me hold her hand all the way to the car. Today was a good day.

After Neala began driving with her permit and getting positive feedback from the driving school instructors, I pushed her to take her behind the wheel test. Neala did better getting to school when she drove. Most days she pulled up to the parking lot, hopped out, and then waved goodbye. I suspected that Neala's sense of empowerment when she drove warded off most of the treacherous morning anxiety battles.

If Neala drove herself to school, my mornings would free up. I fantasized about the liberty I'd have as Neala became self-sufficient. Sometimes guilt ebbed into my secret hopes, but I also knew it would benefit Neala most. She'd have some control, which would likely reduce, perhaps remove, some stress from my life. From all of our lives. But then, I'd maintained my role as a nervous back-seat driver.

"Don't follow so closely! You can't see that far ahead. What if the guy in front of you slams on his breaks? You wouldn't know until too late." I belted out at Neala.

"Mom! I'm going less than five miles per hour. We're in a parking garage, and I am not too close to him," Neala argued.

"Well, it feels too fast to me."

"I'm fine, Mom." Neala pulled into a parking space and turned off the ignition.

"Besides, I don't want to drive anymore, okay?" She tossed the keys at me. "I told you before, I hate your car, and I don't want to take the stupid driver's test."

I was surprised that I wasn't surprised at her comment. I half-expected this conversation to come up weeks ago but I also hoped we might avoid it. Yet, here we were, in the mall's parking garage, Neala threatening not to get her license.

Well, you little a-hole, how do you expect you'll get to and from the mall then? Because I sure as hell will not be at your disposal for the rest of your life! I thought. What I actually said was, "Look, I get how you are nervous, but you're a good driver. You'll do fine. Sure, my car is big, but it's safe, and you handle it well."

"I don't care. I don't want to drive anymore. I don't like—"

"That's fine."

It might be okay to wait for a bit, but the longer Neala put things off, the more difficult it was for her to try again. I searched for words to get Neala to realize what she'd lose if she gave up. It wasn't like quitting Tae Kwon Do, knitting, dog training, or even school. Not getting her license would impact her life in ways beyond Neala's concept. Her already limited world would become even more restricted, and, in all honesty, I was ready to reclaim my free time. I didn't anticipate being Neala's chauffeur for the rest of my life.

"You have the right to make decisions which affect your life, not mine." God! Was that the best I could come up with?

Neala gave me a sideways glance.

"You're growing up, and you have to make choices as you go. Daddy and I are here to help you. However, when you are grown, you'll have to live with the choices you make. You are allowed to change your mind, of course, but you'll deal with the consequences of that."

I will not be driving this kid all over the place.

Then a wave of compassion came over me. Would I ask this kid to drive if her leg was broken? No. Would I ask her to drive if she was feeling sick? No. Then why am I so angry right now?

I looked at Neala. Because having a child who will not drive is one more validation that she cannot cope in the world. I will have to face her disability from yet another angle, and I'm frustrated. Torn between sad and sick about it. Whenever Neala didn't meet my criteria for "normal teenage" behavior, I was forced to face a dark reality.

Sitting in the car stewing about the future, I knew I had to lift my thoughts. It's a good thing you have a sunny disposition, girlie. You have to find some light to shine on this subject and fast!

I silently recited my "gratitude list:" I had two lovely, brilliant daughters. I was blessed to be their mother. Both Neala and I would learn to meet life's challenges. Honestly, it was a fascinating journey—one I never would have had if not for Neala. And, after this outing, I could go home, take a bubble bath—we were, after all, parked at the mall and a short distance away was Naked Luxuries, an organic bath shop.

"Get outta the car bitches; we are going shopping!" I grabbed my purse and opened door.

"Fine."

I heard Neala get out.

"Mom, toss the keys to me," Neala said. She rolled her eyes and added, "When we're done here, I'll drive home."

CHAPTER FIFTY-ONE

NEALA

I reread the text: Laser Tag?

I'd been seeing Slater Green, mostly playing video games online and occasionally hanging-out at one another's house. When we did go out, we went to the movies (the latest showing) or for ice cream. Slater was considerate and usually invited me to quiet places.

His circle of friends spent weekends at arcades, paintball fields, and enjoyed night games of Capture the Flag. Slater politely asked me to join them. Each time, I made an excuse why I couldn't go. This time it was laser tag. The thought of running around in the dark, hiding from opponents, freaked me out.

Each time I made excuses, it dawned on me I felt pressured to go places with him that I didn't want to go. Alina helped me process my need to let this boy have his fun. I would have to decide to let him spend time doing things with his friends with or without me, or be prepared for him to lose interest in me down the road.

I texted: No thanks, sorry. Talk soon?

Maybe it was time to let him go, then again, perhaps he would skip the laser tag outing and would come over to hang out with me. Because he was very sweet, and I liked him a lot, I must think of our relationship. Was I selfish? He was kind to me, but I was bringing him down.

I hit "send" and decided to make a date to break-up. I tossed my phone on the pillow. Tears welled in my eyes. "Anxiety sucks."

CLAIRE

I was in the kitchen, but I heard Neala plunk down the stairs and recognized the tension and heaviness in her steps.

"What's going on?" I hoped Neala wasn't worried about her upcoming school evaluation. I got the email about it a week ago but hadn't brought it to Neala's attention. Maybe the school mentioned it to her. I prepared to tell Neala the testing would be routine, and it would help advance her to junior status next year.

"I don't know, but maybe I should quit seeing my boyfriend. I mean, he is always asking to go places that are uncomfortable for me. He likes to be with groups of friends and hang in crowds. I don't. He wants me to play laser tag with them. Can you imagine that? I really don't like the laser tag place. It's too dark, too loud, and too unpredictable."

"Oh," I said, relieved it wasn't about the testing. My thoughts moved forward: What is this going to mean? How will this set her back? Will it set her back? I should have never let her have a boyfriend to begin with! I was so stupid! My mind raced so fast all of my emotions were spinning. "So, what happens now?"

"Nothing. I just said that I didn't want to see him this weekend—he was disappointed because we are supposed to go to a party at the laser tag complex. This is why I need to tell him I don't want to see him." Neala paused, fidgeting with her hands for a moment. "Mom, do you think it is fair for me to ask him not to go when I don't want to go? It makes me feel bad."

"No, honey, it isn't fair. You shouldn't expect him to forfeit a party just because you can't handle it. I bet it is hard to quit seeing him. I do understand why you don't want him to stop doing stuff or going places because you won't go. That's pretty mature of you, kiddo."

Neala reached across the counter and grabbed a banana from the fruit bowl. "I really like him, but he's more social than me and that's not fair to him. Maybe I can find a guy who likes quieter things." She chomped off the end of the banana.

"Don't be hard on yourself, though. You are a special and terrific person. One day, you'll meet someone who will understand your needs, and they will be patient with your lifestyle—or maybe they will already have the same mellow lifestyle, one to match yours."

Neala bit off another chunk of the banana and thought for a minute. "I mostly feel bad about not fitting in, I guess."

"Come here," I said. I pulled her close and gave her a big mamma-bear hug. "You are my dear." I stood on tiptoes to kiss Neala on top of her head. My daughter was not only becoming mature, but the kid was also passing me up in the height department.

After breaking it off with Slater, Neala spent time holed up in her room, but after a few lonely weeks, she perked up. She spent more time with Nola, and I smiled when I heard laughter around the house again. Nola already had her license, so the Nola-and-Neala duo went out for evening fro-yo runs. Once again, Nola saved the day with frozen treats.

CHAPTER FIFTY-TWO

With Neala's second attempt to pass sophomore year before her, the faculty chose to review her assistance plan. The plan included re-assessing her overall achievements, her current curriculum progress, and her state exam results. A meeting was scheduled to discuss the findings.

Karla brought along a folder and placed it on Principal Whitney's desk. I watched him thumb through about fifty pages. I hoped she'd get closer to graduating, though she still had difficulty getting into the classroom.

For Norden High to offer Neala additional flexibility, the school district's psychologist, Dr. Dolan, recommended a psychoeducational assessment. This evaluation determines if there are underlying learning disabilities, which might have been previously overlooked. Areas of testing included cognitive, academic, and social-emotional. This information would contribute to the goal of Neala advancing to her junior year.

Kane, Neala, and I joined Principal Whitney and the psychologist for this special meeting. We were eager to hear the results. Kane and I were relatively sure Neala would not need special education, but at the same time, we worried that being put into such a class would affect her Exemption Plan. That plan had kept Neala in good standing for the past years. The flexibility helped with the extreme anxiety she experienced.

"Here are the results of Neala's testing," Dr. Dolan said. "I have to note, this report indicates she's in the 'High

Average' with scores of 111-117, in Broad Language and Reading, and 'Superior', a score of 121, for Broad Achievement. This means she rates exceptionally high in communication: reading, writing, speaking, and comprehension."

This didn't surprise me. Neala had compiled an extensive vocabulary and reading—an excellent source for words—was one of her favorite pastimes. She also scored 94, 'Average,' in math which was exciting because her grades had typically been low in that subject.

Dr. Dolan continued to explain Neala's results. "The test scores reflect Neala's well-developed motor skills and shows that she's acquired attainable post-graduation goals. She did not suffer from any severe health issues but, of course, her social-emotional score is high. The 'T Score' of 70 pushes her beyond the 'at risk' mark and crosses into the 'clinically significant' category. This score validates her high levels of anxiety."

"What does this mean for Neala?" Kane asked.

"It means we are not sure what more we can do for her," Dr. Dolan said. "She is bright and has no apparent learning disabilities; her cognitive ability is just fine. There are no physical limitations, so we can't classify her as disabled, in the traditional way, obviously." Dr. Dolan paused. "This test verifies that anxiety is the culprit. Because the anxiety scores are significantly high on her chart, we may be able to accommodate her with a specific special-needs program, though we'll further investigate what to do. This is fairly new territory, but not groundbreaking."

"Will her Exemption Plan stay in place?" I asked.

"Yes." The psychologist looked at Principal Whitney. "We will continue to provide these special requests, which Neala needs to stay in her classes and attend school. It means our school will keep her scholastically engaged in the core curriculum, enabling her to graduate."

Our family declared success after we left the meeting.

"I'm so glad for you, Cookie," I said.

"I knew you could do it." Kane draped his arm around Neala and pulled her in for a hug.

Quiet and reserved, Neala looked timid when she was proud of herself. She didn't slap high-fives or offer fist-bumps. She sometimes looked like the cat who ate the canary. I was used to seeing her sly understatement for satisfaction. Outward confidence wasn't Neala's strong point, but I was glad to see it when she acknowledged her achievement.

We stood outside the main office while I dug in my purse for my keys.

"So, which class do you have now?" I asked.

"Chorus," Neala replied.

"Since it's the last class of the day, do you want me to take your backpack? I'll be back to pick you up."

"Okay, that's cool." Neala removed some papers from her backpack then handed it over. Knowing she wasn't big on physical displays; I blew her a kiss (behind her back) as she headed off to class.

After we left Neala at school, Kane asked me to join him for a cup of coffee. We rode over to the coffee shop in his truck. On our way, Kane spilled his other feelings about the meeting.

"I don't like the idea of Neala being labeled," Kane said while holding the café door open for me.

"I know, hon, I get it. That's why I try to limit the number of meds she's prescribed and keep her appointments going with Alina. I never want Neala to feel that she . . . well, that she is somehow 'less.'"

We sat in a booth near the window, and the waitress jotted down our order and left.

"She is such an amazing person—with debilitating anxiety. I don't think in another time or place she would be asked to conform; you know what I mean?"

Kane stopped fiddling with the silverware and gave me a blank stare.

I looked at his quizzical face. "Let me explain, it's like on that old tv show, *Little House on the Prairie*. Imagine a kid, in those times, who might be farsighted, for example. These days he wears prescription glasses. Back then, imagine what a hunter he would be? He would probably see an elk before the rest of the hunting party, and before anyone else could load their buckshot, Boom! Everyone would eat for a month."

Kane raised an eyebrow.

"Well, maybe not the best example, but you get what I mean?" I said, but Kane continued to stare at me.

"In the past, Neala might not be classified as an anxious person. She would be called 'brilliant or mysterious.' She'd be surrounded by books and always be in deep thought. Perhaps like Victorian-era women rattling around in attic libraries." I smiled. "Or, Christ, she might've ended up in an asylum." I paused for a moment, then said, "I guess it wouldn't matter. Whichever century, she would be deemed odd, and that would be that."

"The way I see it," Kane replied, "is we do our part to keep her in school. Once she has her diploma, she will find her place in this world. She's no dummy. I say we continue to support her as we have been. The school will do their part, we do ours, and Neala will do hers."

"Agreed. You are so sensible." I smiled at my husband. "Besides, those test results proved it to me," I offered. "They scheduled time to evaluate her because she does not attend school the same way 90 percent of the kids do. As if there is an assumption that the problem is her. I'm calling bullshit on that.

"You know what?" I asked. "I am glad Neala lives in these times where she has value as a woman and for her brilliance. I won't let my conception of society's effort to put our square-peg daughter into the round hole of conformity. I appreciate that she is a thinker and not a memorizer." To reinforce my opinion, I raised my voice. "Even though she overthinks stuff."

The waitress returned with two cups, a pot of coffee, and a thick slice of apple pie à la mode for Kane.

We sat in the coffee shop and sipped coffee while we rehashed the meeting. I think we both felt smug despite the efforts, the dramas, the frustrations, and the fears. Our daughter was deemed superior. As if there were ever any doubt.

Kane left our waitress a generous tip, and we returned to pick up our daughter from school.

CHAPTER FIFTY-THREE

CLAIRE

Hitting pause on my Neala thoughts, I made time to indulge in the highlights in Sarah's life. Sarah had graduated from college and found a job doing clinical research. Now living in her first apartment, she was out in the world—and happily engaged to Jeffrey Bell.

Sarah and Jeff met when they went to their friend's Settlers of Catan game night—A game of friendship or rivalry. Yet that night, the strategy included romance. Sarah soon brought Jeff home to meet our family, and Kane and I fell in love with him, too. Yet, it was Neala's seal of approval that stole my heart.

Jeff made a special effort to befriend her. He even asked her to join him and Sarah at other game nights. Neala continued to look forward to evenings when Jeff came around. She liked to play video games with him, especially since Sarah was never interested in them.

That upcoming summer, Sarah and Jeff would be getting married, and Neala would be in their wedding.

"You look amazing in your dress—everyone will think so." I fussed over Sarah, fluffed the full skirt of her bridal gown and then arranged the veil so it cascaded down Sarah's shoulders. We were in the large fitting room at the bridal shop. Standing behind Sarah, I peeked over her shoulder and observed my daughter's reflection in the wall-sized mirror. My heart leaped, and a layer of fresh tears pooled in my eyes.

"Mom, don't cry again," Sarah said with a smile. "You can't keep crying. You will get dehydrated."

I looked for the tissue the salesgirl had handed me earlier.

"I can't help it. You know I'm sentimental, but I really didn't think I would be the kind of mother who cries when she sees her daughter in her wedding dress for the first time." I dabbed at my eyes. I knew it was pointless to avoid smearing my eye makeup. I think it wore off throughout the day's fittings.

"Oh, you look so beautiful, Sarah. I am very proud of you." I carefully hugged her and kept my tear-stained face from brushing up against the gorgeous fabric. "I'll get the dressmaker to see if you need any further alterations, though I don't think you will. I need to check on Neala, too."

I found the seamstress and sent her to Sarah's dressing room, opened the neighboring dressing room door, and found Neala struggling to zip the last half of her bridesmaid's dress. The gown was cut low in the back, making it impossible to reach the zipper's pull-tab.

I came up behind her and said, "Let me help with that."

The soft peach color of the dress complimented Neala's complexion. It looked stunning against her shoulders and brought out the natural blush of her cheeks.

I was both proud of Neala yet nervous. The entire summer had been consumed with preparing for the wedding. Dodging cake tastings, florist meetings, and color swatch comparisons for napkins and tablecloths, Neala still stepped up to do her part. Lately, she stayed in her room when Jeff came over. It wasn't because she didn't like him—I thought she did, mainly because he didn't let her win at video games. But it was evident that wedding talk stressed her out. I wondered how I would make it through the day myself, let alone Neala.

I watched Neala admire herself in the mirror. She scrutinized each line and layer of fabric. I saw her swallow a smile. A sudden flash crossed her eyes, her brows furrowed, and the smile vanished.

"What's the matter?" I asked. "Don't you like your dress?"

"What if I can't walk down the aisle?" Neala whispered, "I will ruin my sister's wedding! What will Jeff think? He might not want to marry her!"

"Sweetheart, let's not think that way. We already talked about it, and Sarah considered your anxiety before she and Jeff asked you to be in their wedding," I said. "She carefully chose a role for you, so you'd be comfortable. You'll have to see how you feel that day, of course, and take it from there."

"I guess you are right," Neala said, sitting down on the large tufted bench in the dressing room. "I heard her tell you her first choice was for me to be her Maid of Honor, but she knew it would be too much pressure. She said no one would notice if she were short one bridesmaid." I watched the flush of embarrassment rise on Neala's face. "But if the Maid of Honor were missing, it would cause a significant disturbance."

"Honey, that's why we all talked about the scenarios together. Sarah felt good about having you in the wedding with a less responsible role only because it would reduce your worries."

"Are you sure, Mom? I don't feel less worried right now." Neala stood and turned her back to me. "Will you unzip this?"

"I want Sarah to see you in it first, okay?" I used the moment to reassure Neala.

I interrupted Sarah and the seamstress. "Sarah, come see your sister in her dress. She's gorgeous," I called.

I winked at the shop girl then whispered to Sarah, "Please say something to encourage Neala. She's concerned about ruining your day."

"Sure, Mom," Sarah said, and then excused herself from the garment maker. I followed Sarah. She rapped on Neala's dressing room door and, without waiting for a response, opened it.

"Neala Byrnes, you simply cannot wear that dress on my wedding day!"

Neala looked startled at Sarah's comment.

"You will steal the day in that gown. You look absolutely breathtaking." Sarah smiled her warm big-sister smile. She clutched Neala's hand and sat on the broad bench with her. "It is important to me that you are at my wedding. I am proud of you and all that you are. It won't matter if you walk down the aisle with me or attend the ceremony from the altar or the pews. I don't want you to worry about a darn thing. What I do want is for your presence and to feel included. At least for as long as you can stay." Sarah shifted in the layers of her gown. "I love you, and I hope you will have a wonderful day like I will, so do what you need to do that day, and don't stress over it today. Got it?"

"Yeah, I get what you mean, Sis," Neala said, hugging her sister, then let out a sigh.

"Sarah," Neala smiled a crooked smile, "All of this wedding talk has kept the relatives from asking about my life. I'm glad about that. One more question from them about what I am going to do when I graduate would probably put me over the edge."

Sarah and Neala giggled.

I adored them from the threshold, and I searched for the damp tissue to wipe my eyes one more time.

NEALA

I found summer relaxing—not just because the trauma of getting dropped off at school was gone, but also the long evenings felt laidback. I could lie around in my room all afternoon, yet it was still light enough to walk Lady after dinner without Mom worrying about us.

Summer was busier because of Sarah's wedding. I helped her make wedding favors. She chose traditional Jordan Almonds and brought them to the living room along with circles of tulle and ribbons. Together, we watched a

Supernatural marathon and made about a hundred favors. I was in a better mood than usual because I didn't have to go to school in the morning. Sarah and I got along well, considering there were ten years between us. She was nice to me when I was little. The closer I came to graduating, the more it felt like I was catching up with her.

Her fiancé, Jeff, was cool, too. I enjoyed hanging out with her and Jeff at their place, especially when their friends came over to play board games. We all played video games, too, and I always felt safe. They might be older than me, but they're nifty. Mostly, we talk about nerdy stuff, but when it came to knowing about superheroes, like Captain American—or pretty much any Marvel hero (or villain), I could hold my own.

When I was little, people in my family thought I was jealous of Sarah. I used to hide in my room when Sarah threw parties. God, it sucked. Sarah reached milestones, and I had to be present at each one. And now a wedding! But the problem wasn't Sarah; it was the noise. Sarah's friends were rowdy. The girls always said, "Oh, my God!" really loud, and the boys chased the squealing girls up and down the stairs. It was stupid.

Then there were the relatives. When they came around, they compared me to Sarah.

"You are taller than Sarah was at this age."

"Sarah was so smart."

"Sarah is going to do wonderful things."

"What about you, Neala? What will you do?"

Well, I hid in my room, that's what I did. I gathered my "stuffies" and told each teddy bear and dog just how much I hated every sound echoing through the house. I would pretend my toys helped me by placing them around my head to stifle the noise. And I stayed like that, waiting for everyone to go home.

The worst was when my cousins, especially those my age, banged on my door begging me to come out to play. They slid notes under my door and taunted me to join them. I wrote "Go away" on them and shoved them back under the door. Then they would say that mom wanted me to go downstairs for cake, or some other thing. I refused to go, so I would scream, "Leave me alone." I felt bad if I hurt their feelings. I know they only wanted to play with me and my toys.

My feelings confused me, and I didn't have words to explain the pain in my body or the rushing in my brain. Especially, the aching disappointment in myself.

I loved my family and felt safe with them. But sometimes, I wished the madness would stop. If everyone would hold still and be quiet, my head could catch up. But they didn't stop. The chaos continued, and it scrambled my thoughts. It turned my mood. My body trembled with the amount of fear that had built up inside my chest.

Now, it was the wedding. I was genuinely happy for Sarah and Jeff. It made me feel good to see the diamond ring on my sister's hand; I could tell Jeff loved her by the way he'd be sweet to her. I hope someone will love me enough to get me a ring that pretty someday.

The thought of Sarah being married didn't weird me out, but the idea of a wedding—the full summer of preparing and then the day of the wedding made me want to throw up. It was hard to swallow sometimes.

Alina had been helping me plan for the occasion. We broke down the schedule of events—we devised a plan so I'd get a few minutes to myself throughout the big day. I'd know when I should help, and when I could escape. Alina assured me this event was a test for me to learn just how far I had come. She had faith in me, and I would remember that on the day of the wedding. I'd slip her encouragement into the toolbox we'd been building to guide me through stressful situations.

CHAPTER FIFTY-FOUR

CLAIRE

When the day of the wedding arrived, we completed our preparations for the ceremony and reception. Neala's main task was to be dressed, show up on time, and be ready to walk down the aisle. We crossed our fingers and hoped for her comfort. Kane was prepared to drive Sarah to join her bridesmaids for photographs before the wedding guests arrived.

A half hour before the ceremony, Neala and I headed to the church to meet the florist who was the dad of Sarah's friend. He brought gorgeous arrangements. Blossoms filled the bouquets with sweet smells. Baby's breath looked like lace throughout, and decorative feathers peeked from behind the blooms. The boutonnieres for the men were elegant—a single peach rose. The grandmothers' corsages were floral tributes to their wisdom and grace.

I cried when Neala pinned the mother-of-the-bride corsage on my gown. It was one more detail that validated that my firstborn would soon be a married woman.

The morning passed quickly, and before I knew it, it was time to start the ceremony. The girls in the bridal party, including Neala, gathered in the church's narthex. Next came Jeff's mother, Vivian, then me. The wedding planner stood at the entry, waiting to give us our cues.

Jeff's brothers arrived to escort the honorary mothers to our seats.

I arranged for Sophia to sit by me in the front pew.

Everyone was seated. Jeff and the groomsmen lined up at the altar with the reverend. The music began, and my stomach lurched. I wasn't sure if it was because Sarah was getting married, or anxiety about Neala. Perhaps I was overcome with emotion by the event itself. She will do just fine, I told myself, speaking those words for both of my girls.

Music bellowed from the church speakers, and in succession the bridesmaids' arrival announced the ceremonial rites had begun. Neala, being tall, was positioned just before the flower girl. I saw Neala take careful steps down the aisle. She kept her eyes focused on the large cross at the front. Within seconds, Neala reached the altar. I exhaled—it was at that moment I realized I'd been holding my breath.

The flower girl, a four-year-old princess, looked like a peach fairy as she sprinkled rose petals, and pranced her way to the altar. The Maid of Honor came next and then, the music changed. Everyone stood up from their seats and waited for the bride. I reached for Sophia's hand and watched Kane—so elegant in his tuxedo—escort our beautiful daughter. Sarah took confident steps, her arm wrapped around Kane's elbow, as she gazed toward her groom.

I drew in a sharp breath and squeezed Sophia's hand. Sophia squeezed back. My friend had been present in Sarah's life from the beginning. She was at my house when the doctor called to confirm the pregnancy. When I told Sofia that Sarah would be married, I saw Sofia's whole life with Sarah flash through my eyes. But it wasn't death, not at all; it was a new beginning. A new life.

I made the right decision asking Sophia to sit by me during the ceremony. Without Sophia or Kane, I didn't know how I would have managed. Sophia was my best friend, Sarah's godmother, and the Byrnes family's saving grace.

Reaching their destination, Kane lifted Sarah's veil, gave his stepdaughter a kiss, and shook Jeff's hand. He placed Sarah's hand in Jeff's and released them to the reverend. I heard the words of love, faith, devotion, and commitment but only listened to the voice in my head. The one that praised my daughters and congratulated them for a successful day. Once the happily married couple shared their first kiss, I knew the rest of the day would be a breeze.

It wasn't until midway through the reception that Neala came to me in tears. The music and loud noises, along with boisterous activities, bugged her.

"I tried to fight it, Mom, but I feel overpowered."

I searched the room for Kane. I frowned when I located him at the bar, beer in hand, apparently getting drunker by the sip. He would not be able to help. I went to the ladies' lounge, found my purse, and searched for the tranquilizers I'd packed for Neala.

I offered one to her and then sat with her a few minutes until it took effect. Once Neala calmed down, her cousin, Lexy, came over and offered to sit with her, and I returned to the role of hostess.

After several celebratory toasts, the serving of the cake, and a few designated and obligatory dances, the wedding and reception were over. Neala was wiped out from the excitement and the tranquilizer. I wanted to complain to Kane about his overindulgent drinking but chose to revel in the luxury of having our daughter's wedding behind us. In the back of my mind, I rejoiced in the thought of our next big event. I hoped Neala's graduation would top the list.

JUNIOR YEAR

CHAPTER FIFTY-FIVE

NEALA

I filled my backpack for my fourth "first day" of high school. Just this year and then next year to go. Only eighteen more months of school, and I will be free from this hell. Looking down at my new shoes, I was pleased I had chosen the black Converse with the white piping. For some reason, adding a color, even if the amount was small and the color was white, made me feel accomplished.

Prepared to begin my junior year, I felt like I was in two grades. I identified myself with different groups—my current class, and the seniors.

The day worked out well. First period classes were alongside a bank of classrooms, which were accessed by a nearby driveway. Mom and I got permission to use that area as my drop-off spot. That way, I could avoid the high-traffic area of the quad. I felt comfortable with Blaze Johnson and was glad he helped me. This year he was a leader at the NAMI meetings held on the campus. He not only understood anxiety and how it manifested differently in people, but he also helped remove the stigma.

I was also glad Mr. Buckley spent most of his time in the quad; my odds of avoiding him were strong. I listened to the excitement from upperclassmen about dances, senior portraits, cut day, yearbooks, elaborate field trips, and the prom. I didn't envy any of the activities or feel like I was missing out until Karla announced on the PA that seniors should order caps and gowns if they haven't done so already. Hearing the announcement was the first impact of my reality.

I would not be graduating. All I could do was to stay on track. I had to march on through, like the soldiers I read about in History, and accomplish my mission. Eighteen months to freedom.

It was impressive how my first week flew by. I was organized, a skill I had recovered. Last year, I'd relied less on Jill, and this semester we arranged to work together on an as-needed basis. I could do my regular assignments, some being online, but Jill would help me if I needed her for larger projects and reports.

During the last two years, Jill clarified the content of work and untangled confusing directions from more than one teacher. It wasn't because teachers couldn't help me, there were just too many students for a single teacher to take me under their wing.

Even Mom was happy that Jill intervened when needed. Jill confronted the problematic teachers who challenged my ability to complete my work. When Jill validated the harshness of some faculty members, my insecurities dissolved, and I felt braver about turning in assignments.

I could tell that Mom worried about my lack of socialization, but I was too tired at the end of the school day to do more than nap. Part of the reason was the hefty dose of Zoloft, I suspected, but I also knew it was hard to keep alert and "on" during school hours. By the time last period ended, my body relaxed a bit. My shoulders fell, and my chest wasn't so tight.

After three years of turning down offers to hang out after school, I didn't get many invitations to socialize. When Mom asked who my friends were, I could sense her sadness because there were so few. I was comfortable with my limited social life.

At home, with Lady by my side, I closed my eyes. I felt safe in my toasty bed with the blackout curtains banishing the afternoon sun. Peacefulness swept through me. Sleep was my best natural drug. Being the only one home after school, the quiet of the house provided shelter from the chaos of dealing with people.

I read about soldiers who came home from war, freaking out because they thought the enemy lurked behind every corner. They fell apart with exhaustion. I felt no different. Oddly, I considered the soldiers fortunate because they knew who their enemy was. For me, it was the infinitely, dark cavern of the unknown.

CLAIRE

Before the school year even started, anger and stress rose within me the moment I thought about dropping Neala off at school. Summer break usually meant less rushing out the door, but for me, it also brought emotional relief. This summer, I anticipated that with her progress, Neala would get herself to school. Drop-off drama caused a knot to twist in my chest. Since Neala refused to get her license, I knew that I'd have to enforce tight boundaries.

"You will have to start driving yourself to school this year, Neala. My hours are going to change at work in a few months," I warned. "If you don't get your license, you will have to walk. Otherwise, you'll have to figure out transportation to and from school."

Neala looked terrified at the thought of getting herself on campus. I caved and told her I would drive her but only to the back bank of classrooms.

"For the next couple of weeks, if you refuse to get out, I am taking you home. No more waiting in the parking lot."

It would be up to Neala to either walk to school or find a ride from a friend. Even in the rain. Though I harbored compassionate feelings about Neala's disabilities, I swore I would enforce the challenge. I would make Neala responsible for herself. Satisfied with my choice, and more pleased when Kane supported me, Neala agreed to the terms.

School started, and I put my threats into action. The new routine worked. For the most part, Neala exited the car and went to her homeroom without a hitch. A few days—the first ones were hard on both of us—Neala couldn't get out. But I just kept cruising along the bank of classrooms until she gained the confidence to do it. It was only a matter of a few minutes at this point, not painful hours-long bouts of darkness and fear.

There were hints of hesitation, but clearly, Neala conquered her fears. Once she was out of the car, I headed to work. I worried less often about my cell phone buzzing or getting calls for help. I smiled more knowing Neala became assured while walking her own path. She applied caution with her every step, but she was making the journey.

CHAPTER FIFTY-SIX

CLAIRE

I made it to the office early for a meeting with a couple of interns, on loan to our department, to help organize and count inventory. According to Finance, the overspending on duplicated items needed to stop, and this new project would help track items to replace them. This never made sense to me. We ended up using all we had, only to order more another day. Oh, well, who am I to question it? Even if I am behind on other tasks, I guess I get paid either way. But my stress mounted.

Fortunately, this morning, Neala exited the car with minimal anxiety. Thank God for small favors.

I gathered last month's purchase orders and inventory request slips from the staff. I was prepared to present the paper trail to the interns when my cell phone rang. I deposited the paperwork on the large workspace near my desk and grabbed my phone. The ringing stopped, but now the landline rang. Caller ID on the desk phone showed Neala's cell number.

My chest tightened. My throat, suddenly dry, made it hard to breathe. I opened my mouth as if ready to bite my way through the thick air. My vision tunneled and darkened. I grabbed the arm of the desk chair to steady myself. In the throes of a panic attack, I experienced a brief, overwhelming sense of doom. A sheen of sweat broke out over my body.

The phone continued to ring. Shrill. Loud. Although I felt about to pass out, my lungs struggled for air. I commanded myself to keep calm and breathe.

I swiveled the desk chair around and sat in it. As if sitting on the bottom of a swimming pool, the ringing echoed. I pushed my feet to the floor, grounded myself, and picked up the receiver.

"Hi Neala-Girl, what are you doing?" I attempted to sound chipper, but I could hear how flat and disconnected my voice was. Each word exposed my anxiety.

A quiet "Hi, Mom" drifted over the phone line.

I tried to swallow. "Hey, can I call you back? I have some people I have to meet with right now—"

"No, Mom, don't go," Neala blurted.

"Okay." I leaned forward in my chair, but I continued to push my feet into the ground and dug my nails into my palm.

Silence.

"What's going on? Where are you?" I chided, fighting to sound calm. Visions of death came creeping up my spine. I noticed a tingling sensation in my hands and feet; probably from lack of oxygen (or a stroke? Stop!), I began some grounding practices. I looked at my reflection in the computer monitor, tried an awkward smile. You are not going to die. If you do, your co-workers will have to clean you up. That thought had my smile broaden a bit, and I dismissed the gruesome thoughts of death that swiped at me.

"I'm in the front office, and I am really scared, Mom. I don't know why. I'm starting to feel a panic attack coming on," Neala muttered.

I could hear her erratic breathing and her shaky voice. I felt terrible for Neala because I was suffering right then, too.

"Okay, but there must be collective panic in the universe right now. Today, on this random Tuesday, because I feel like I'm going to die right now, too," I said and then began to describe to Neala how my physical sensations of panic held my body hostage.

"You know that darkness we see coming around the corner of our vision? It's because we're not getting enough oxygen, right?"

"Uh-hm," Neala replied.

"So, take a deep breath, but do it slowly." I wished I could offer Neala an aromatherapy oil to smell. "Hey, I have an idea. Do you still have the orange you packed for lunch, or did you eat it already?"

"I still have it."

"Okay, take it out of your backpack and roll it around in your hands for a minute. Get it warmed up a bit."

I heard clattering as Neala rifled through her backpack for the fruit.

"Got it."

"Now, when it's warmed up, bring it close to your nose and inhale. Do you smell the citrus? Rolling it around helped to release some of the fruit's oils. Is it on your fingers, too?" I also drew a breath and imagined the citrus scent.

"Yeah, I do."

"Good, keep on smelling it but make sure to take long, deep breaths. Don't rush, just go slowly. It will help you get some air back inside of your body. That relieves the panic."

I kept imaging I was smelling the orange. Inhaling deeply I felt my body respond. I began to relax.

"Just keep breathing for a few minutes. In . . . and out . . . and in . . . and out."

"Okay," Neala said.

I heard Neala's voice become steady and her breathing less ragged.

"Here's the deal; you keep on breathing in the nice orange smell, and if you start to feel worse, just peel the orange and take some small bites. You can use all your senses to get your grounding back. For now, just keep breathing the orange smell. I don't care how weird you look sniffing an orange." I tried to make Neala laugh.

"It's working, Mom. I feel better. I think I can go back into the classroom."

A sigh of relief escaped my lips. "Good girl. I'm so proud of you, Neala." I smiled even though I knew Neala couldn't see me. I suspected she could hear the satisfaction in my voice, just as I could imagine hers. I was amazed at how connected we were.

"It's a mystery as to why our bodies get these scared feelings," I said. "But I do know that sometimes I feel like this when something good is going to happen, too. Try to remember, this is what it feels like to be excited, not necessarily afraid. Do you think you can remember that? Instead of feeling like something terrible will occur, maybe think about what amazing thing is coming next."

"Yeah, okay, I'll try. I love you, Mom," said Neala.

"I love you, too, sweetie. Call me again if you need to, but otherwise, have a good day. I'll see you when I get home."

After we hung up, I took a moment to think. The fact that I'd talked Neala off the ledge, so to speak, also calmed me. My breathing sounded normal again. Letting out one last exhale, I picked up my pens to color coordinate the inventory lists then headed toward the workspace to meet the interns. Getting this financial mess out of the way was the "something good" I could look forward to.

CHAPTER FIFTY-SEVEN

CLAIRE

The semester continued at a pace our family hadn't felt in years. The household developed a routine. Neala began to thrive. Kane and I sought time together, taking Sunday drives and going to dinner. Neala continued to avoid such outings but asked us to bring a meal back for her.

The time we spent together was meant to bring us closer. Our dates were to keep us focused on our future and on our relationship. I fantasized about what we'd do once Neala graduated. I enjoyed going out and living it up with Kane. Maybe we could travel. It felt good to not worry about Neala so much, but when we went out, I developed a new and curious sensation. A caution I hadn't felt in a while, a red flag poked at my gut.

Kane boasted about business getting better, listing potential jobs, while his bank account dwindled. I thought it strange that Kane found money to splurge for extravagant lunches and his after-work beer. The economy was down, and though his days were long, work was slow. The power hadn't been paid, and the water was turned off more than once, but Kane found enough money to party.

I suspected he was doing a financial balancing act because Kane made excuses that he couldn't get to the bank and then asked me for cash from my stash so he could get fuel. I let the warning slip by. Caring for Neala the last few years drained what little energy I had. Confronting him seemed massive, but I decided not to go along with his cavalier ways any longer.

Sitting in the living room, I relaxed with my Sunday morning coffee and a good mystery. Kane asked me to join him for yet another drive and dinner. This routine developed recently, every Sunday he'd take me out for a late lunch or early dinner.

"Your income has slowed," I said. "How can we have enough money to indulge like this?" I listened to my intuition screaming inside of me. I couldn't help but notice that something was amiss.

"I got it covered, don't worry so much. You always bring me down," Kane snapped.

"Someone has to be responsible, Kane, and I don't think you have your priorities straight."

"Look, I have work coming in. We might be behind in some areas, but I will handle the bills. I need to relax. You can come along, or not, but I am going out."

I couldn't decide what to do. After a few cocktails, I'd forget about how nasty he was. Sometimes, I chalked the misery up to him being a big baby who needed to get his way. This time, I followed my inner voice, and I called his bluff.

"Go ahead. Have fun by yourself. I don't want to contribute to the fall of the house of Byrnes."

I went back to my book and pretended to read while he went upstairs, presumably to change for his day out. Go ahead, be an ass. It's gonna catch up with you, Kane, wait and see! I heard the shower, and when he was through, he stomped passed me. I ignored him.

"Mark and I are going to Riverbend," Kane said.

I disregarded his comment and continued to stare at my book, rereading the same line for the fifth time. God damnit Kane. Why are you doing this?

Kane didn't come home until after eleven p.m. As he boasted about the day he'd relished without me, I could barely stand the reek of alcohol. He then ranted about him being superior to everyone who crossed his path.

As if in agreement, I nodded, but secretly, I knew his unbecoming behavior was growing worse. This strange attitude used to emerge on Friday nights, then the occasional weeknight, but now showed up pretty much every day, including our "special" Sunday date. His drinking had accelerated, adding more to our problems.

I was about to find out just how big that problem was.

I asked Sophia and some of our mutual friends to celebrate Sophia's birthday. Kane had standing plans at his car club, so I invited everyone over for dinner at my house for the party.

All the women, except Sophia, had left when Kane called me. He said he was done with his meeting, "Is the coast clear?"

"Oh, you know us, we're just getting started," I laughed, knowing how Sophia and I could go on for hours.

"Okay, I'll hang out with Mark a little longer and be home soon."

"Sounds good, drive safe." I looked at the clock and realized it was getting late.

A couple of hours passed. Sophia insisted on helping me straighten up. I wiped the countertops down one last time.

"Sophia, it's time for you to go home," I said, waving the dishtowel at her. "You can't be the guest of honor and do the dishes."

Sophia said, "I'll go as soon as I get the rest of the glasses in from the dining room." As she turned, she looked back at me. "Thank you for such a fun time tonight. You make birthdays easier."

"My pleasure, birthday girl, now bring me those glasses." I smiled back at my friend.

Minutes later, Sophia and I had the house back in order. Sophia accepted some leftovers to take for her lunch then went home. I crept upstairs to check on Neala who was engrossed in a *Supernatural* marathon.

Neala agreed to watch it on WebSeries with Nola. "We're watching the hunky demon hunter series from the beginning on WebSeries. We can both watch it in our own home, but I am face-timing her. I want to watch her drool over Jared Padalecki," Neala said.

"You two are so funny. Hi Nola," I said to Neala's smartphone.

Nola smiled.

"I'm turning in, you should as well; it's getting late." I kissed Neala on the top of her head.

"Night, Mom. Love you," Neala said.

I put my clothes away and glanced at the clock. 1:00 a.m. What the hell? Where was Kane? Then the sound of the garage door rumbled.

Kane boisterously called up the stairwell, "Hey, anybody home?" I heard his footfalls on the steps. Somewhere in my primal self, I sensed fear. Not panic or anxiety, but fear. As if all the panic attacks I'd experienced had been practice drill for this moment.

"How was your little party?" Kane asked. He stunk of beer, and the edge in his voice was mean.

"Fine, it went well," I answered. I dodged by him and headed to Neala's room. She and Lady were cuddled together, just falling asleep.

Kane followed me down the hall, leaned down to say goodnight to Neala, and he shoved her shoulder. In the past, he'd scoffed that it was just a tickle, but Neala complained it hurt, especially when she was tense.

"Stop!" Neala yelled at her dad. She shoved him away and yelled, "STOP!"

"Hey, don't do that to me," Kane sneered. "Don't talk to me that way!"

At first, I thought he pretended to sound hurt, but then I realized he was furious by his tone. The hair on my neck stood up.

"Leave her alone, Kane, she needs to go to sleep." I tried to turn him away from Neala.

Kane turned around and lunged toward me.

I stumbled back.

Raising his voice, he lashed out at me, "You stay out of this. You always get involved. I'm tired of the two of you teaming up against me!"

Lady jumped off the bed and ran out of the bedroom.

I recognized the scared face and tail between her legs as she brushed by. "Kane, go to bed. You need to get out of this room," I demanded.

"I want Lady! Dad, you scared her." Neala sobbed.

A rush of fear for Neala coiled in my belly.

Kane left Neala's room and snatched Lady by the hindquarters. Marching to her room, he lifted Lady and threw the dog, making her bounce on Neala's bed. "Here's your precious damn dog. Too bad nobody around here thinks of me like they do this damn animal." Kane spat out his words and left Neala to calm a trembling Lady.

Within seconds his tantrum began. Kane stomped back and forth in the master bedroom. He started throwing things off the dresser. He broke one of my porcelain dolls, kicked the laundry basket—freshly folded clothes now a jumbled heap on the floor. I feared he would strike out at me next. I ran downstairs. I grabbed some cash from my stash and started my return for Neala. Kane stood at the top of the stairs.

Pacing, he blocked the stairway to keep me from approaching. Terrified for our safety, I longed to get the hell out of there, but Neala was upstairs, and Kane continued to rant and stride, above me on the landing. Maybe I could run to Chuck's, see if he'd be able to talk sense into Kane. But I knew I couldn't leave my daughter alone with him. I grabbed my cell phone and texted Neala.

Me: We're leaving

Neala: I'm scared.

Me: I know. Get a bag of clothes, your backpack together, and meet me in the front yard.

Neala: When?

Me: When he goes to his room. I will open the garage door without the opener, so he won't hear me. Hurry. Be ready.

Neala: What about Lady?

Me: Take her. I'll get her leash and bowl.

I put the phone in my pocket, disconnected the automatic door opener, hoisted the heavy door, and let the car roll into the driveway. When I was done, and sure Kane didn't know what I was doing, I quietly lowered the garage door.

I sat with the key in the ignition, time ticking. Images of Kane—eyes flaming with malice, came to mind. What the hell was happening? I reached for the phone to text Neala but put it away when I saw her and the dog come into view and dash toward the car.

Once Neala and Lady were safely with me, I drove away from the house without looking back. We turned the corner and my body started to shake. A lump formed in my throat, and I couldn't breathe. I focused on the road, but unsure where to go; I just drove.

"I am so sorry, Neala. Jesus, what the hell happened in there?" I heaved.

I drove around town and up and down the boulevard a couple of times. Where could we go? Thoughts raced through my mind. I'd saved some money, (years ago, our marriage counselor shook her head and advised me—always have a to-go bag and cash when he's drinking). A hotel? The idea seemed extreme. "I don't know where to go, sweetheart. I don't know where to go." Tears streamed down my face. I was sick to my stomach and felt vulnerable, victimized, and in shock.

Finally, Neala had enough.

"If we can't go to Chuck's, then how about the police. Can we just tell cops?" Neala begged. "He drinks too much."

"No, we are not in immediate danger; they can't help us," I explained to Neala, but to make her feel better, I drove to the police station. I was relieved to notice the parking lot was well lit. "We can sit here where it is safe and until we choose a destination." After a few rejected proposals, we decided the best option was Sophia's house. We agreed we were too frightened to go home. We didn't know if Kane knew we'd left. Had he passed out? We weren't prepared to take any chances.

"You know you have a best friend when you can literally show up in the middle of the night with your kid and your dog, and she takes you in." I sipped herbal tea and leaned back on the couch.

Telling our tale of terror to Sophia was traumatic. I kept Neala close to me, and even though she dozed, I was careful of what I said.

"Kane's relationship with alcohol is intensifying," I confided. "It's become his way to escape. I partly understand, but this . . . I'm livid. Tonight, he really lost his shit."

Kane's drinking forced me to be the only person Neala could rely on. Understanding this, I realized why Neala sometimes clung to me. Kane's drinking provoked Neala's stress. No wonder the kid hated parties. She watched the monster unleash with every sip Kane drank. Puzzle pieces began to gravitate toward each other, and the ones locking into place scared the hell out of me.

For three days after the incident, Kane texted intermittent reports that he fed the animals, brought in the mail, and left other benign messages. Then he sent a text that startled me. Kane wanted to meet me.

I'd been going back and forth to the house to get clothes, but only when his truck wasn't in the driveway—the only time I felt safe. I rushed through, grabbing things for Neala, too. We couldn't keep living like this, so I agreed to see him.

"I don't want to meet you at home. I want to meet in public," I said.

He was already at Dee Dee's when I arrived. He looked like shit, and I was glad.

"Hey," he said. His voice sounded rough. "I am glad you came."

"It isn't easy to be here with you. What the hell?" I said.

"I'm so sorry," he started. I tuned out what I felt was an empty apology. Cutting him off, I mentioned we should place our order. He went to the counter to order and pay, and I let him go without thanking him.

I was pissed, scared, vengeful, and hurt, yet I felt sorry for the poor guy, too. He was family, and I could see his hurt. I was mad at myself for feeling compassion edge its way into my heart. I decided I should just shut up and listen to what he had to say.

"I . . . uh . . . I am . . . I stopped drinking. For good."

I just looked at him. "I saw a counselor yesterday, and . . . uh . . . I think she will help me." He sipped his coffee, but he kept his eyes on mine.

"I hope you get the help you need. This bullshit has been hard on Neala and me." I didn't tell him I was staying with Sophia. He probably figured it out, but neither of us confirmed it.

"When will you come home?" His voice nearly cracked.

Before I left to meet him, Sophia warned me not to go back to Kane right away. "I haven't thought about when, so much as how, Kane. We won't be back until you quit drinking, which you say you have. I want a little more time to think about this—how this will play out between us. It won't be easy for you." I looked at my cup.

We both sat in silence, feeling each other's pain. Apprehension hung for a while, but it subsided once I saw how scared he was. He had the most to lose, and he knew it.

I told him I wanted to stay away for a little longer, but I would drop the dog back home. I didn't mention Lady was taking a toll on Sophia's yard.

"You know you don't have to leave yet," Sophia told me.

"I know, thank you so much. We can't stay here much longer. Neala and I need to go home sooner or later. When I spoke to Kane, he said he'd stopped drinking. He's gotten into counseling and may check out AA." Was this my new vocabulary? I looked at my hands. They were red from wringing them for the past few days. "For our family's sake, I have to go back. Give it a try. He knows though, one fuck-up and we are so gone."

I joined Neala at her subsequent counseling appointment to talk about our current events. Alina didn't seem surprised; she seemed prepared for this conversation. I appreciated Alina's support in Neala's life, and now in mine.

I experienced validation when I chose to leave, and Alina helped me to admit that. She agreed to help support Neala with this new information and discuss how Neala might learn to rely on herself and not let Kane's and my problems become hers.

The next few weeks our family lived on eggshells. Kane did his best to be polite and stay calm. Although I longed to lash out at him, I kept my snide comments to myself.

Neala appeared to be the same. She was quiet and in her room most of the day. When we first got home, Kane sat down with us and apologized profusely for his behavior and his violent actions. He gently befriended Lady again, and we all half-heartedly smiled when she excitedly accepted a dog biscuit from him.

For a couple of months, all went reasonably smoothly until late one night, Kane called me on his way home from his club meeting. My heart fell when I heard the slur in his voice; he'd been drinking. I felt a flutter in my gut. How could he do this? I couldn't let this happen to us again. "Don't come home." My words were lined with disappointment and rage. "You can't sleep here tonight," I said and hung up on him. I ignored the phone when it began to ring repeatedly.

I contemplated calling Chuck but decided against it. I wasn't ready to expose Kane, not yet. Instead, I double-checked all the doors to make sure they were locked and re-locked the entry door's deadbolt. Once again, I disconnected the garage door—this time to keep him out—and turned off all the lights. I checked on Neala and Lady, who were sound asleep, then I crept back downstairs and sat near the front window and called Sophia.

"He's drunk," I said.

"What? Is he there?" Sophia asked.

"Not yet. He's on his way, I think."

"Well, I'm glad you called. I will stay on the line with you." Sophia's calm voice reassured me. "Is Chuck home? Can you go there?"

"Honestly, the thought crossed my mind, but I don't want to drag him into it," I said.

Why am I such a chicken shit? He'd be here in a minute to talk to Kane, to protect Neala.

We stayed connected while Kane arrived. "Oh, God. I see his truck. He's pulling into the driveway," I whispered, my voice shaky. "I unplugged the garage door, so it won't open, he's gonna try the front door. . ." I inched toward the doorway.

"Stay calm, honey, I am right here. When he tries to unlock it, hold the bolt closed and remind him he is not supposed to be drunk around you or Neala. Ever. Period," Sophia coached.

I grasped the lock. Then I remembered, thank God, Kane never put the deadbolt key on his keyring. It was still in the kitchen junk drawer, left there from when they installed the new door years ago. This time his lack of follow-through was to my advantage. The wooden door seemed flimsy; I wondered if he was belligerent enough to try to kick it down.

Why didn't I call Chuck?

The panels vibrated as Kane pound. "Hey, someone let me in!" Bang! Bang! Bang! "Open up in there," he shouted.

I braced myself at the front door and held the bolt the way Sophia told me to. "Were you drinking tonight, Kane?" I shouted.

Sophia coached me with what to say.

"Yeah, a few beers," he said.

I was sickened.

I'd put Sophia on the phone's speaker. I guess she heard his yells through the phone because she coached some more, "Remind him of the rules."

"You know the rules. No drinking." Damn him, this is awful! "How can you think it would be okay with us?"

I heard a shuffle and glanced up the stairs to see Neala above me.

"Mom?" Neala looked at me with woeful eyes. She stood on the landing, holding her stuffed dog. Wow, she looked vulnerable. I needed to protect her. Feeling a surge of strength, I tightened my grip on the deadbolt.

"What am I supposed to do if you won't let me in?"

"Maybe now you will get to see what it was like for us to flee in the middle of the night without a plan. You'll figure it out." I grinned—I didn't need coaching for that. I just let him have it, my rage vibrated in every word. It was then that I realized that I was no longer afraid. Power, as strong as steel, surrounded me. I thought of Neala and shot her a look of confidence.

"Okay," he mumbled and went back to his truck. I watched him sit in the cab for a few minutes before he finally started the engine and drove off. The fact that he was driving drunk flickered through my mind, but he had told me time and again that "he was a big boy," and he could handle what came his way.

Tonight, I was mad and scared, and I didn't have the energy to worry about him or his consequences. Staying strong for myself and Neala were my priorities that night.

"He's gone," I told Sophia. "I think he won't come back. God, I need to go to bed."

"Okay, but keep your phone nearby. If he comes back or you need anything—I'm here."

After that night, Kane quit drinking for good. He followed up with his counselor and learned he used alcohol to get through tough situations, including socializing, and his own anxieties. A beer before the event, who knows how many beers at the event, and always one for the road. The habit of cloaking his feelings of unworthiness and awkward social skills took over and sent him crumbling down.

I decided I couldn't help but love this humbled version of my husband and found him more desirable for being vulnerable and honest. Perhaps I could stay in the marriage and work with him if he continued to be sober and decent. With that choice, Neala and I began to witness recovery in action.

CHAPTER FIFTY-EIGHT

CLAIRE

I arranged for a day off. Errands had piled up and needed to get done. This included sweet-talking us out of late fees for some overlooked bills. Fortunately, I dropped Neala off at school without much resistance. Because I got home on the earlier side—no two-hour wait today—I indulged in a long, hot shower before starting my chores.

I wiped the steam from the mirror to apply my makeup just as my cell phone vibrated. It was Neala. Sighing, I picked up the phone and hesitated. What should I say to convince Neala to stay at school? I didn't want to deal with Neala's anxiety nor forfeit my free day. A barrage of excuses lined up on the tip of my tongue, each one tasting of deceit.

Before Neala left for school, she'd agreed to turn in assignments. She reported having a tough time getting them to the teacher. If this call was about the homework, I'd convince Neala to turn them in and get the current assignments to keep her from falling behind. If I were to cave in and pick Neala up, first I'd demand some progress.

"Hi, kiddo," I cheerfully answered the call.

"Hi, Mom." Neala sounded stressed.

"What's up?" I refrained from jumping to conclusions and waited to see what the problem was. Today though, I was pretty sure Neala would ask for me to get her. I could feel the vibe.

"I'm having a really tough day. People are all around me," Neala said. "They all want to talk to me, and I can't do it."

"I know, sugar, it happens sometimes. All the kids are in the halls at the same time. It'll pass."

"No, Mom, I'm freaking out."

"Look, all you have to do today is to turn in your work. You promised you would. After that, you can move along with the rest of your day—"

"Mom, not today. I just . . . it's too hard."

"Well, you have to get it turned in and then—"

"Mom! I don't want to come home, okay. I only called because I needed to hear your voice."

I stopped mid-thought. Here I was ready to argue with Neala—better turn in your work or else—when I realized Neala was in fact, working up to it on her own.

"Oh," was all I could say.

"Yeah, so I just need to talk with you," said Neala.

I let out a breath. "In that case, what do you want to chat about?"

"I don't know."

"Okay, I will get some goodies at the store, so we can make a yummy snack after school. I'll pick you up today. You won't have to walk if you'd rather have a ride."

"Okay," said Neala, her voice now calmer.

"And now the cat just jumped up on the counter." I began a cat-commentary to lighten the conversation. "He knows I'm trying to get out of here."

Neala giggled. "I love him, Mom. He's so sweet."

I scratched Beans under his chin. "I'm petting him now. He's purring, so I think he wants me to say 'hi' to you. Ouch! The little shit just bit me."

Neala laughed. "It was a love-bite, Mom. He likes you a lot."

I heard Neala's voice calm, the stress had lessened. Chatting about the mundane lifted her mood. I tucked that bit of knowledge away to use the next time Neala called me in a panic.

"Okay, love me or not, this cat is going outside for the day. I need to head out of here. I'll see you after school then?"

"Okay. Yeah, so pick me up today?"

"Yes, at the usual spot."

I sent Neala a kiss over the phone, and Neala said goodbye.

When I clicked off, I confirmed Neala had made enormous strides by taking control of her anxiety. She reached out for help without running away—even stayed at school to face another level of "getting through."

My shoulders fell. I realized I'd braced myself to be on the defensive when it came to keep Neala in school. I fought a constant battle, which we both had to face. My daughter's worries transferred to me, and it became a burden I hadn't realized I carried. After the phone call, I noticed that maybe the time had come for me to up my level of confidence in Neala, too.

With this conscious thought, I gave my shoulders a roll and stretched my neck. I am Wonder Woman. The best mom ever—my silly, but positive affirmations. I applied my lipstick and smacked my lips. And I am quite lovely, too. I winked at my reflection in the mirror. Fortified with new strength, I left the house with the confidence to take on the world.

CHAPTER FIFTY-NINE

CLAIRE

Neala and Nola planned to hang out at our house after school. In the evening, they planned to attend the senior's English class production of Shakespeare's Romeo and Juliet. A four-hour window between the last bell and the play allowed the girls time to relax, freshen up, and to make dinner plans.

I grew to appreciate Nola's company. Nola made me laugh with her vocal opinions about school and the students. Her frankness was refreshing, and I knew I could count on Nola to keep me informed about the goings-on at school.

After a delicious dinner of Kane's barbequed ribs, Neala's tossed green salad, Nola's doctored corn on the cob, and my special cherry cake, everyone cleared the table to get ready for the play.

"I can't believe they picked a tragedy for the senior play," Neala said, then added, "Speaking of tragedy, I'm going upstairs to change my shirt. I have sauce on this one."

"Nice way to avoid kitchen duties," Nola called to Neala, who'd already left for her room.

"I hope you ate enough for dinner, Nola," I said. "I need your list of toppings that you put on the corn; it was terrific."

"Don't tell anyone, but I start with paprika and then use what looks interesting in the spice cupboard. It is different every time."

"You don't say! Well, your secret is safe with me." I paused and peered into Nola's eyes. "I don't get to tell you often, but Nola, I am forever grateful Neala has you for a friend. I mean, I benefit, too, of course." I smiled and gave Nola a wink.

"I love hanging out with Neala. We get along, and we have so much fun together. We share opinions, and some of them are salty, I think it's what makes her fun. She makes me laugh, too." Nola said. "Who would have thought a common interest in *Supernatural,* and the cute demon hunters, would lead to a lifelong friendship."

I laughed at Nola's remark. "I appreciate how you help her at school, too."

"I am happy to help her and stick up for her." Nola paused. "Sometimes, though, I don't know what to do so I do nothing. You know? I am not sure if I should help her get out of the car or just avoid the situation. Neala knows I am not ignoring her though," Nola quickly added.

"I understand. Having someone on her side is important, and I am glad it is you. I'm happy we're friends, too," I said and leaned over to hug Nola. "What do you mean stick-up for her?" I pulled back but left my hand on Nola's shoulder.

"Well, Mrs. Byrnes." Nola paused and looked over toward the stairs. "Sometimes, I have to defend Neala. More than once, this jackass—oh! I'm sorry!" Nola covered her mouth, "I mean, this kid who was in our Biology class, well, one day Neala was having a tough time and went to the office. He sarcastically said that he had anxiety, too, so he should be excused from class and get reduced homework passes like Neala does."

I lowered my hand and searched Nola's eyes, imploring her to continue.

"I told him he was a jerk, and that Neala has special privileges because she has a disability. Just because he can't see it doesn't mean it isn't there."

My eyes probably revealed sadness, but I gently smiled at Nola. "Thank you for being there for her, even when she isn't in the room. That's awfully kind of you, Nola. And yeah, I think it's safe to say he is a jackass." I smiled and changed our pace. "Now, on to the play so I can tell him to break a leg."

We were still cackling up at our joke when Kane and Neala joined us.

Later that night, after Neala was asleep, images of the wonderful people Neala attracted to herself fluttered through my mind. Nola was, though the best, one of many of authentic and mature friends that supported her. Then it dawned on me how the world would be a better and peaceful place because of the kids of this next generation—minus the occasional jackass or two—who showed more kindness and compassion than many of the adults.

CHAPTER SIXTY

CLAIRE

"I have an early meeting on Wednesday, and you've been leaving for your job earlier than usual, Kane. Maybe we should plan on Neala staying home from school that day," I suggested.

"Works for me. Neala will catch up on other work and avoid a rough morning. Maybe it would be good for her."

I heard Neala rustling around in the family room—the sounds of her pulling out her art supplies from within the trunk-style coffee table in front of the couch. "Hi, Mom," Neala said when I came into the room.

Neala looked up and noticed me—a good indication Neala's mood was relaxed.

"Hey, going to do some painting?" I spotted the oils and brushes scattered on the floor. "I always ask the obvious, don't I?"

Neala crossed her eyes and we laughed. I was relieved Neala understood my humor. Unsure how Neala would react to my offhand remarks, I tried to keep things light. I learned from experience that Neala's response might be negative.

Neala's adverse reaction would pour out of her mouth, and I would take the brunt of it. I made an effort to understand but didn't always know how she would respond.

I figured Neala knew that when she lashed out at me, she was really screaming at the world. Although a pretty good sport about it, I secretly cried when she was brutal. Neala's fits landed on me the most because she knew it was me who aimed to make life better for her. Especially those times when all she wanted to do was give up. Through her fury, I grasped this and did my best to stay grounded.

I believed Neala trusted me. I was Neala's soft place. When the world was mean to Neala, Neala was mean to me. I tossed the unwarranted anger aside when I could, but sometimes the hurt became intense, and I lashed back.

I watched Neala's face while she painted and wondered what was going on in my daughter's mind. She looked adorable, like her younger self, amongst her art supplies. It would be as good a time as any to approach the subject of getting herself to school. Or not.

"So, I was thinking," I said as if nonchalant, "I have to be at a meeting first thing on Wednesday, and Dad has to leave early, too. Neither of us can drive you. Maybe we can plan on having you stay home? On Wednesday, I mean . . . unless you want to take a stab at it by yourself."

I searched Neala's face for any indication of worry; making changes could bring up the weirdest phobias. Gosh, Claire, you just tossed a whole conversation, answers and all at her, let her think a moment!

"No, I don't want to try to make it there without you. I'll stay home on Wednesday," Neala said.

I wasn't surprised at the quick response.

"Okay, but Dad and I want you to check in with your teachers for class assignments. You can catch up on past work and study for some tests. I'll call in and say you are sick that day." I winked at Neala then headed back into the other room.

NEALA

I collected my painting materials and brought them to the large crafting table on the other side of the room. The picture window let in natural light—good for color choice. Accustomed to body checks, I scanned my body to identify any uncomfortable feelings. I felt unruffled. Serene. I credited some of the tranquility to Wednesday—a day I'd have to myself. No summoning of the energy necessary to go through the rigors of getting to school.

Choosing the yellow paint tube from the array of colors, I squirted some onto my pallet. Without having planned it, I made the outline of a bouquet. Yellow petals emerged from the abstract blobs in the shape of full flowers. I smiled as I painted the cheerful arrangement.

CLAIRE

When I arrived at the wine bar, Sophia was already there. She put her menu down and slid off her bar stool. "Claire, it's been a while," Sophia said, enveloping me in her arms.

I relaxed into Sophia's warm embrace. "I'm so glad to be here! What a day!" I let my arms fall to my sides, releasing the hug. "This is just what the doctor ordered, happy hour with you!"

We sat at the table, scanned the wine list, and decided to split a bottle of a local vintner's chardonnay. With that, we chose some savory bruschetta amongst select cheeses and fresh fruit.

"How are you, really? And Neala?" Sophia asked.

"We're hanging in there. You?" I replied, thinking about how much Neala and I had begun to heal. With support from Alina and Sofia, we'd learn to set boundaries. But even so, my gut still clenched whenever I thought of how my daughter and I'd fled to Sophia's for safety.

"I'm splendid! And how are the newlyweds?" Sophia's smile was sly. "Immersed in marital bliss?"

"Jeff and Sarah are doing well. Jeff got a promotion last month, and Sarah started house hunting. She mentioned they found a place, not far from us, but not too close either." I laughed; glad Sophia changed the subject. I smiled thinking how happy I was that Sarah chose to stay near.

"And Neala? She's handling junior year, okay?

"Yes, this year we seem to have figured it out. Not so much pressure," I said. "I'm really having fun with her. We go to the craft stores, bookstores—she enjoys quiet places. We're getting along great lately. She has changed and grown in many ways."

"How does Kane do with all this? Is he coping better since his last binge?"

The waiter came by and set the wine glasses down and then poured the wine. We both acknowledged his service with a nod. Then I went on.

"You know Kane, he's got depth. Not much shows on the surface. Some days I still feel like he is out of touch. Now he deals with his own stress and unpredictability instead of numbing himself with alcohol. He doesn't share much about his therapy, but I think it is helping. I can tell he's beginning to understand more now that he is enlightened and fighting his own battle." I felt a flicker of happiness cross my brow. "He is more attentive, and I noticed he feels things by the way he displays empathy. It's kind of sexy."

"I am proud of Kane. You really got through to him. Sounds like you are all doing better."

"Thanks, Sophia. I do need validation and to be reminded occasionally. It keeps me encouraged. Especially since our goal is to have Neala complete school with a diploma. I am eager for her to graduate and enjoy that achievement. And get her driver's license. And get a job." I stopped. "Oh, listen to me! I think I may be part of the problem," I chuckled. "We hope she will take a summer job, so wish us luck!" I sipped my wine and settled into the seat. Rolling my neck, I said, "It feels good to relax with you. Thanks for getting together with me, I don't know why we wait so long between visits."

"Me either," said Sophia, "But we need to change that!"

CHAPTER SIXTY-ONE

CLAIRE

Kane switched on the news, and I switched my focus from the TV to the laptop. I clicked on Facebook and noticed posts of Neala's classmates in formal wear for the prom and senior pictures. There were boasts about college acceptance and internships. Filled with sentimental blues, I sighed. There were the girls from Brownies, T-Ball, and the kids from middle school, and Neala's classmates from Norden. Their once cherubic faces were now mature and esteemed. My heart swelled with pride for the moments I got to share with them. At the same time, seeing these posts taunted me because Neala was no longer part of their group.

A pang of torment and longing struck through my belly. Knowing Neala's classmates were moving on was bittersweet. I realized Neala might be behind in other things, not only her grade. She wasn't driving yet, nor had she ever held a part-time job. No experience with interviews, social etiquettes, nor going on a proper date. My twinge sent the nagging feeling to my chest, where it sat like a lump of guilt. With all the efforts to get Neala to school, I had overlooked teaching Neala life skills.

Alina worked with Neala on managing her feelings and holding herself accountable in her interactions with others. The tune-ups came, ensuring Neala grew with her experiences, but at the same time, Neala faltered in other accomplishments. Neala's world was narrow, and it dawned on me even with further achievements, it may remain small.

I decided to speak to Neala about volunteering; it seemed the logical place to start. Later that evening, I called Neala down to the family room. She sat next to me on the sofa, pulled her legs up on the couch, chose a pillow, and hugged it to her belly.

"Mom, I want to try something, but I might need your help."

I was speechless as Neala divulged her grand plans for summer break. "There's a possibility to earn a full scholarship toward a trade school because I'm enrolled with an exemption plan and take special courses. A guidance counselor thought I should try to go to beauty school."

"Beauty school?" Where did that come from? Staring at Neala's blue hair, the starry-eyed vision of pink-haired Frenchie, the beauty school dropout from *Grease*, popped into my head, but I kept quiet and listened.

"I could shadow at the salon where Dad gets his hair cut," Neala explained. "I want to learn about the beauty industry before I apply for the scholarship."

I was impressed with Neala's forethought, but I scolded myself for jumping to conclusions. What if she found out she hated working in a salon? I didn't have the heart to question Neala about the clatter and noise of chatter, music, and hair dryers in a beauty parlor.

"How can I help?" I asked.

"I don't want to call Jolene. Will you call her for me? See if we can meet her?"

"Done," I said. I put my arm around Neala, but she pulled back.

"Stop, Mom," Neala said. "I'm going back upstairs."

I let her go, satisfied enough with Neala's idea.

NEALA

A few weeks before school was out, Mom and I stopped by the beauty shop and met with Jolene, the shop's owner.

"I'd love to have you, Neala," Jolene said. "Let's look at my schedule. Okay, hmm . . ." Jolene flipped the pages in her appointment book. "I'd be more than happy to have you come in on a part-time basis to shadow." Jolene looked at me, and I smiled back at her. "Looks like I could use your help at least three mornings a week. What will work for you?"

I was excited and looked forward to volunteering in the salon. A favorite pastime was to watch YouTube clips with how-to hints. Makeup and nails were my favorites, but I wanted to try to work with Jolene in the hair salon. Jolene's kindness and bubbly personality made me feel good when I went with Dad for his haircut. And Jolene was the only stylist who trimmed his mustache evenly. I could tell when he went to someone else, the sides of his mustache were a disaster, and I called him on it every time. "I guess Jolene's was closed, huh?"

Each day, I counted down the days for school to end. The problem was, the closer summer got, murky tendrils of fear invaded my excitement.

I endured Mom's gentle reminders, as well as all-out threats to contact Jolene about shadowing. The pressure grew so much, I withdrew from the decision to shadow. I knew it was not a good time to confess to Mom that I let the trepidation take over, but I couldn't sleep with it on my mind anymore.

I went to the family room where Mom was watching television and drinking some of her orange-spiced tea. Just like the night I'd mentioned my summer plans, I sat on the same couch and explained how I wasn't able to summon the courage to follow my passion.

Mom put her teacup on the table and turned to me. "I'm concerned about your lack of follow-through." Mom sounded stern. "It seems you can't complete what you start, and that is not a good trait to perfect. At this point, I worry about your ability to hold down a job."

I read confusion and judgment on Mom's face.

"I think you need to go to bed, young lady, and you better think about how you are going to make it in this world. Something's gotta give." Mom turned away from me. She snatched the remote, and clicked the TV off, picked up her tea, and went to her room.

If she tried to hug me tonight, I surely would let her. I struggled to sniff the tears away, but they still trickled down my cheeks.

CLAIRE

Fear dragged its talons along my spine as I envisioned my 36-year-old daughter still living in my house, playing video games on my couch, surrounded by Domino's Pizza boxes, and coming home to twelve cats. I tossed Kane into the picture—hanging out at The Corner Bar, avoiding the situation.

I stopped mid-thought. Kane was changing. He would be here for us, not at the bar. I might begin by talking to him. It had been a long time since I'd felt my partner at my side.

The day began with inner turmoil over what to do, which led me to Kane. What were his thoughts regarding Neala's summer?

Kane sipped his coffee and read the newspaper app on his smartphone. I looked at him and noticed how much he resembled his father, Bill. I hesitated. Now was as good a time as any.

I poured myself a cup of coffee and explained what Neala had said the night before. After a few sips, I offered my conclusion. "She'll be a senior this year. Next summer, she'll either have to enter the workforce or be enrolled for college in the fall."

Kane seemed to be taking more than a slight interest.

"At the current rate," I continued, "I'm betting on the workforce, but now, this lack of interest on Neala's part concerns me." I took another sip. "That's why I figured it was time to bring in reinforcements—a big, handsome, though perhaps formidable, kind man." I got up and wrapped my arms around his neck.

"Okay, let me think about this," Kane said earnestly. Then he looked at his watch, "I gotta go, but let's talk tonight."

After Kane left, I tried to let it go. All the scenarios I came up with left either me or Neala crying, and it wasn't how I wanted summer to start.

That evening, after dinner, Kane suggested I take the dog for a walk. "I want to speak with Neala," he said.

"All right," I said. "If that's what you want."

Lady was leashed, and we headed out the door. I'd asked if he would talk to Neala, and now it was going to happen. Would he come on too strong or be scary? But that was what dads were for. Moms could make the world a happy place, but dads, well, dads would tell you how it is.

When I returned from the walk with Lady, I half-expected to see Neala crying at the kitchen table, and Kane looming over her. He'd be telling how the world worked. To my surprise, the house was quiet.

I unleashed Lady, hung up the lead, and ventured up the stairs. Lady was at my heels. All I could hear was Kane gently snoring from our bedroom. So, whatever happened, he was at peace with it.

Tiptoeing past the master bedroom and down the hall, I found Neala in her room painting her nails a different shade of black than they were the day before. How is that even possible? I questioned Neala about that, but when Neala held the nail polish bottles side by side, they were in fact, two different shades of black.

"Lady!" Neala scolded when Lady jumped up on the bed. The dog quickly went to the foot of the bed, circled once, and laid down.

"Well, how'd it go with Dad?" I asked.

Without looking up, Neala nonchalantly shrugged her shoulders. "This summer I'm going to work with him. He said he would pay me. That way I can buy a car and save up for what I want to do next summer."

"That sounds . . . fun." I felt an unexpected wave of relief but was stunned they came to this decision. Kane would keep her safe at work, teach her excellent work ethics, and she'd get to earn a little money.

I only hoped it would work out and be enough for Neala to want more. Secretly, I savored the fact she'd be with Kane all week long. This meant the house would stay clean, and I'd have respite, something I'd lost touch with.

Reeling in my comments, I reminded myself to keep quiet, primarily since I was unsure what I could add. I didn't want my excitement to ward off whatever magical charm was cast upon Neala. I told my daughter what a great idea it was, and kissed her on the head. I returned downstairs and practiced minding my own business.

CHAPTER SIXTY-TWO

CLAIRE

At the end of Neala's junior year, the education staff suggested she try an alternative high school. The faculty made it clear to Neala that it wasn't because they didn't want her enrolled in Norden, but they were concerned their senior year program would be too rigorous and cause disruption in her progress. They advised it was not a good idea to risk graduation without another option in place.

Though Neala had many positive qualities, it was obvious she continued to exhibit this learning disability and emotional struggle, which would hinder her progress. Her anxiety remained the culprit—panic attacks brought on by overstimulation during her earlier education years were the probable culprits.

Guilt for missing these earlier signs haunted me, but Kane took the initiative with this decision. He and Neala went to the school district and enrolled Neala in Areta High School, an alternative program located on the Laughton campus. Areta offered more significant opportunities for students like her.

The student body—fewer than 70—would enable her to focus on her work without facing common stressors. Teachers were skilled and able to recognize problems and address them early. Then they would discuss these issues, whether personal, social, chemical, or otherwise, and create proactive steps with the student (and family), thus ensuring resolutions and success.

"As far as I'm concerned, it doesn't matter to me. My friends graduated last year. Going back to Norden in the fall would be terribly lonely," Neala told me.

"Also, I'm pretty sure my friend Brody goes there. You remember him, Mom. We both hated the after-school club."

While touring the campus at Areta High School, Neala didn't see Brody, but she hoped he still attended. I hoped his presence would make the transition pleasant. She was already halfway through the last semester of junior year. Neala agreed Areta would be an excellent place to complete her public education. And the campus was about three blocks from Norden—she'd still be within walking distance from home.

The program at Areta was developed to encourage students to stay in school while addressing their scholastic inhibitors. A big plus, for Neala, was the ability to get to classes from a back entrance—less traumatic than maneuvering through a sea of students. Next year might not be so bad.

NEALA

"I can't believe we will both leave this place at the same time and move on to bigger and better things," Nola said.

We sat outside by the vegetable garden, and already I missed her. This time I knew exactly where my blues and nervousness stemmed from. Nola was graduating, and I would be going to a new school for my senior year. Talk about freaking out! I wondered about Brody. I hadn't seen him since fifth grade, but if he went to Areta and lives in the same place, he could easily soothe my apprehension.

Nola encouraged me to feel better by taking a smashed zucchini and tossing it at me.

"Stop it!" I ducked and laughed. I wanted to wallow in sadness, but Nola was unwilling to give me that luxury.

"You'll be sorry," I threatened, taking a stance at the compost pile.

"You wouldn't dare," Nola pressed on.

I rummaged around the fermenting vegetables, found a tomato with enough resiliency to withhold a good toss, and catapulted the rotting tomato at her. I knew I'd better run for my life once the burnt-orange blob flew from my hand.

Nola raised her hands in front of her face to block the tomato, but just as she did, it hit her forehead. The mush splattered; seeds were sticking to her hair.

"This means war, Byrnes," she screamed at me. Running at me with full force, Nola slammed into me, shoving me smack into the stinking heap. We sat on the withering vegetables laughing, doing our best to make the most of our last days at Norden. Just as we were about to get sentimental and confess how sorry we were, Harvard approached us.

I glanced toward Nola, but before I could stand or throw her an insult, Nola called out, "Food fight!" She pushed me back into the mound, held my kicking legs, and leveraged herself to stand.

"Harvard, will you take our picture?"

The preppy Ivy-Leaguer obliged. Since he was part of the Senior Memory Gallery, he submitted the picture for the assembly slideshow.

CLAIRE

The Byrnes family summer had started off well. Overall, Neala was chipper even if the mornings continued to expose her usual grumpiness. Working with Kane kept her energetic because she was active throughout the day. It was hard to sit around at your job when your dad made you the gofer at construction sites. She even found herself walking several blocks to buy lunch on days they'd left too early to make them. Neala good-heartedly grumbled about the time she walked uphill to fetch their meal, only to turn around to go back for bottled waters. Once again, she survived the uphill climb, especially with the heat.

I witnessed comradery and knowing glances between the cohorts. Neala and Kane's relationship deepened. My mind swirled with new hope, and an exhilarating warmth surrounded my heart.

Sometimes the two of them got home several hours after me, so I used the free time to make gourmet meals for them. The word, "rush," was no longer in my vocabulary, and the tension in my neck and back melted away. I got back into crafting and making time for myself. I made appointments for manicures with the gals after work because there wasn't any reason to feel guilty or to hurry home to keep Neala company.

Two weeks into the summer's routine, I began to realize how much Neala's ailments had encroached for years on my own health and wellbeing. I suspected Kane wouldn't develop any discomfort having Neala around. The more I looked at the two of them, the more I realized they were cut from the same cloth. The cloth was caramel-colored construction coveralls, and they were adorable.

SENIOR YEAR

CHAPTER SIXTY-THREE

CLAIRE

Four years of searching for answers: constructing coping mechanisms for anxiety, developing breathing and focusing techniques, and learning to care for herself led Neala to a place of acceptance. Ready to emerge from her darkness to see what the world offered; she could reach for the stars. In the past, the stars were terrifying and threatening and kept her from seeing their light.

"I feel hopeful for Neala," I said to Kane as we walked through the campus parking lot after our tour of Areta High.

"Me, too."

I could tell he was immersed in thought. A reflective man, he would take his time to digest the environment, weigh it for Neala's sake (and for me, too), and would arrive at his own conclusions. His counseling had helped him get in touch with his feelings, and I kept quiet to let him process them on his own.

Several weeks after school began, Kane told me that Neala and I seemed different. "There are fewer problems in the morning," he said. The days he offered to drop her off, Neala had gotten out of the car without a hitch.

While I remained proactive with the teachers, I also set up a strategy with Mr. Kyle, Neala's homeroom teacher. When mornings were rough, I sent a text to alert him. This simple plan eliminated the threat of her late arrivals from being considered tardy. This act alone relieved pressure.

Homework was an issue for some students, so at Areta, all course work was done in class. That policy alleviated

Neala's evening stress and offered the break she needed. Areta's program worked for both Neala and our family. The results instilled confidence in each of us.

One afternoon, Kane called to let me know he'd seen Neala walking after school, but in the opposite direction of the house. "I was on my way home when I saw her. I pulled over to pick her up, but she said she was meeting some kids, Brody and Paisley, at the square—that little area where the deli is," he said. "I gave her a twenty and said, 'Careful not to spend it all in one day.'" He chuckled. "Neala accepted the money and put in the front pocket of her hoody. She remembered to thank me." He paused a moment. "It felt terrific to see her being social."

"Sounds like we made the right choice for her. Areta is helping her blossom," I said. Before we hung up, we agreed to have a dinner date, and if she was willing, Neala could join us.

NEALA

I couldn't believe what I heard at school. A kid I'd known since elementary school had gone missing. Cops asked questions because Landon Carey didn't come home over the weekend. They searched for his bike, music player, and any sign that might indicate where he might have gone.

Three days later, they found Landon. It appeared as though he'd been murdered, which terrified the shit out of me. But knowing a kid that died was much worse. I went to grade school with him, and now he was gone.

The mystery seemed surreal. I became hypervigilant and aware of my surroundings because if someone did harm him, they could be someone I know. That freaked me out. It's kind of strange, too, that other kids felt uneasiness for the first time. Now they identify with how I dealt with life most of the time.

Mom has been extra kind to me. I'm not sure if it is her fear for my safety or if she feels sorry for me, or both.

Months passed and there were still no arrests nor leads for Landon's murder. Even so, his parents held a memorial for him. The community was welcomed to attend.

"Mom, I want to go to Landon's memorial on Friday," I said.

Mom turned to me, a surprised look on her face. "Sure. Are you going with someone, or do you want me to come with you?"

I could tell Mom was upset. Last night she'd said something about the agony his parents must feel.

At the memorial, I signed the visitors' book and placed flowers on the food table.

"I feel awful for his mom," I told Mom.

The community hall was decorated with items remembering Landon and how he'd touched many lives. Art and stories from grade school, yearbooks, jerseys, and skateboards filled the hall.

"God, he was so young . . ." Mom started to sob.

I found a tissue—containers were pretty much all over the place—and handed it to her.

"Neala, sweetheart, I am so, so sorry," she said.

CHAPTER SIXTY-FOUR

CLAIRE

The girls had been shopping for nearly four hours, and I didn't get one phone call or text from Neala asking to come home the entire time. I was partially frantic, but another part of my mind didn't worry too much, even with the unsolved murder.

I had met Paisley and her parents at Areta's Back to School Night. They were well known in Pleasant Hills and seemed friendly. When Neala asked if she could go shopping with Paisley and her mom for the upcoming 70s dance, I was thrilled to grant permission.

Paisley had some of the same anxieties as Neala, but Paisley fell behind in school when she developed type one diabetes. Another invisible disease many kids are faced with today.

Neala and Paisley were a good match. Paisley befriended and accepted Neala's anxiety as part of the "Neala Package." She wasn't put off when Neala got cranky and often stayed with Neala on tough days.

Neala paid attention to activity levels with Paisley. Her caring side emerged, and with it, her confidence in the friendship grew. It pleased me to see the two spend time out of the classroom and away from home. Perhaps this glimpse of freedom might encourage Neala to go for her driver's license.

Just as I set the last fork on the dinner table, I heard the girls come into the front entry. "Sorry we're late, Mom, we dropped Brody off," Neala said.

Surprised they had taken Brody with them; I was glad they were all getting along. Lady perked up at the sound of Neal's voice and she followed them to Neala's room to snoop at their loot. They were excited to model their thrift shop garb. Paisley found a vintage Gunne Sax dress, a bargain at $25.00, and Neala found platform boots with hip-hugger, bell-bottomed jeans, and a tie-dyed top.

"I can get a pair of cheap mod-looking glasses at the dollar store and a headband to complete my outfit."

Neala seemed to glow.

"Mom, do you think Dad has any cool stuff left from high school for Brody to borrow?" Neala asked.

"Pretty sure I tossed a lot of that when we moved from our first apartment," I said but noticed Neala wasn't too discouraged.

"My aunt says she has some platform sandals I'm sure I can borrow," Paisley chimed in. "Maybe she has something for Brody. I'll ask."

CHAPTER SIXTY-FIVE

CLAIRE

Two weeks before the dance, the girls experimented with their hair and perfected their "flower-child" look. Kane demonstrated the Hustle, and Paisley pointed out it was a lot like the Electric Slide.

"My dad does that move to country music!" She laughed. "Neala we can do it, it's not too hard to remember, just stand behind someone and follow their moves."

The night of the dance, Paisley came down the stairs in her Gunne Sax dress followed by Neala in her bell-bottoms and tie-dyed shirt.

"Kane, come quick, I'm having a flashback," I laughed. "You two look great. Nice job on the hair, Cookie. I don't think I have ever seen it that straight."

The girls posed at the bottom of the staircase for pictures, but I had to promise not to post it on social media. I stretched my neck to reach up to kiss Neala on the cheek because her platform shoes gave her another three inches in height.

The doorbell rang. In walked a young man who could have been Vinnie Barbarino's twin from *Welcome Back Kotter*. If anyone could pull off John Travolta, it was Brody. A handsome kid, he was dressed in blue jeans and a T-shirt.

"Whaaaat?" he asked, splaying his fingers and shrugging his shoulders.

"Ready ladies?" Kane asked, jingling the car keys. "Oh, hey!" he said, viewing the crowd. "Look who's here!" He introduced himself to Brody, and I snapped another picture.

Before Kane walked out the door, he leaned into me and said, "I'll drop them off and be right back. We get the house to ourselves. Can you dig it?" He winked at me. Then he was off to escort the kids to the dance.

"Dream on," I said with a smile.

NEALA

The band's tempo pulsed from beyond the gymnasium doors and strobe lighting flashed through the windows. Kids hung out by the front doors while waiting for friends to join them.

Paisley led the way, followed by Brody and me, but he stopped to flirt with several girls as we passed by. I fell behind though I didn't feel uncomfortable. I'd packed a couple of Ativan, just in case. But it was like the doctor told me. Sometimes just having the medicine with me was enough to keep the panic at bay. I hoped that would work for tonight.

When we reached the check-in, the PTA moms checked our student IDs.

"Wow! They have a disco ball, how far out is that?" Paisley said when she peeked into the building.

"As far out as your mom." I kiddingly roasted her; it was what we did to "act chill."

At first, we cruised the border of the gym and noticed all the other kids and their funky outfits. On our second round, we stopped at the refreshment table to get Mountain Dew.

We relaxed into the scene, started engaging with others, observing, and commenting on the outfits and the disco music. The strobe lights projected a bazar effect, and a strange sensation tried to overcome me. I paused, pulled in some relaxing breaths, and engaged in the fun again. I decided it was a good thing that Paisley and Brody were able to convince me to come.

After the fifth set of songs, the Renunciation cover band played the 1978 hit, Own Sweet Way. Because about every teen there was made to suffer through their parents' blaring this oldie on the radio, quite a few of us knew the song. We began moving to the beat and singing along. I watched as kids filled the floor in pairs. Brody danced with two girls, and Paisley was asked to dance.

Alone by the bleachers, I stood and listened to the music, rocking back and forth to the rhythm. I joined the crowd by singing the lyrics. I was getting into it, ready to take on the second stanza, when a finger tapped my shoulder.

"Hey, uh, do you wanna dance with me?" a boy said.

I turned my head, the big hoop earrings swung with my long, straightened hair, and I saw him. A dark-haired boy wearing a jean vest with lots of anti-war patches sewn all over it. He smiled but kept his head tipped down just a bit. It made him look a little shy.

I remembered what dad said a few years ago when he danced around the house with me: Be kind when a boy asks you to dance. "No matter how shy you are, or how dumb you think you will feel dancing with him. It takes a whole lotta courage for a boy to ask a girl to dance. Don't be afraid to say yes. Then continue to dance until the song is over, say thanks, and walk back to your friends. If you like him, then linger, and he may ask you to stay for the next song. But," he stressed, "this is only advice for dancing. Never go off with anyone strange or who makes you uncomfortable. Keep within sight of your friends."

I sucked up my courage. I noticed how black his eyes looked in the dim light, but they sparkled. He wore a crooked smile and had perfect teeth. My heart did a flip, and my palms heated with sweat. Before I knew what I was doing, I said, "Sure."

I followed him onto the dance floor. He chose a spot near the speakers. At first, the loud noise annoyed me, but then I realized it might be a good thing because it would be too loud to talk over the music.

Facing each other, we began to sway to the beat. Some kids' actions were obnoxious, but I didn't mind, their behavior gave this dark-haired boy and me something to look at besides each other. When the melody slowed, he kept ahold of my hand and we continued moving around in a slow circle. Most of the other kids left the floor, there were only a few couples slow dancing, but I was compelled to put my arms around his neck, and his hands loosely rested on my hips.

I was extra careful to avoid stepping on his toes with my platform shoes when I noticed he was taller than me—even in towering shoes. When the song ended, I was surprised when we just stood there, lingering.

After a few awkward seconds, he thanked me for the dance. We chatted a bit. He said he was new at our school, his name was Griff Baker, and that he was into visual arts and alternative rock.

"I enrolled in Areta because it is hard for me to tolerate large groups," he offered, "which is weird because I'm not shy."

Suddenly his phone chimed. After checking the screen, he told me his dad was there to pick him up. "So, maybe I will catch you on the flip side." He grinned at the old term. Then he was gone.

Paisley appeared and said, "Who was that Casanova?"

Brody looked at me with a what's-up expression.

"Griff Baker," I said, but I'm pretty sure my eyes said a lot more.

"You are in love, star-struck, outta your mind, outta sight, and feeling groovy!" Paisley teased.

"Crazy, man, crazy," I replied. "I wonder if he knows about Dee Dee's."

Brody, Paisley, and I left the dance, and her dad drove us to the diner.

"I don't see that guy here, Neala, sorry," Brody said.

I surveyed the diner when we walked in. No such luck, the young man in the anti-war denim vest was nowhere to be seen.

Monday night, I was loading the dishwasher and shooing Lady away from table scraps when I saw an old green Nova pull into our driveway. I looked at my reflection in the kitchen window before I closed the dishwasher door.

The doorbell rang, Lady barked, and Dad answered the door. I held my breath so I could hear better. Men's voices came through the hall, followed by nervous laughter and the mention of my name.

I peeked around the corner—oh my God, it was Griff! My heart fluttered. He stood in our living room with Dad and my stomach filled with butterflies. The stir made me wish I hadn't eaten so much at dinner.

"I tracked Neala down," I heard him say.

I could see through the doorway and noticed his proud grin. "I'm thinking of being a private investigator." He laughed.

"Well, you're off to a good start," Dad said with a wink.

Griff explained to Dad that he was new to Areta, and I had been kind to dance with him. "She's a sweet girl and easy to be with," he said politely. "I want to hang out with her, learn more about Areta, and hear about some of the art programs."

"I'm sure you'll like the school," Dad replied.

After a slight pause, Griff asked, "Could Neala come with me to get frozen yogurt?"

I felt like I could fly. He invited me out for yogurt!

Dad called me into the living room. "Neala, I hear you know this young man?" he asked. "Says he wants to take you for a fro-yo."

"Yeah, that sounds okay," I said, trying to be nonchalant as I walked toward them. Of course, I wanted to go! I grabbed my purse from the entry hall and without hesitation, flew out the door.

"Be back by eight," I heard Dad shout while Griff held the car door for me.

CLAIRE

Within a couple of weeks, Neala and Griff were inseparable. Griff brought a new kind of energy into our household, which revitalized the whole family. Kane and I noticed Neala flourishing. Griff made an effort to keep Neala comfortable and helped her through any anxiety that popped up. He had a fun sense of humor and was gentle with her. And he owned a car. He drove Neala wherever she wanted to go, and he seemed to enjoy it.

I was pleased to hear Griff's plans to attend the Middleton Art Academy. He planned to work toward a degree in graphic art design. A realist, he mentioned that he was confident he could sell his art to earn a living in the art world, without selling his soul. I respected that about the kid.

Cautious that Neala didn't have any negative influences, I monitored their relationship. I checked to ensure Neala was safe and joyful, but not spending too much time with Griff. I didn't want Griff filling my role as Neala's caretaker.

After all, he was driving Neala everywhere, and I noticed he encouraged her to expand beyond her comfort levels. Not in a creepy controlling-boyfriend way, but as a person who sincerely cared for her. Still, I kept a close eye.

Griff encouraged Neala to study French because, in Europe, it was spoken as much as English and Spanish. He embraced her dream of traveling to Europe, and he supported her independence when he could. Griff was turning out to be a great guy for my daughter.

I was aware most mothers would not want to have their daughter fall in love so early in life. As parents, they might invoke higher education, career, and then family. But Neala was different. She began and ended with family. That was her challenge, her path, and her blessing.

CHAPTER SIXTY-SIX

CLAIRE

I was grateful my last meeting for the day was close to home. This meant no traffic. I'd get home earlier than usual. I coveted the luxury of an hour in the house by myself to reflect on the early days when I'd imagined my house empty at this stage of my life. Neala would be out with friends, driving to a part-time job, volunteering—yet, overall, Neala stayed home often since she'd started high school.

Kane accepted projects nearer to home, so my imagined routine was out of sync with reality. This left me craving time for myself in a quiet house—just to think and be.

More jobs came in and Kane worked hard most days, but when he was home, he turned on the TV and fell asleep in his chair. Like most teens, Neala stayed in her room with her electronics and social media. For some, being alone meant being lonely, but for me, it was like a crisp glass of champagne, a cup of hot spicy tea, or smooth chocolate—a luxury to indulge in and savor.

A whole hour! I chose not to call the list of new psychiatrists I was supposed to interview. Dr. Teller's retirement was more of a bummer than I thought it would be. I'd learned to trust him, and I really liked him. His receptionist, Lindsey, was personable and efficient. When it came to changing prescriptions or dosages, Lindsey was like a magician. She worked things out with insurance companies and pharmacies. Enough about that, this is my "me time" not my "I-should-be-doing-this-or-that" time. Learn to chill, girl!

Shrugging off my outfit, I put my clothes into the "okay to wear again without washing" pile in the walk-in closet. I slipped on my jeans—they were broken in and stretched as comfortable as sweats. I pulled on a snuggly sweater and headed to the kitchen for a cup of tea.

During one of our excursions along the coast, Neala and I stumbled across a quaint tea shop. The exotic aromas enticed us to overindulge in a variety of flavors. Validation came with fruity, floral, and spicy scents wafting in the air when I opened the cupboard. I could use a strong but relaxing cup of spiced tea. Something citrus and warm. Cinnamon Orange, perfect.

I set the electric kettle to boil and prepared the tea the way the shop owner had shown me.

"Let it steep in the boiled water for 3-5 minutes for the perfect cup," I said to Lady, reciting what I'd learned. In the past, I would have thought that packing tea into the strainer was ridiculous, but as it turned out, it was not only worth it, but the preparation of the drink became my new ritual. The focus broke worries and stresses. Brewing a perfect cup of tea became a relaxing task.

The electric teapot boiled then automatically shut off. Kane's favorite feature.

"One time, Claire forgot about a teapot and left it on the stove. She was in the shower and didn't hear the whistle. The water boiled out, and the damn thing nearly set the kitchen on fire." He'd told the story more than a few times. "The teapot melted onto the burner. What a stench!"

These days, automatic shutdown removed one more worry from my list.

Pouring the hot water over the tea and orange rinds, the steamy aroma filled my nostrils, and my shoulders fell with the inhale. Lady followed me into the living room and sniffed for a cookie when I set my tea down.

"No cookies today," I said to my companion. I tossed one leg up over the sofa's armrests and piled the pillows behind my head. The Smithsonian always had cool items for sale. I hadn't even gotten the catalog open or drank a half a cup of tea before Lady settled at my feet, and Beans crawled up onto my lap. Snuggled together, the animals and I fell asleep.

The phone blared. Not the cell phone, the home landline phone, and the caller ID announced Neala's number. I rolled off the couch, the cat hit the floor, and I knocked the receiver from its cradle and onto the carpet.

Before I could see straight or say hello. I heard Neala's voice. She sounded like the eight-year-old girl she once was. It never ceased to make my heart melt.

"Mom, MOM. I can't move. I'm stuck." Hearing this level of Neala's desperation pulled me into her worry.

"What? Where are you? How are you stuck, what do you mean?"

"I'm in the quad. I'm frozen. Mom, I need you to help me."

"What?" I said, still groggy.

"I was on my way to the library. I thought I could make it, but my legs won't move. I started to freeze up halfway there."

I heard Neala let out a long breath.

"I am stuck in the quad, and I need you to get me."

I started to grasp her urgency. "All right, let me think. Is there anyone near you?"

"No!"

"Okay, stay on the line. I gotta get my cell phone." I carried the landline with me to my cell phone which was charging in the kitchen. I clicked open the mobile. I searched for the number and quickly called Areta High.

"Hello, Areta High School, will you please hold?" said a cheerful secretary.

"Actually, no, I can't hold. It is an emergency." I said, looking at the remote phone, hoping Neala was still on the line.

"All right, go ahead, how may I help you?" the secretary asked. She sounded concerned.

"It's my daughter, Neala Byrnes. She has terrible anxiety, and she is immobile in the quad area. Can you send someone to help her? Please, she's frightened."

"Oh, dear, absolutely. Where is she in the quad?"

"Neala, where are you," I asked.

"She's near the gym, heading toward the library," I told the secretary.

"Okay, I have Laura, one of the campus supervisors, on the way. She has a golf cart, so she'll be there fast." the secretary said.

I held both phones to my ears as I waited for something, perhaps a miracle, to happen. I heard a woman talking to Neala, and Neala agreeing to get into the cart. "Mom, someone is here to help me. I will call you when we get to the office." And then, Neala disconnected.

"She got help, and they are on the way to you. Thank you so much," I said to the nameless secretary. "Will you ask her to call me when she gets there?"

Within minutes, Neala called. She said she would sit in the front office and try to make it to her next period class. I was astonished. Extensive help for Neala wouldn't have been available at her other school. This school was affiliated with a larger campus, so it had more staff to accommodate Neala, and they helped her to feel secure. This was a good move for her.

I didn't hear from Neala again until lunch. Neala texted that she was fine, but she wanted me to pick her up from school at the end of the day. She didn't think she'd have the energy to walk home.

"And so you rode in the golf cart to the office?" Kane asked, laughing at the story.

"Yeah," Neala said, relaxed with her tale. "Some kids thought I hurt my leg or something, so I just let it go. But

Laura was so friendly. She also kept snacks in the cart, so that was cool."

"Well, I am glad you have Laura's number now, so you can call her anytime when you need help at school," I added.

I was glad Neala reached out, and with this new level of confidence, I felt that Neala would be okay and would learn to make her way in the world.

CHAPTER SIXTY-SEVEN

CLAIRE

"I hate parties, Mom. I really don't want to have one." Neala scoffed at my suggestion to celebrate her eighteenth birthday. What Neala didn't know was there were plenty in cahoots who wanted this memorable celebration for her.

I couldn't let this milestone go. I chose to invite only close relatives to wish Neala "happy 18th" with a small surprise party. Griff wanted to do something special, too, but with just a few people and planned another celebration with close friends for another day. We hoped it would keep Neala from being overwhelmed.

Griff said his parents would let him hold her soirée at his house. I worried about two parties in one week, so I changed the family party to a cake party. Grandparents, aunts, uncles, and cousins would come over one night for cake and presents.

"I'll try to do it, Mom, but only for two hours. Cake only. No other food or festivities, okay?"

"You got it. Let's do it on your actual birthday—Tuesday night. No one will stay late on a work night," I said.

Neala's celebration went well. She helped pick out a beautiful chocolate cake with blue frosting, which matched her hair. The family came, and she got a few cards with cash in them. I was grateful when the relatives got the cue to leave right after the cake was devoured. Even Pat enjoyed the moment and seemed to have come to terms with Neala's quirky behavior.

"It was worth it, Mom. And not just for the money-stuffed birthday cards, either," Neala confessed. "Thanks for the party."

"You are welcome, sweetie. There was no way I was going to let this special day pass without a celebration. One day you will look back on these years. Maybe you won't have anxiety as much as you do now, and I wanted you to see how much everyone loves you. There is so much you already missed, things you'll never ever get back. I understand having the party was trying, but it was the right thing to do." I hugged Neala close. "In fact," I continued, "I hope you will consider walking down the aisle at graduation this year."

"Mom," Neala blurted and pulled away.

"I'm only asking you to think about it, not commit to it," I said.

NEALA

Mom might have been flexible about my birthday, but Griff wasn't going to let the opportunity to pull off something big pass by. Once again, Griff and I were on a dance floor—a small platform of plywood Griff built in his parent's backyard for my close-friends-only birthday party. He invited Paisley and her latest heartthrob, Keenan; Nola and Steve, a sweet guy she met at the junior college; and Brody, who was welcome to bring a date, but had a crush on Paisley, so came solo. Just enough people to keep me from going over the edge.

Nola baked a giant chocolate chip cookie and served it with ice cream. Paisley's mom made a cheese and fruit platter for snacks. I smiled, thinking about how much my friends were willing to do for me.

At the end of the evening, Nola's date, who established the role of DJ, played all the top hits for the night. All of us rocked following along with the dips and swells of the tunes. Griff asked to save a special song for last. As soon as I heard the interlude, I knew Griff picked it for me, "Own Sweet

Way." The old ballad was about letting go of other people's expectations and living and fighting for what you believe in.

"I believe in you, Neala Byrnes," Griff whispered in my ear.

I hugged him tightly and smiled.

"I'm glad I met you when I transferred here," Griff whispered.

I was glad I'd worn my new perfume. "Me, too," I replied.

We danced a few more bars. "You know, after graduation and the summer, I will be at Middleton Arts. I want you to continue to be my girl, though. Maybe you can visit me there."

"I agreed to work for my dad again this summer, and maybe some of next year, so I won't be going far after school. I think he'll allow me some time off. Perhaps I'll save some of my money to visit you," I said while beaming up at him. "I still plan to visit Europe one day, but . . ." I sighed. "I have a lot of hours ahead of me in those ridiculous coveralls before I can afford to travel."

"Good, but I may have to take measures to make sure you stay protected while I'm away," he said.

I saw his smile and once more admired his straight teeth. I wondered how I got so lucky to be in the same time, space, and place as this dude. He was pretty awesome.

He pulled me closer to him, and a wave of excitement washed over me. I heard about kids who would "Netflix and Chill," but with all the thoughts I did have, I hadn't thought about going all the way with anyone. Before Griff, how could I have known I would care this profoundly or be so close to anyone? But here he was, this warm, smart guy with genuine feelings for me, too.

We'd talked about sex, but I got mad when I heard Mom's words coming out of my mouth. The ones about making decisions and owning up to them. I knew I would not have any regrets if I were to sleep with Griff.

Little did I know that Griff prepared his parents and his room in the expectation of bringing me there once our guests departed. We were awkward but sincere as we climbed the steps toward his bedroom. I hadn't talked to Griff about having sex after the party, but my body stirred with passion and sentiment. When we got to Griff's bedroom door, it was closed.

Nervous and wondering what to do, I called on the therapy tricks I had learned. I was well-practiced in rehearsing events before they happened to prevent freaking out. I had fantasized about this moment, but, I hadn't done the headwork to prepare, emotionally or physically, for "doing it."

"Go on, open the door," he invited, gesturing his hand toward the knob.

I lightly touched the handle, and the door slowly swung open.

The dimly lit room had rose petals on the floor that led to the bed and completed in the shape of a heart on the center of the comforter. I felt Griff watch me as I absorbed it all. He smiled, I'm sure, at the quizzical furrow on my brow. Then my eyes softened, a smile spread across my mouth. I looked at him and shouted, "Oh, my God! A puppy!"

In the middle of the rose-petal heart was a little Corgi. He was mostly tan with white accents on his ears and tail. I wanted to hug Griff, but I rushed over to scoop up the puppy instead. Ever-so-gently lifting him to prevent startling the pup more than I had.

"I've been calling him Sir Lancelot, but he prefers plain Sir," Griff said.

I continued to stroke the puppy, bringing it up to my face, and kissing its brow. "Uh, so you know, I okayed this with your mom and dad. We thought it up when we were talking about how hard it would be for Lady to move to Europe, and if you do go one day, this little guy would like to visit his homeland."

"Oh, Griff, I never expected such a beautiful dog."

"I told you I would take measures to protect you. What were you expecting?"

"Let's save it for another day, okay?" I said. Then I began with a barrage of questions. After an hour of cuddling the puppy and learning Griff got him from a rescue, not from a breeder—which was one of my strong sentiments—I hugged Sir. He fell asleep in my arms.

Shortly afterward, the Bakers came home, an indication it was time to end the evening. Before we left, I made sure to thank the Bakers for keeping the puppy a secret and for their part in surprising me.

CHAPTER SIXTY-EIGHT

CLAIRE

There she is!

My heart swelled with pride as I watched Neala walk down the center aisle. She kept pace with the high school band's march. The sleeves of the gown covered most of her hands, just her black nail-polished tips dangled out. Her hair lifted in the breeze, and her eyes were focused toward the designated seating for the latest senior class.

After going through five years of behavior therapy, medications, and countless episodes of frustration, I held my breath as the band began another round of Pomp and Circumstance.

Because Areta's program was located on Laughton's campus, the two schools joined together for the promotion. I was glad Neala accepted the excitement of graduation without being overcome by anxiety. Neala learned to clarify her feelings, and this event showed me how far Neala had come since freshman year.

Across the field, through the glare of the setting sun, I looked above the sea of orange and black to find the one cap with a golden retriever pasted on top. Neala. She wore her gown with pride, draped with a white sash indicating she was an Areta graduate.

I watched the parade of students pass, and when Neala came into view, I noticed her flip-flops. I wasn't surprised. We'd lucked out finding the perfect dress—a black sundress with white polka dots. It was a retro copy of a dress from the fifties. Neala said she would wear the flip flops because they were more comfortable than the strappy sandals I'd pushed for. Neala's first choice as an adult was to wear casual beach shoes to a formal event. Oh, well. That's my Neala.

Student after student climbed the stage and then I heard the loveliest sound. The name Neala Jeanne Byrnes came from the loudspeakers. I watched Neala cross the podium to accept her diploma.

A joyous and wild sensation surged through my body. My skin prickled, and a giddiness took hold of my heart. This is what heaven must be like. Heaven, answered prayers, pride, joy, the ultimate bliss! This was it. I was proud of my daughter. Every step of Neala's life propelled her to this moment, this first huge success. I was sure many others would follow.

NEALA

I made my way down the aisle to my seat. I could not believe my stroke of luck. Too bad Robby Jackson broke his ankle last night at the grad dinner, but good for me to be placed next to Tommy Darrin second cutest boy in class next to Griff.

When we sat, I looked down at my feet. I should have listened to Mom and worn the strappy sandals. No, it wouldn't have been cool. I didn't want to go through the ceremony worrying about tripping on the field. Worse than Robby breaking his ankle. I was glad I paid attention to Mom about the importance of walking with my graduating class.

I passed on the senior breakfast and didn't request a permission slip for grad night, but I did decide to walk. At first, I wasn't going to bother with it.

"You know, Neala, if you don't walk at graduation, you'll miss the chance to feel pride in yourself, which you truly deserve. You worked harder than any kid I know to earn your diploma. If you pass this up, well, you will never get another chance to experience it. No matter how many good things come your way, you won't have this opportunity again."

Mom always knew what to say to get her point across. It worked, because here I was, sitting amongst all these other students. Don't think about it too much, or you might have to run away. I accepted the emotions and let myself feel the goodness of it all for a few seconds. And it did feel good.

I conceded it had been a long five years. I heard the principal speak and then the valedictorian. What I perceived was the noise, but I listened to the voice in my head. The one praising me. The one thankful to have made it through school—leading me to this very day. I was grateful for Mom and Dad, for Alina, and I was indebted to Lady. I thought about Nola, Paisley, and Brody, and of course, Griff. There were the teachers, and Jill, and even the horrid Mr. Buckley.

If it weren't for Mr. Buckley being such a bully, I would not have pushed Mom to seek alternatives for my education. I realized the people one meets in life are beacons of light who lead and guide you toward a safe harbor.

Once I heard my name called the world was a blur. One minute I was walking to the stage, the next I was holding my high school diploma. I swallowed and let the rush of success cascade over me.

The ceremony concluded, and the new graduates tossed their caps. There were tears and laughter as each student sought out family and friends. Pictures were taken and uploaded to social media within seconds. Mom made her way to me and threw her arms around me. "Kane take our picture, I feel like I graduated, too!"

My smile was broad and sincere.

"Mom, Griff, Nola, and I want to go to the grad party at Nikki's house, can we go? I'll be home before my graduation dinner party, I promise."

CLAIRE

Kane and I were delighted that Neala preferred to be with friends and agreed to let her go. We saw a new Neala transitioning before our eyes. She chose to be social. It was a big step, and we didn't want to ruin the momentum. The graduation dinner would be small: Nola, Griff, Bill, Pat, Sarah, and Jeff, and of course, Sophia.

Filled with admiration, we watched our new graduate laughing with her friends as the kids headed toward their cars.

As we trekked across the football field, Kane found my hand and gently squeezed it. I squeezed back. We reached the car, got in, and patiently waited for all the other parents to exit the parking lot.

Kane turned to me. "You did it, hon. You helped Neala make it through high school. I am so proud of you. You are a strong woman, and I'm glad I am married to you. You're the best mom a kid could ever have." He looked down for a moment. "You saved my life, too. I am a lucky man, and Neala is a fortunate kid. Claire, you kept this family from falling off the track." He looked into my eyes, "Not only do I love you madly, but I'm also grateful for you."

I must have blushed. "I love you guys. You, Neala, Sarah, and Jeff. You are all mine to care for, and I am so proud of you, too. Your changes have made a big difference in Neala's life." I leaned over and kissed his cheek.

"When Neala gets home, I am gonna frame her diploma and nail it up over the fireplace," Kane boasted. "Whenever anything seems unattainable in this family, this diploma will be our reminder that nothing, nothing is impossible." Then, as the traffic line came to a complete stop, he pulled me close and gave me a tender and meaningful kiss to seal the deal.

The car behind us honked and ended our kiss. I sighed and sat back in the seat. The traffic started to move along, and Kane turned on the radio. Our family theme song filled the air—

EPILOG

CLAIRE

The second week after she graduated, Neala retook her driver's permit test (the first one had expired) and set up her behind-the-wheel driving test. She passed with a perfect score. To celebrate, Kane and I surprised her with her own car. It was second hand, and Neala called the color "Granny Gold," but it was safe. It got her to and from work, out for coffee with her friends, and shopping at the mall for occasional makeup binge purchases. Being able to come and go as she pleased lowered her incidences of anxiety, and she gained confidence with her independence. It was decided, even though she was doing very well, she would continue to see Alina.

Kane kept his vow to quit drinking and focused on balancing his budget. Having more time, I signed up for cooking classes and expanded my healthful and creative culinary talents. Kane and I enjoyed each other's company—hiking, dancing, and dining without drinking. We secretly looked forward to an "empty nest," which no longer seemed so far away.

Once she was able to drive herself to and from the jobs, Kane asked Neala to work in his office. This offer required that she attend junior college and take some business courses. Though he liked having her on the job with him, he surmised he needed help in the office. Neala demonstrated terrific attention to detail, so having her take calls, answering emails, and doing payroll would be good for their bottom line.

The first night of her class at the junior college came, and Neala worried. She hesitated for a while but gathered her courage. With that, she got into her car and drove off.

A few hours later, I heard Neala come home. "Well, how was it?" I asked.

I think Neala was glad I waited up for her. I was in the living room with Sir, who was sitting on my lap. Neala smiled when she noticed that the dog and I had bonded.

"Class was just like you said, Mom, a bunch of forty-year-olds and me," Neala said as she passed by and headed to the fridge for a drink. "The teacher is nice; she's a lot like Nola's mom, so I was comfortable. I can do this. But I still want to look into getting my certificate in dog training and handling."

For the first time in a very long time, Neala revealed a desire to go to school and further her education.

"I know you can do whatever you decide upon," I said. As for now, you have car insurance to pay, a job to keep, and a mouth to feed." I indicated the dog as I handed Sir over to Neala.

Neala bent down so I could kiss her on the top of her head. Afterward, I went to bed. I fell asleep knowing the worst was now behind us, and Neala would always find her way. Her own sweet, perfect way.

Dear Reader,

Growing up isn't easy for anyone, and it's especially hard when you have an undiagnosed anxiety disorder. What was seen as acting out or being defiant when I was young were actually all the little quirks of social and separation anxiety. Quirks like going from tired to exhausted at the drop of a hat, asking to be excused every morning in your first-grade class to call your mom, or separating yourself from friends and family at parties just so you can form a single thought. The list goes on.

Anxiety is different for everyone and has many symptoms such as inexplicable bouts of anger or irritation; clinging to or pushing away; crying uncontrollably or feeling nothing at all. What's important is to remember that it won't be this way forever. It *will* get better.

Anxiety isn't all hyperventilating and going cold in an instant, (which does happen, but only at the climax of an attack; again it's different for everyone). It can start the minute an assignment is handed out in class, or your classmates start chattering away. Round a corner and see a hoard of people in the street and the beast might raise its horrific face. It can come unexpectedly—you're sitting on the couch watching cartoons.

Suddenly your arms and fingers go numb, your legs feel like lead, and your heart thumps like the heart of a prize-winning horse at the end of the race. All the while, you won't be able to form a clear thought, your breath will catch in your throat, and the tears will pour from the depths of your soul.

If you suffer from anxiety and someone has told you "Don't worry, it's all in your head," I want you to know that they're right. It's controlling you from the inside out. Sure, it's all in our heads—but not like others may think. The symptoms aren't any less real. Nor the fear. Mental illness is an authentic illness and should be treated as such. I hope my story can help you fight your battles.

If you don't suffer from an anxiety disorder, I'm still happy you've found your way here. Listen to your friends and family if any of them say that they are struggling. All we ask of you is that you listen. I hope my story can help you understand what it's like to be afraid of an everyday task.

Anxiety is manageable, and there are ways to make peace with this monster.

It really does get better.

Much love,

Neala

Author's Note About Anxiety

To worry is normal, but excessive worry or anxiousness is not. You may not die from an anxiety or a panic attack, but it feels like you will. A sense of doom surrounds you, and your body gets an unexpected fight-or-flight message. Are you going to stay and fight, or are you going to flee? Maybe you'll freeze. Unrecognized or undiagnosed symptoms will cause poor health, depression, acting out, and loneliness. Those factors certainly will contribute to a heartbreaking quality of life, and sometimes premature death.

Anxiety sucks.

It sucks the fun out of everyday events. It sucks relationships dry and sucks energy from a person. There are multiple symptoms a person might exhibit if they have anxiety. Some of the signs and how they manifest are:

Panic, fear, and uneasiness

Anxiety might emerge as antisocial or withdrawn behavior, or the inability to move. Reluctance to finishing a task—such as not turning in schoolwork. The fear of not doing well builds in the belly.

Sleep problems

It might present itself by making the person seem lazy or stays up too late. Maybe falls asleep in class or takes naps . . . a lot. Maybe they are restless at night.

Not being able to stay calm and still

Fidgeting, toe-tapping, impatience, irritability, can all be symptoms. Or they become combative, picking fights, or lashing out.

Cold, sweaty, numb or tingling hands or feet

If the person is frequently rubbing their hands or their legs, or say they feel "frozen and unable to move," it could be anxiety.

Shortness of breath

Some may need a paper bag to slow down their breathing, seem overexcited, or perhaps trying to catch their breath.

Heart palpitations

Hard to see, but the face might become flushed. The person mentions their heart is slamming inside of their chest.

Dry mouth

An anxiety-ridden person might be unable to swallow and might drink a lot of water or other beverages. The person may even chew a lot of gum or suck on candy.

Nausea

Complaints of frequent stomachaches or having "butterflies" in the stomach is often mentioned.

Tense muscles

Perhaps the person rubs the back of their neck, shoulders, legs, or hands repeatedly.

Dizziness

The person might stop short, choose to stay behind or remain seated.

Noises

Habitually whimpers, sighs, or even growls when they are provoked.

Indecisiveness

The person may be reluctant to agree to anything you offer. No matter what you suggest, the answer is "no." It also looks like they're combative, but the person might be afraid to choose and then worry about being stuck with an undesirable outcome.

Withdrawal

Declining invitations to events, like parties, dances, hanging out, or other activities often shows up. Perhaps they even use their hoody, like Neala, to hide.

Tunnel Vision

Another symptom: shallow breathing or holding their breath or breathing too fast. When this happens, vision becomes blurred or tunneled.

Flashbacks or Post Traumatic Stress Disorder (PTSD)

Reliving frightening experiences might bring on an anxiety attack. Neala experiences this when she goes to parties. The fear of not having control stems from PTSD.

When a person feels one or more of these signs, they might begin to panic. It may lead to a **panic attack,** (this is when the body may release chemicals to fight or flee. Many symptoms of anxiety might bombard a person all at once) which usually stems from being afraid of having a panic attack. Panic attacks can be terrifying for the person and may be intimidating for you to see, but do your best to stay calm for them and yourself. Get someone to help you if you need.

If you suspect you or someone you love has an anxiety disorder, seek the help of a doctor. It seems like it would be easier to self-medicate with drinking or drugs—even over-the-counter medications, but bad habits and addictions may lead to greater anxiety. At the very least, talk to someone, a trusted friend, co-worker, teacher, or counselor. Even your boss, they may be willing to help.

Simple but effective ways you can help someone with anxiety:

- *Believe* the person. Their symptoms are real.
- *Stay* with them if they ask you to or stand back if they ask you to go away.
- Remind them that *they are okay*.
- Offer a *five-sense exercise*: touch, taste, look, listen, smell. If they engage their senses, it will help ground them. (Like the scent of an orange peel.)
- Offer to do **Square Breathing** with them. Breathe in for four seconds, hold your breath

for four seconds, and breathe out for four seconds. Repeat four times.

- Most importantly, be supportive by ***keeping a good sense of humor*** and relax knowing that the episode *will* pass.
- And lastly, ***never give up!***

Be open to begin a dialog and start a conversation about anxiety.

A person with an anxiety disorder will find comfort because you listen and believe them. Talking shows that you are there for them, and you support them.

If you care for someone with anxiety or other invisible diseases be sure to take care of yourself, too. Seek support and respite as needed. You are worth it.

Resources:
National Alliance for Mental Illness **www. nami.org**
Al-Anon **www.al-anon.org** (you may also search for Ala-teen meetings at this site)
Alcoholics Anonymous **www.aa.org**
Emotional Support Animal (EAS) Registration **www.nsarco.com**

Your local government office of Health and Human Services

If you are a student, investigate resources available to you through your school district.

Join the Facebook group. **In Spite of Anxiety**, to see how others succeed in spite of their anxiety.

Suggested Book Club or Class Discussion Guide

Types of anxiety disorders

1. Generalized Anxiety Disorder (GAD)
2. Panic Disorder (PD)
3. Social Anxiety Disorder (SAP)
4. Separation Panic Disorder (SP)
5. Phobias (fears)
6. Obsessive Compulsive Disorder (OCD)
7. Post-Traumatic Stress Disorder (PTSD)

Tell about character situations in the book which might cause your anxiety to develop

1. Neala: restaurant, school authority figures, homework, her dad's anger
2. Claire: being late, worrying about Neala, taking care of her family
3. Kane: not confronting his own anxiety, his concern for his family

Discuss three types of *responses* to anxiety disorders

A. Fight
B. Flight
C. Freeze

   Give an example from the book where Neala experiences the Freeze response

   Give an example from the book where Claire experiences the Flight response

   Give an example from the book where Kane demonstrates the Fight response

Discuss these symptoms of an anxiety disorder:

1. **Stomach Pain** including indigestion, gas and bloating, abdominal cramps and pain, and irritable bowel syndrome
2. **Difficulty Breathing** including a choking sensation, hyperventilation, asthma attacks and coughing fits
3. **Negative Thoughts** including anticipating danger and catastrophe around every corner, frequent feelings of inadequacy or impending failure, or believing that something bad will happen if certain things aren't done a certain way
4. **Feelings of Worry** which may result in edginess and physical trembling or shaking
5. **Heart and Chest Pain**
6. **Low Appetite or Binge Eating**
7. **Insomnia**
8. **Feeling Detached or Surroundings Seem Unreal**

Sometimes anxiety might make the person appear:

1. Mean
2. Lazy
3. Uncaring
4. Defiant
5. Entitled

Discuss what you can do to help someone who is having an anxiety attack?

1. Stay with them or stand back if they ask you to leave
2. Remind them that they are okay
3. Offer a five-sense exercise: touch, taste, look, listen, smell
4. Offer to do Square Breathing with them

How can you help someone who has anxiety disorder?

1. Believe the person, their symptoms are real
2. Be supportive, show trust
3. Continue to be their friend; keep inviting them to events, call or text, reach out and just be there, and like Nola, defend your friend when needed

What things might you <u>avoid</u> saying to someone having a panic attack? Why?

1. "I know what you mean. I had a panic attack once"
2. "Snap out of it." or "It's all in your head."
3. "Calm Down." or "You're embarrassing yourself."
4. "Are you OK?!" (Repeatedly)
5. "Why aren't you seeing a therapist about this?" or "Don't you have medication?"

What are Claire's worst fears about her daughter's condition? Why?

1. That Neala will not graduate, that she might drop out
2. That Neala might self-medicate with alcohol or drugs

Are Claire's worries valid? Discuss.

A high school dropout earns less than a high school graduate because of: Loss of employment

1. Financial losses (job loss/divorce)
2. Dropout have more criminal charges
3. Loss of family and relationships
4. Possibility of becoming a life-long addict
5. Someone who drops out will earn less money
6. It may be harder to go to college

Share about a time or experience when you felt worried or anxious:

Did you experience Fight, Flight, or Freeze?

What did you do to feel better?

How do you take care of yourself, so you worry less?

Where can you get help if you think you or someone you know has an anxiety disorder?

1. Parents
2. Doctor
3. Therapist
4. Teacher
5. School District
6. Additional Ideas and Suggestions

ACKNOWLEDGMENTS

I respectfully thank my editor, Robbi Sommers Bryant. It's a pleasure to collaborate with her. Her expert guidance enabled me to tell this story in its best way. I am also thankful for my cousin and fellow author, Sheryle Bauer. Her courage to tell her story enlightened me and gave me the voice to disclose mine. A big thank you to my readers: Gloria Azevedo, Apryl Lopez, Mona Mechling, Linda Severietti-Torrez, for you helped me connect all the dots.

One's Own Sweet Way is my true account of how our family handled our daughter's anxiety disorder, her remedies, and therapies. I am grateful for the Rohnert Park Cotati School District and Credo High School for allowing my daughter, Mia, to have Bella (Mia's Emotional Support Animal) on campus and for establishing best practices for Mia's education. Great gratitude to Phoenix High School Program at Rancho Cotate High School for exceptional support and encouragement received from Phoenix teachers Mr. Samuelson and Mr. Carp, and additional faculty. Also, a big thank you to Laura Deffendall and her golf-cart chariot! Because of their collaborative efforts, Mia achieved her goal and obtained her high school diploma.

Additionally, I thank Mia's Behavioral Therapist who presented her with ways to verbalize her fears and the tools to conquer them and her tutor for guiding her through her courses while she battled her dragon, and Connie Bartlett, Performance Paws Dog Sports, for her support for both Mia and Bella.

I also thank my village of friends including Nancy Dew, Cathie Poncia, Janet Silvashy, Christine Sleight, Jenni Teague, and my sister, Tami (Tt) Bender and the cousins, Ash, Ants, and Lex. They knew when to listen, support, kick my ass, hug me, and love both Mia and me through those five uncertain years.

I am ever thankful to my manager, Maria Larsen, for allowing me the flexibility to do my job and care for my family without losing my balance or my mind.

I am genuinely appreciative of my loving husband, Brian, our children, and for our families for honoring us to do what we needed to do and of course, I am forever beholden to Bella, our official ESA.

ABOUT THE AUTHOR

When author CM Riddle's teen daughter suffered from severe anxiety disorders, Ms. Riddle was compelled to share their courageous journey. Uniquely told from the experiences of both mother and child's point of view, Ms. Riddle offers compassion, humor, and hope to those who suffer from anxiety and other invisible diseases.

The author has additional work published in anthologies and magazines. With several other books on her horizon, she shares stories which touch the human heart and awaken the soul.

She raised her young family in Novato, CA, where she provided quality home childcare. As her children grew, she continued her work in the childcare field with the local Child Care Council and Child Care Food Program. After moving to Sonoma County, where her youngest was born. Tina then worked as an American Heart Association Basic Life Support CPR and First Aid Instructor and training center coordinator.

Learn more about One's Own Sweet Way and Anxiety Disorders at:

https://spark.adobe.com/sp/design/page/0f40f7e9-614b-4193-a6dc-b8c414b143de

CM Riddle is an Ordained Priestess, Women' Circle and Apprenticeship Facilitator, Anxiety Disorder Facilitator, Author, and Mother. Learn more at **priestesstina.com**

When asked what is her all-time favorite job? She says it has been to raise her children, Lorenzo, Natalie, and Mia, along with her stepdaughters, Andrea, and Hilary. Ms. Riddle resides in Sonoma County with her husband, Brian, and their family pets, Bella, Buddy, and, Mitty.